T0213055

## Whitestein Series in Software Agent Technologies and Autonomic Computing

Series Editors:
Marius Walliser
Stefan Brantschen
Monique Calisti
Stefan Schinkinger

This series reports new developments in software agent technologies and autonomic computing, with particular emphasis on applications in a variety of scientific and industrial domains. The spectrum of the series includes research monographs, high quality notes resulting from research and industrial projects, outstanding Ph.D. theses, and the proceedings of carefully selected conferences. The series is targeted at promoting advanced research and facilitating know-how transfer to industrial use.

## About Whitestein Technologies

Whitestein Technologies AG was founded in 1999 with the mission to become a leading provider of advanced software agent technologies, products, solutions, and services for various applications and industries. Whitestein Technologies strongly believes that software agent technologies, in combination with other leading-edge technologies like web services and mobile wireless computing, will enable attractive opportunities for the design and the implementation of a new generation of distributed information systems and network infrastructures.

www.whitestein.com

**Radovan Cervenka**
**Ivan Trencansky**

# The Agent Modeling
# Language - AML

A Comprehensive Approach to Modeling
Multi-Agent Systems

Birkhäuser
Basel · Boston · Berlin

Authors:

Radovan Cervenka
Whitestein Technologies
Panenska 28
811 03 Bratislava
Slovakia
rce@whitestein.com

Ivan Trencansky
Whitestein Technologies
Panenska 28
811 03 Bratislava
Slovakia
itr@whitestein.com

2000 Mathematical Subject Classification: 68T35


Library of Congress Control Number: 2007923777


Bibliographic information published by Die Deutsche Bibliothek
Die Deutsche Bibliothek lists this publication in the Deutsche Nationalbibliografie; detailed bibliographic
data is available in the Internet at <http://dnb.ddb.de>.


ISBN 978-3-7643-8395-4 Birkhäuser Verlag AG, Basel · Boston · Berlin

© 2007 Birkhäuser Verlag AG
Basel · Boston · Berlin
P.O. Box 133, CH-4010 Basel, Switzerland
Part of Springer Science+Business Media
Printed on acid-free paper produced from chlorine-free pulp. TCF ∞
Printed in Germany
ISBN 978-3-7643-8395-4            e-ISBN 978-3-7643-8396-1

9 8 7 6 5 4 3 2 1                 www.birkhauser.ch

# Preface

Today, in 2007, the field of study known as multi-agent systems has been in existence for more than 25 years. However, only during the mid-1990s did the field begin to draw widespread attention as the hype-curve approached its zenith. Now as the first decade of the 21st century begins to wane, we find the field ever more active with branches in a myriad of disciplines and aspects of multi-agent systems theory and engineering in use throughout multiple application domains and business sectors. However, one important aspect of multi-agent systems that still lacks complete and proper definition, general acceptance and practical application, is that of modeling, despite the substantial efforts of an active research community.

In short, software agents are a domain-agnostic means for building distributed applications that can be used to create artificial social systems. Their facility for autonomous action is the primary differentiating property from traditional object-oriented systems and it is this aspect that most strongly implies that standard UML is insufficient for modeling multi-agent systems.

The focus of this book is thus on an approach to resolving this insufficiency by providing a comprehensive modeling language designed as an extension to UML 2.0, focused specifically on the modeling of multi-agent systems and applications. This language is AML—the Agent Modeling Language—the design of which is informed by previous work in this area while explicitly addressing known limitations relating to managing complexity and improving coverage and comprehension.

But why modeling in the first place, and moreover why model multi-agent systems? Software modeling is now a pervasive technique used to simplify the view of a software system by offering abstracted perspectives and hiding non-essential details. In fact one of the key benefits of traditional object-oriented modeling is the availability of easy-to-use semi-formal modeling languages such as UML. As a result, almost all contemporary software development processes make use of UML modeling for visually documenting aspects of requirements capture, software analysis, design and deployment. And so given that multi-agent systems are essentially a paradigmatic extension of object orientation principles, it is clear that a properly formulated extension to UML is feasible for software agent modeling. AML offers such an extension by addressing the particular characteristics associated with multi-agent systems including entities, behavior abstraction and decomposition, social aspects, mental aspects, communicative interactions, observations and effecting interactions, mobility, deployment, services and ontologies.

But the availability of AML alone is not in itself sufficient to assist adoption; methodological support is also a critical concern. Therefore AML is supported by a software development methodology called ADEM (Agent DEvelopment Methodology) which provides guidelines for the use of AML in general software development processes. ADEM follows the Situational Method Engineering approach to provide flexibility in defining concrete methods customized to specific conditions of particular system development projects. One other critical aspect of modeling language utility is tool support, without which widespread adoption is essentially an unobtainable goal. In recognition of this, AML is supported by implementations of its UML profiles for several well-known UML CASE tools including IBM Rational Rose, Enterprise Architect and most recently, StarUML.

As AML is still quite new, adoption is still in an early phase but it is hoped that the public availability of the specification, methodology, tools and of course this book will help encourage widespread use. Currently Whitestein Technologies is at the vanguard of adoption having recognized a strong business need for AML and thus supported its creation and evolution. Whitestein, as a leading vendor of multi-agent systems applications, now actively employs AML throughout their product lines spanning telecommunications, logistics and business process management.

As a final note, the objective of this book is to familiarize the reader with the Agent Modeling Language by explaining its foundation, design principles, specification, and usage. The book however makes no attempt to educate the reader in the techniques of software modeling and thus a reasonable understanding of object-oriented design principles and especially UML is recommended.

# Acknowledgements

Very special thank goes to Dominic Greenwood, not only for the precious discussions and advice which have inspired and shaped many ideas, but also for his generous and unfailing help concerning language refinements and wording polishing. Without his encouragement this book would hardly be published.

We are indebted also to the AML technical reviewers, namely Stefan Brantschen, Monique Calisti, and Giovanni Rimassa, for their fruitful comments and suggestions which have substantially influenced the current version of AML.

We would also like to thank professor Branislav Rovan for his encouragement and valuable contribution to the form and content of the work.

Thanks to Whitestein Technologies for their support and provision of sufficient time, team of professionals, and other resources which we utilized in our work.

We are also obliged to Hilary Greenwood for her thorough proof reading of the final text resulting in substantially improved legibility and understandability.

Our thank belongs also to the members of the FIPA Modeling and Methodology technical committees and AgentLink AOSE technical forum groups for the discussions about various topics of agent-oriented modeling and agent-oriented software engineering.

Last, but not least, to our families for their love, unconditional support, and patience.

# Contents

# Chapter 1

# Introduction

## 1.1 Overview

**Agents and multi-agent systems**
Agent-based systems are one of the most vibrant and important areas of research and development to have emerged in information technology in recent years, underpinning many aspects of broader information society technologies [82].

The underlying concept of agent-based systems is an *agent*. Jennings, Sycara and Wooldridge in [65] propose a classical definition of the term agent[1], where the central concept is autonomy:

> "An agent is a computer system, *situated* in some environment, that is capable of *autonomous* actions in this environment in order to meet its design objectives. ...
>
> Situatedness means that the agent receives sensory input from its environment and that it can perform actions which change the environment in some way.
>
> By autonomy we mean that the system should be able to act without the direct intervention of humans (or other agents), and that it should have control over its own actions and internal state."

Beyond these fundamental properties of an agent, there are also several additional capabilities that allow the formation of special classes of agents, called *intelligent agents*. The following list of capabilities was suggested by Wooldridge and Jennings in [160]:

**Reactivity**
Intelligent agents are able to perceive their environment, and respond in a timely fashion to changes that occur within it.

---

[1] From now on we will use the term *agent* to talk about software agents, unless another meaning is noted explicitly in a particular context.

**Proactiveness**
> Intelligent agents are able to exhibit opportunistic, goal-directed behavior and take the initiative when appropriate.

**Social ability**
> Intelligent agents are capable of interacting with other artificial agents and possibly humans.

Agents rarely exist alone. To provide the required functionality and to solve problems they are dedicated to, agents are socialized into larger groups. Environments, in which communities of agents exist, mutually interact, and possibly also cooperate, are known as *Multi-Agent Systems* (*MAS*).

Multi-agent systems are based on the idea that a cooperative working environment comprising synergistic software components can cope with problems which are hard to solve using the traditional centralized approach to computation. Software agents with special capabilities (autonomous, reactive, pro-active and social) are used instead to interact in a flexible and dynamic way to solve problems more efficiently.

**Applicability of agents** The features provided by multi-agent systems predetermine their applicability in development systems that are open, heterogeneous, highly dynamic, unpredictable, and complex. Agents are a natural metaphor to model social structures that are within the sphere of interest of information systems, artificial social systems, simulators, etc. MAS architecture can be successfully applied to environments with distributed data, control or expertise. In such environments to build a centralized system would be extremely complicated or even impossible.

Multi-agent systems have already found their place in a diverse range of information technology sub-disciplines, including networking, software engineering, agent-oriented programming, artificial intelligence, human-computer interaction, distributed and concurrent systems, mobile systems, telematics, computer-supported cooperative work, control systems, mining, decision support, information retrieval and management, and electronic commerce. It has been recognized that agents appear to be a promising approach to developing complex applications in several business and industry domains, for example, business-to-business exchange, supply management, manufacturing, logistics, telecommunications, or traffic control.

**Agents as a design metaphor** Agents provide designers and developers with a way of structuring an application around autonomous, communicative elements, and lead to the construction of software tools and infrastructure to support the design metaphor [64]. The use of agents as an abstraction tool, or a metaphor, for the design and construction of systems provided the initial impetus for developments in the field. On the one hand, agents offer an appropriate way to consider complex systems with multiple distinct and independent components. On the other hand, they also enable the aggregation of different functionalities that have previously been distinct (such as planning, learning, coordination, etc.) as a conceptually embodied and situated whole. Thus these notions provide a set of technology areas that relate directly to these abstractions in the design and development of large systems, of individual agents, of ways in which agents may interact to support these concepts, and in the consideration of societal or macro-level issues such as organizations and their computational counterparts [83].

Many specialists believe that agents represent the most important new paradigm for software development since object orientation.

**Agent-oriented software engineering** However, building large-scale multi-agent systems is a very complex problem. To design, implement, test, and maintain distributed and concurrent systems built up of possibly many autonomous, rational and proactive entities (agents) is a challenge. The problem becomes more complicated in open multi-agent systems, where the developers have to cope with problems such as *heterogeneity* (agents may have different and possibly conflicting goals, are created by different people, etc.), *communication problems* (agents use different communication protocols and/or ontologies, etc.), *security problems* (e.g. authorization, rights, trust, or communication and data storage security), etc.

To cope with these problems, very active research in this area has been ongoing for almost twenty years to determine abstractions, languages, methodologies and toolkits for modeling, verifying, validating and finally implementing applications of this kind. These activities resulted in forming the *Agent-Oriented Software Engineering* (*AOSE*) domain, which is the one of the most recent contributions to the field of software engineering. AOSE is being described as a new paradigm [78] for the research field of software engineering. But in order to become a new paradigm for the software industry, robust and easy-to-use methodologies and tools must be developed.

The main goal is to determine how agent qualities affect software engineering, and what additional tools and concepts are needed to apply software engineering processes and structures to agent systems. The purpose of AOSE is to create methodologies and tools that enable effective development and maintenance of agent-based software [145].

Luck, McBurney and Preist in [82] identify the following specific areas of AOSE's interest:

☐ requirements engineering for agent systems,

☐ techniques for specification of (conceptual) designs of agent systems,

❑ verification techniques,

❑ agent-oriented analysis and design,

❑ specific ontologies for agent requirements, agent models and organization models,

❑ libraries of generic models of agents and agent components,

❑ agent design patterns,

❑ validation and testing techniques, and

❑ tools to support the agent system development process (such as agent platforms).

To date, this work has largely concentrated on analysis and design methods, development tools and languages for programming and communication [153].

AOSE has made a substantial progress in recent years, and nowadays is becoming ready for the process of transformation from the predominantly academic environment, where it was originally invented, to the mainstream software industry. However, further achievements (such as wider application to the development of real-world systems, creation of reliable agent-based technologies, standardization, etc.) are necessary to overcome the current problems with AOSE and to provide high-quality solutions for software engineers.

**Agent-oriented modeling languages** *Modeling* is a crucial aspect of all software engineering methodologies. Methodologies generally aim at building a collection of models which describe various aspects of the system being considered. A *model* is a simplified view of a system, which shows the essentials of the system from a particular perspective and hides the non-essential details [56]. The development process can be understood as a successive transformation of one model to another. Starting from a model of requirements, through models of analysis, design, implementation, until a model of testing. Models and their parts usually represent artifacts of methodologies and the underlying modeling concepts are used to describe the development process (workflow).

In order to capture specific features of agent-based systems, specific modeling languages had to be created. Traditional software engineering methodologies are insufficient for use in the development of such systems because of the particular characteristics of autonomous agents [9].

Several agent-oriented modeling languages and modeling approaches have appeared in past few years, for instance, Gaia [161,168], AUML [7,8,9,10, 92,93,96,113], MESSAGE [40,86], TROPOS [12,143], Prometheus [111,112], PASSI [25,26], TAO [128], and AOR [150,151]. They are mostly developed as parts of methodologies, but we can encounter also "stand-alone" agent-oriented modeling and specification languages.

In spite of quite a considerable effort in the area of agent-oriented modeling, we can observe that currently available agent-oriented modeling languages do not adequately support the features required by potential industrial application of AOSE. In many cases they are often deficient with respect to qualities of traditional modeling approaches represented, for instance, by Unified Modeling Language (UML) [102, 104]. As Cervenka et al. identify in [22], current agent-oriented modeling languages are often:

☐ Insufficiently documented and/or specified.

☐ Using proprietary and/or non-intuitive modeling constructs.

☐ Aimed at modeling only a limited set of MAS aspects.

☐ Applicable only to a specific theory, application domain, MAS architecture, or technology.

☐ Mutually incompatible in concepts, metamodel, and notation.

☐ Insufficiently supported by CASE[2] tools.

Achievements and problems of the current MAS modeling approaches are further discussed in section 2.7.

**Industry challenges** Unfortunately, existing agent-oriented modeling languages do not address a sufficiently wide community of software engineers. Some of the reasons relate to the problems mentioned previously and their elimination is one of the hot topics in the AOSE community.

The solution lies in creating a new unified modeling language that overcomes the identified problems. This language should intentionally incorporate solutions to the problems into its design, and be based on solid theoretical foundations of MAS and practical experiences in the areas of agent-oriented and object-oriented modeling. This will provide an effective modeling means to software engineers. There are intentions within the AOSE community to design and consequently standardize such a language, similarly to UML in the area of object-oriented modeling. Unfortunately these activities have not succeeded to date, resulting in no widely accepted MAS modeling standard yet being available. However, it is generally expected that a MAS modeling standard emerge within the next few years, that would be a next important step toward industrialization of AOSE and dissemination agent-oriented modeling (and subsequently also architectonic concepts and technologies) into a broader community of software engineers.

---

[2] Computer-Aided Software Engineering.

## 1.2  Goals of this Work

**Goals**    In this book we present the results of more than 6 years of intensive
**summary**  research and practice in the area of AOSE and MAS modeling in particular. During that period our activities were driven by the following
goal:

> To design and specify a semi-formal[3] visual modeling language,
> called **Agent Modeling Language** *(AML), for specifying, model-*
> *ing and documenting systems in terms of concepts drawn from*
> *MAS theory.*

The modeling language had to be designed to address and resolve the
deficiencies of the state-of-the-art and practice in the area of MAS
modeling languages identified in the previous section.

The most significant motivation driving the development of a new
modeling language stemmed from the extant need for a ready-to-use,
complete and highly expressive modeling language suitable for the
industrial development of real-world software solutions based on
multi-agent technologies.

**Rationale**   Michael Wooldridge said in one of his papers [158] published in
**behind the**  1997: "Unless researchers recognize that agent-based systems are
**goals**       about computer science and software engineering more than they are
about AI[4], then within a decade, we may well be asking why agent
technology suffered the same fate as so many other AI ideas that
seemed good in principle."

We believe that the results of our work can contribute to the today's
efforts of the AOSE community to obtain a generally accepted and
widely (even commercially) used language for modeling MAS applications, a possible candidate for industrial standardization.

Our intention is to provide software developers with a high-quality
modeling language. The first properly documented, consistent, unambiguous, and comprehensive general-purpose "out of the box"
agent-oriented modeling language supported by CASE tools, which
achieves qualities of existing object-oriented modeling solutions, like
UML.

By successful achievement of the stated goals (see the results later in
the book) we see a real potential for contribution to the AOSE in the
following ways:

---

[3]  The term "semi-formal" implies that the language offers the means to specify systems using a combination of natural language, graphical notation, and
formal language specification. It is not based on a strict formal (e.g. mathematical) theory.

[4]  Artificial intelligence.

☐ **Encourage the growth of the MAS tools market.**
By enabling vendors to support a modeling language used by
most users and tools, the industry benefits. While vendors can
still add value in their tool implementations, enabling interoperability is essential. Interoperability requires that models can be exchanged among users and tools without loss of information. This
can only occur if the tools agree on the format and meaning of all
of the relevant concepts.

☐ **Help to define new MAS development methodologies.**
AML can become a modeling language used for MAS development
methodologies. Particularly, AML would provide the concepts and
MAS abstractions which can be applied in defining the methodology process, and the AML models and their parts can directly become artifacts.

☐ **Accelerate convergence of existing MAS modeling approaches.**
Unification of divergent modeling concepts from different agent-
oriented modeling languages into one language should aid "con-
version" of software engineers to a new modeling language that
provides richer modeling possibilities. This is applicable especially in the case that the unified modeling language is standardized.

☐ **Support standardization.**
AML itself or some of its modeling concepts have the potential to
become standard(s) in the area of MAS modeling.

☐ **Contribute to wider dissemination of AOSE.**
Having a high-quality agent-oriented modeling language available would encourage software engineers, tool vendors, technology developers, and software companies to use it and/or to produce
supporting technologies. This would be an important step toward
acceptance of agent-oriented modeling, but also MAS, AOSE,
agent-based technologies, etc. in a broader community of software engineers.

## 1.3 Outline of the Book

The remainder of the book is structured as follows:

**Part I:** Background Information—This part presents, in **Chapter 2,** a
survey on existing agent-oriented modeling languages. In order to
demonstrate the current state-of-the-art in this area we focus only on
the most frequently discussed languages which significantly influenced the MAS modeling discipline. In **Chapter 3** we then declare, in
terms of quality criteria, the requirements which were used in the development of AML as the mandatory criteria that our solution had to
unconditionally adhere in order to achieve high quality.

**Part II:** Solution Summary—This part describes the main concepts and design principles which guided us in the development of AML. **Chapter 4** explains the main motivational and design aspects which influenced the construction of AML, and describes the overall language architecture and principles of its extensibility mechanisms. In **Chapter 5** we outline the fundamental concepts used to describe an abstract metamodel of MAS, which were then used as a basis for the design of AML. In **Chapter 6** the core AML modeling constructs are explained and demonstrated by examples. In **Chapter 7** we discuss activities that were not originally included in the goals of this work, but relate to introduction of AML and its underlying ideas into practice, namely: implementation of AML in CASE tools, creation of a software development methodology based on AML, application of AML in concrete software development projects, and standardization activities related to AML.

**Part III:** AML Specification—This part contains a detailed technical specification of the AML metamodel, notation and demonstrates the defined modeling elements using examples. **Chapter 8** specifies several presentation options to some UML elements in order to provide a more intuitive and comprehensive notation. In **Chapter 9**, the overall package structure of the AML metamodel is presented. **Chapters 10, 11, 12, 13,** and **14** contain specification of all packages from the AML Kernel (Architecture, Behaviors, Mental, Ontologies and Contexts), their sub-packages and metaclasses. In **Chapter 15** we discuss the AML-related extensions of UML. **Chapter 16** contains the specification of the AML-specific diagrams and diagram frames, and **Chapter 17** definition of AML extensions of OCL.

**Part IV:** Final Remarks—This part provides a summary of the achieved results in **Chapter 18**, and outlines the possible directions of further development and application of AML in **Chapter 19**.

# Part I

# Background Information

This part provides a survey on existing agent-oriented modeling languages, summarizes applied modeling mechanisms, and states the requirements put on an agent-oriented modeling language in general.

# Chapter 2

# Survey on Agent-Oriented Modeling Languages

In this chapter we give an overview of the work that has been carried out on the development of agent-oriented modeling languages. These languages are intended to assist first in gaining an understanding of a particular system, and, secondly, in designing it.

Since the mid-nineties, when the first tentative agent-based methodologies and their modeling languages started to appear, there came into existence quite a large number of languages for analysis and design of agent systems. We selected the ones that significantly influenced the domain of MAS modeling and that can demonstrate different modeling approaches. All the presented agent-oriented modeling languages have been taken into account for designing the concepts and modeling principles of AML, see Chapter 4.

Our main intention is to introduce the basic underlying concepts and modeling constructs for each of the presented languages, in order to understand their scope and the main modeling principles. For details about the semantics, notation, modeling guidelines or the modeling process of a particular language we refer to the respective literature.

## 2.1 Gaia

Introduction Wooldridge, Jennings and Kinny present in [161] the Gaia methodology for agent-oriented analysis and design. The requirements capture phase, independent of the paradigm used for analysis and design, is not included in Gaia. Gaia is a general methodology that supports both the micro-level (agent structure) and macro-level (agent society and organization structure) of agent development; however, it is not a "silver bullet" approach, since it requires that inter-agent relationships (organization) and agent abilities are static at run time. The motivation behind Gaia is that object-oriented methodologies fail to represent the autonomous and problem-solving nature of agents; they also fail to model agents' ways of performing interactions and forming organizations. Using Gaia, software designers can systematically develop an implementation-ready design based on system requirements.

**Modeling concepts** Analysis and design can be thought of as a process of developing increasingly detailed models of the system to be constructed moving from abstract to more concrete concepts. Abstract entities are those used during analysis to conceptualize the system, but which do not necessarily have any direct realization within the system. Concrete entities, in contrast, are used within the design process and will typically have direct counterparts in the runtime system. See Tab. 2-1.

| Abstract concepts | Concrete concepts |
| --- | --- |
| Roles | Agent Types |
| Permissions | Services |
| Responsibilities | Acquaintances |
| Protocols | |
| Activities | |
| Liveness properties | |
| Safety properties | |

**Tab. 2-1** Abstract and concrete concepts in Gaia

Gaia, in its analysis model, specifies the *roles* in the system and the *interactions* between the roles identified. Roles are described in terms of: responsibilities, permissions, activities and protocols. *Responsibilities* are of two types: *liveness properties*—the role has to add something good to the system, and *safety properties*—prevent and disallow that something bad happens to the system. *Permissions* represent what the role is allowed to do, in particular, which information it is allowed to access. *Activities* are tasks that a role performs without interacting with other roles. *Protocols* are the specific patterns of interactions described in terms of purpose, initiator, responder, inputs, outputs, and processing. Gaia provides formal operators and templates for representing roles and their attributes; it also has schemes that can be used for the representation of interactions.

In the Gaia design, the analysis models are refined by the *agent model* (specification of various agent types in terms of a set of roles they play), the *service model* (identification and specification of services associated with the roles), and the *acquaintance model* (a directed graph identifying the communication links between agents types).

**Summary** Gaia is appropriate for the development of systems with the following main characteristics:

☐ Agents are coarse-grained computational systems, each making use of significant computational resources (think of each agent as having the resources of a Unix process).

☐ It is assumed that the goal is to obtain a system that maximizes some global quality measure, but which may be sub-optimal from the point of view of the system components. Gaia is not intended for systems that admit the possibility of true conflict.

☐ Agents are heterogeneous, in that different agents may be implemented using different programming languages, architectures, and techniques. Gaia makes no assumptions about the deployment platform.

☐ The organization structure of the system is static, in that inter-agent relationships do not change at run time.

☐ The abilities of agents and the services they provide are static, in that they do not change at run time.

☐ The overall system contains a comparatively small number of different agent types (less than 100).

Due to the above-mentioned restrictions, Gaia is of less value in the open and unpredictable domains; on the other hand it has been proven as a good approach for developing closed domain agent-systems. As a result of the domain restrictions of the Gaia method, Zambonelli et al. [168] propose some extensions and improvements with the purpose to support the development of open MAS applications, i.e. the systems in which agents are not designed to share common goals, have been (possibly) developed by different people to achieve different objectives, and the composition of which can dynamically change as agents enter and leave the system.

Further extension of Gaia toward larger scope (specification of requirements, domain knowledge, the execution environments, etc.) and more precise models (advanced models of roles, interactions, individual agent characteristics and social aspects, system decomposition, etc.) is represented by the ROADMAP methodology [68].

## 2.2 AUML

**Introduction** Bauer, Odell, and colleagues designed the agent-oriented modeling language *Agent UML (AUML)* [7,8,9,10,92,93,94,95,96,113,116] as an extension of UML. Exploiting the extension mechanisms such as stereotypes, tagged values and constraints, AUML provides specific agent modeling mechanisms over object-oriented ones. The core parts of AUML are interaction protocol diagrams and agent class diagrams, which are extensions of UML's sequence diagrams and class diagrams, respectively.

**Modeling** *Interaction protocols* was the first aspect of multi-agent system design
**concepts** that the AUML community considered. The original idea proposed in
[9,10] was to use the UML 1.x sequence diagrams to represent message exchange between agents. The UML sequence diagrams were en-
riched by explicit specification of the formal *protocol parameters*, representation of *communicative acts* by UML messages (performatives as
message names and payload as the parameters), specification multiplicities for sending and reception of messages, *threads of interaction*,
and *nesting protocols*. Either the communicating agents or their roles
were modeled as interaction lifelines.

In a new version of AUML [7,54,93], based on UML 2.0, the threads of
interaction were replaced by UML standard combined fragments and
the protocol nesting by the interaction reference. With significant
updating of the UML interaction diagrams from version 1.* to 2.0,
most of the original AUML extensions became redundant, and only a
few specific modeling elements have remained, such as protocol parameters specified as a note, multiplicity of lifelines and messages,
*blocking constraints*, and extended notation of continuations.

To model types of agents and their features, Bauer in [8] first proposed the extension of UML class diagrams. In this approach an *agent
class*, in addition to a UML class, can also contain a set of roles its instances can play, state description, actions, capabilities, service descriptions, a set of supported protocols, constraints, society names,
and a reference to the "agent head automata" (an extended state machine).

In the new version of AUML, presented e.g. in [91], a new metamodel
for the agents, roles and groups is introduced. The metamodel defines
the *agent classifier* as a specialized UML classifier. There are two specialized agent classifiers, *agent physical classifier* and *agent role classifier*. *Agent* is defined as specialized UML instance specification and
*group* is defined as a special UML structured classifier. Two kinds of
groups are defined: *agentified group* (inherited also from the agent
metaclass) and *non-agentified group*. Even if the metamodel is not
complete and does not define concrete modeling language, it basically explains the main AUML concepts.

Poggi et al. in [116] also introduce extensions of the UML deployment diagrams used to model the agent platforms, deployment of
agents, and a static models of the agent mobility.

**Summary** AUML is probably the best-known representative of the agent-oriented modeling languages based on UML. But we can observe several
deficiencies. Despite of few attempts, AUML has no clearly defined
metamodel so far.

One of its main drawbacks, though, is the absence of precisely specified semantics for defining the different modeling elements, which can lead to misinterpretation of AUML models.

AUML also needs to populate a set of diagrams. Initial work on AUML focused on interaction protocols and agent design. The newer version also provides static structure diagrams for modeling internal and external aspects of agent types, agents, role types, and groups.

However, the metamodel defined for AUML class diagrams is just an explanation of the basic concepts, but it does not represent specification of the language used. AUML interaction diagrams are not specified in terms of a matamodel at all.

Another of AUML's drawbacks is the absence of modeling tools dedicated to it.

Finally, it is necessary to challenge the AUML notation against industrial and real-world applications to verify its completeness. This is a very difficult task, because it's hard to find proper real world industrial applications. Nevertheless, the AUML community is encouraging companies to participate in its efforts to develop a strong and useful agent-based modeling language.

## 2.3 MESSAGE

**Introduction** *MESSAGE (Methodology for Engineering Systems of Software Agents)* [40,86] is an agent oriented software engineering methodology, developed in particular for the needs of the telecommunications industry. However, it covers most of the fundamental aspects of the MAS development, and it can also be thought of as a generic methodology applicable to other domains.

**Modeling concepts** MESSAGE modeling language extends UML 1.* metamodel with 'knowledge level' agent-oriented concepts, and it uses the same metamodel language as UML for description of its abstract syntax.

The MESSAGE modeling language uses the following concepts (modeling elements):

*Agent*—an atomic autonomous entity that is capable of performing some (potentially) useful functions. An agent can play roles, provide services, perform tasks, achieve goals, use resources, be a part of an organization, and participate in interactions and interaction protocols.

*Organization*—a group of agents working together to a common purpose. An organization can provide services, achieve goals, use resources, be a part of another organization, group subordinates into one collection, and participate in interactions and interaction protocols. Behavior of an organization is achieved collectively by its constituent agents.

*Role*—a concept that allows the part played by an agent to be separated logically from the identity of the agent itself. A role describes the external characteristics of an agent in a particular context. A role can be played by agents or organizations, provide services, perform tasks, achieve goals, use resources, be a part of an organization, and participate in interactions and interaction protocols.

Agent, organization and role are commonly called *autonomous entities*.

*Resource*—a concept used to represent *non-autonomous* entities such as databases or external programs. A resource can be used by autonomous entities.

*Task*—a unit of activity with a single prime performer. Composite tasks can be expressed in terms of causally linked sub-tasks. A task can be performed by an autonomous entity and is causally connected to other tasks or goals.

*Interaction*—an act of exchanging messages among participants in order to achieve some purpose.

*Interaction protocol*—defines a pattern of message exchange associated with an interaction.

*Goal*—an intention of an autonomous entity to achieve some desired state. Goals are "wished" by autonomous entities, can be decomposed into sub-goals, and can imply execution of tasks.

*Information entity*—an object encapsulating a chunk of information.

*Message*—an object communicated between agents. Transmission of a message takes finite time and requires an action to be performed by the sender and also the receiver. The attributes of a message specify the sender, receiver, a speech act (categorizing the message in terms of the intent of the sender) and the content (an information entity).

In addition to the basic concepts, MESSAGE defines a number of views (or perspectives) that emphasize different aspects of the full model. Each view focuses on a limited but consistent aspect, but together they provide a comprehensive view of the whole system. The following views are defined:

*Organization view*—this view shows concrete entities (agents, organizations, roles, and resources) in the system and its environment, and the coarse-grained relationships between them.

*Goal/task view*—this view shows goals, tasks, and the dependencies among them. Goals and tasks can be linked by logical dependencies to form graphs that show, for instance, that achieving a set of subgoals implies that a higher level goal is achieved and how tasks can be performed to achieve goals.

*Agent/role view*—this view focuses on the individual agents and roles. For each agent/role it uses schemata supported by diagrams to its characteristics such as what goals it is responsible for, what events it needs to sense, what resources it controls, what tasks it knows how to perform, 'behavior rules', etc.

*Interaction view*—this view shows interactions, the binding of interaction participant roles into concrete agents/roles, the relevant information supplied/achieved by each participant, the events that trigger the interaction, and other relevant effects of the interaction (e.g. an agent becoming responsible for a new goal).

*Domain view*—this view shows the domain specific concepts and relations that are relevant for the system under development. MESSAGE uses UML class diagrams for this purpose.

**Summary** MESSAGE modeling language represents one of the best of today's agent-oriented modeling languages. It enables modeling of at least the fundamental elements of a MAS, and it is applicable across several domains and MAS architectures. Furthermore, the provided notation is relatively comprehensive.

However, MESSAGE modeling language does not cover all aspects of MAS, deployment, mobility, internal structure of entities, social dynamics, etc.

One of the main community-related deficiencies of MESSAGE is that it is no longer developed and supported.

## 2.4 Tropos

**Introduction** *Tropos* [12,143] is an agent-oriented software development methodology which is founded on the concepts of goal-based requirements adopted from *i\** [4,163,164] and *GRL* [51,80]. Tropos deals primarily with modeling needs and intentional aspects of the agent system, from the early requirements analysis to the late design.

**Modeling concepts** Tropos applies actors and goals as fundamental modeling concepts to all phases of the software development process. It adopts concepts from organization theory of strategic alliance to model MAS architectures. Tropos defines the following modeling elements:

*Actor*—an entity that has strategic goals and intentionality within the system or the organizational setting. An actor represents a physical or a software agent as well as a role or position.

*Goal*—a strategic interest of an actor. *Hard goals* are distinguished from *soft goals*, the second having no clear-cut definition and/or criteria for deciding whether they are satisfied or not.

*Plan*—represents, at an abstract level, a way of doing something. The execution of a plan can be a means for satisfying a goal.

*Resource*—a physical or an informational entity.

*Dependency*—a relation between two actors, which indicates that one actor depends, for some reason, on the other in order to attain some goal, execute some plan, or deliver a resource. The former actor is called the depender, while the latter is called the dependee. The object around which the dependency centres is called dependum. Dependum can be either a goal, a resource, or a task.

*Contribution*—a relationship between goals or plans representing how and how much goals or plans can contribute, positively or negatively, in the fulfillment of the goal.

*Decomposition*—a relationship between goals or plans representing AND/OR decomposition of root goal/plan into subgoals/subplans.

*Capability*—the ability of an actor to define, choose and execute a plan for the fulfilment of a goal, given certain world conditions and in presence of a specific event.

*Belief*—the actor's knowledge of the world.

Tropos also defines the following specific diagrams:

*Actor diagram*—describes the actors, their goals and the network of dependency relationships among actors. This diagram type is used either to define needs and intentional relationships of the business actors or users of the system (a kind of a "goal-based requirements business model" built in early requirements phase) or to show intentions of and relations between the inner system's actors (representing architectural requirements and organization).

*Goal diagram*—shows the internal structure of an actor—its goals, plans, resources and relationships among them.

In the detailed design phase Tropos, to be able to also cover other aspects of MAS architecture, uses class diagrams, activity and interaction diagrams from UML, or sequence diagrams from AUML.

**Summary** Tropos is an interesting approach resting on the idea of using requirements modeling concepts to build a model of the agent-based system.

However, specific Tropos models provide just a restricted view of the system. The agent architecture, behavior, and deployment are described insufficiently. Furthermore, improvements of the existing modeling concepts would also help to create semantically richer models, for example, better logical structuring of goals (constraints), or better definition of still fairly unclear concepts about plans, capabilities and resources.

## 2.5 MAS-ML

**Introduction** Silva et al. contribute to the set of agent-modeling languages based on UML by their language *Multi-Agent System Modeling (MAS-ML)* [127, 130]. Based on the *Taming Agents and Objects (TAO)* [128] conceptual framework, the MAS-ML extends the UML metamodel describing new metaclasses, extending the class and sequence diagrams and proposing two new diagrams: organization and role diagram.

**Modeling** TAO (MAS-ML) defines the static and dynamic aspects of MAS. The
**concepts** static aspect captures the system's elements and their properties and relationships. The elements defined in TAO are:

*Object*—a passive or reactive element that has state and behavior and can be related to other elements.

*Agent*—an autonomous, adaptive and interactive element that has a mental state (such as beliefs, goals, plans and actions).

*Environment*—an element that is the habitat for agents, objects and organizations. An environment can be heterogeneous, dynamic, open, distributed and unpredictable.

*Organization*—an element that groups agents, which play roles and have common goals. An organization hides internal characteristics, properties and behaviors represented by agents inside it.

*Role*—defined in the context of an organization, a role is an element that guides and restricts the behavior of an agent or an object in the organization. The social behavior of an agent is represented by its role in an organization. MAS-ML defines two types of roles:

> *Object role*—guides and restricts the state and behavior of an object. It may restrict access to the state and behavior of an object but may also add information, behavior and relationships to the object that plays the role.

> *Agent role*—guides and restricts the behavior of an agent by describing its goals, beliefs, and the actions that an agent must and/or may perform while playing the role. An agent role adds new goals and beliefs to the set of goals and beliefs associated with an agent and describes duties, rights and protocols related to an agent while it is playing the role.

TAO also defines a set of relationships that link the mentioned elements, namely *inhabit, ownership, play, specialization, control, dependency, association*, and *aggregation*.

The dynamic aspects of TAO are directly related to the changes of relationships between the elements in time. The dynamics of MAS involve the creation of the elements, the destruction of the elements and the interaction between the elements. The elementary dynamic processes defined by TAO are domain-independent dynamics that are the basis for other higher level dynamic patterns and domain specific behavior.

MAS-ML transforms the TAO concepts into the corresponding metaclasses extending the UML metaclasses. MAS-ML extends the set of UML static diagrams with organization and role diagrams.

*Organization diagram* models an organization, showing the environment it inhabits, the roles it defines and the objects, agents and sub organizations that play those roles.

*Role diagram* defines the relationships between agent roles, between agent roles and object roles, between object roles and roles and the classes that they use/define.

MAS-ML extends the UML sequence diagram to represent the interaction between agents, organizations and environments. The extensions proposed to the UML sequence diagram were based on the domain-independent dynamic processes described in [129].

**Summary**  MAS-ML allows modeling of the static as well as the dynamic aspects of a MAS, and defines the modeling elements based on a well-defined set of concepts from TAO. From the conceptual point of view (because of TAO), the MAS-ML is one of the best specified agent-oriented modeling languages.

However, the concrete modeling mechanisms and the way they are defined do not reach this quality. MAS-ML extends the UML metamodel and defines its UML profile in a relatively strange way, for example, not all MAS-ML-specific metaclasses are represented by stereotypes, there are some stereotypes defined without corresponding metaclasses, and some constraints from the TAO metamodel are not preserved by the MAS-ML metamodel. Furthermore, not all elements from TAO are reflected by the MAS-ML metamodel. Notation of the MAS-ML elements is quite non-standard and difficult to draw.

Due to the problems with defining the MAS-ML metamodel, UML profile, and its notation, it would be very difficult (if even possible) to implement MAS-ML in a UML-based CASE tool.

## 2.6 AOR

**Introduction** Wagner in [151] suggests an agent-oriented approach to the conceptual modeling of organizations and organizational information systems called *Agent-Object-Relationship* (AOR). AOR proposes a conceptual framework for agent-oriented modeling that is based on a set of 19 ontological principles, including those of *Entity-Relationship* (ER) modeling, and a corresponding diagram language called *AOR Modeling Language* (AORML).

In [150] Wagner presents a UML profile for AOR. Casting the AOR metamodel as a UML profile allows AOR models to be notated using standard UML notation.

**Modeling** In the AOR, an entity is either an agent, an event, an action, a claim, a
**concepts** commitment, or an ordinary object. Special relationships between agents and events, actions, claims and commitments supplement the fundamental association, aggregation/composition and generalization relationship types of ER and UML class modeling.

In the AOR approach, behavior is primarily modeled by means of interaction patterns expressed in the form of reaction rules that are visualized in interaction pattern diagrams. It is also an option to additionally use UML activity and state machine diagrams.

There are two basic types of AOR models: external and internal ones. An *external AOR model* adopts the perspective of an external observer who is observing the (prototypical) agents and their interactions in the problem domain under consideration. An *internal AOR model* adopts the internal (first-person) view of a particular agent to be modeled.

Typically, an external AOR model has a focus, that is an agent or a group of agents, for which we would like to develop a state and behavior model. In this external-observer-view, the application domain consists of various types of agents, communicative and non-communicative action events, non-action events, commitments/claims between two agent types, ordinary objects, various designated relationships, such as send and do, and ordinary associations. An external AOR model may comprise one or more of the following diagrams:

❑ **Agent Diagrams**—depicting the agent types of the domain, certain relevant object types, and the relationships among them.

❑ **Interaction Frame Diagrams**—depicting the action event types and commitment/claim types that determine the possible interactions between two agent types (or instances).

❑ **Interaction Sequence Diagrams**—depicting prototypical instances of interaction processes.

❑ **Interaction Pattern Diagrams**—focusing on general interaction patterns expressed by means of a set of reaction rules defining an interaction process type.

In an internal AOR model, the internal view of a particular agent to be modeled is adopted. In this view the domain of interest consists of various types of: other agents, actions, commitments towards other agents to perform certain actions, events (many of them created by actions of other agents), claims against other agents that certain action events happen, ordinary objects, various designated relationships, and ordinary associations. An internal AOR model may comprise of one or more of the following diagrams:

❑ **Reaction Frame Diagrams**—depicting other agents (or agent types) and the action and event types, as well as the commitment and claim types that determine the possible interactions with them.

❑ **Reaction Sequence Diagrams**—depicting prototypical instances of interaction processes in the internal perspective.

❑ **Reaction Pattern Diagrams**—focusing on the reaction patterns of the agent under consideration expressed by means of reaction rules.

**Summary** AOR, by virtue of its agent-oriented categorization of different classes, allows more adequate models of organizations and organizational information systems than plain UML.

The author identifies the following main strengths of AORML with respect to conceptual modeling:

1. AORML has a richer set of basic ontological concepts, allowing it to capture more semantics of a domain, as compared to ER, UML and AUML.

2. AORML includes and unifies many of the fundamental domain modeling concepts found in enterprise modeling approaches such as CIMOSA and the Eriksson-Penker business extensions.

3. Unlike UML, AORML allows the integration of state and behavior modeling in one diagram.

4. AORML allows the inclusion of the deontic concepts of rights and duties for organization modeling in an ER/UML-based information model.

5. AORML seems to be the first approach that enables the systematic distinguishing between external and internal models and accounts for the phenomenon of internalization.

6. AORML seems to be the first approach that employs and visualizes the important concept of reaction rules for behavior modeling.

However, weaknesses of AOR modeling in its current form include:

1. The entire development path from analysis to implementation is not yet fully defined.

2. AORML does not currently include the concept of activities. It will be added, however, in future work.

3. AORML does not include the concept of goals which is fundamental in several other approaches, such as [39,166].

4. AORML does not allow modeling of the proactive behavior of agents. This type of behavior, which is the focus of Artificial Intelligence approaches to agents, is based on action planning and plan execution for achieving goals.

## 2.7 Summary of Today's MAS Modeling Languages

**Achieved results** In the last few years we were witnesses to rapid progress in the area of MAS modeling. A considerably large number of agent-oriented modeling languages came into existence as reaction to the urgency of application of an organized way of development agent-based systems.

In general, most of the existing agent-oriented modeling languages share the common basic concepts coming from solid foundations of MAS theories, such as the concept of agent, role, or interaction. However, the current modeling languages differ in their approach to modeling these concepts. Several MAS modeling and specification paradigms used in various (AI, MAS, and computer science) theories and software engineering approaches are reflected by the current modeling languages, including logic-based, knowledge-based, requirements-based, BDI[5]-based, UML-based, etc. languages.

The majority of the current agent-oriented modeling languages were developed by people with mostly academic backgrounds. This fact, on one hand, generally assures the creation of theoretically sound solutions, but on the other hand, results in insufficient testing and the lack of proof of their applicability in modeling real-world problems. There are only a few known examples of successful application of MAS modeling approaches in development of large-scale real-world systems.

**Deficiencies of existing approaches** In spite of interesting results in the area of agent-oriented modeling, the currently available agent-oriented modeling languages, in general, are:

---

5  *Belief-Desire-Intention*—an agent architecture based on the notion of agents as *intentional systems*. Introduced by Rao and Georgeff in [119].

❐ **Insufficiently documented and/or specified.**
It is difficult to correctly understand and properly use a modeling language described informally, without exact specification of syntax and semantics of the comprised modeling constructs.

❐ **Using proprietary and/or non-intuitive modeling constructs.**
Exploiting modeling constructs which are not natural abstractions of the particular MAS concepts in a modeling language can decrease the level of its comprehensibility and usability. People might learn and use it with difficulties and undesirable overhead.

❐ **Aimed at modeling only a limited set of MAS aspects.**
The smaller set of aspects of a system that can be expressed using a modeling language, the narrower applicability and usability that language has. Those languages which cover just a limited set of modeled aspects are restricted in providing complex models of systems.

❐ **Applicable only to a specific theory, application domain, MAS architecture, or technology.**
Many modeling languages are not *generally* applicable, but only within the scope of a particular theory, application domain, MAS architecture, or technology. Even though such modeling languages may be used to create fine quality models, the range of modelable systems is usually restricted.

❐ **Mutually incompatible in terms of concepts, metamodel, and notation.**
We identify three problems connected to this fact: (1) The lack of agreement among agent-oriented modeling languages discourages new users from entering the agent technology market and from undertaking agent-oriented modeling. (2) It might be difficult, or even impossible, to interchange artifacts and information between MAS development teams using different modeling languages and to transform models from one language to another. In this case a modeling language fails to represent a common communication and interchange language. (3) Producers of tools are discouraged from entering the agent modeling area because of the need to support many different modeling languages and means of interoperability.

❐ **Insufficiently supported by CASE tools.**
Success in the practical usability of software modeling languages is empowered by the CASE tools provided for modeling, model maintenance, validation, forward and reverse engineering, etc. Languages that do not provide automation support of sufficient quality are significantly weakened. Even existing MAS-specific modeling CASE tools, for instance, ISLANDER [60], INGENIAS IDE [59], or Prometheus Design Tool [117], mostly do not achieve the level of quality required of industrially applicable tools.

**Conclusions** Existing agent-oriented modeling languages represent the first step in defining high-quality, generally accepted and practically used MAS modeling solutions, applicable not only in academia, but also in the area of industrial software development.

But still, due to the existence of many divergent MAS modeling approaches and their insufficient industrial quality, none of them have achieved general acceptance and use in wider community of software engineers. Current agent-oriented modeling languages either remain practically unused, or are being used just by isolated groups of software developers, usually closely cooperating with the authors of the particular modeling languages. Therefore, the wider community of software engineers is not yet aware of the current MAS modeling approaches. "Agent-orientation" is still usually perceived as "yet another buzzword" from the side of traditional software engineers still mostly focused on the object-oriented approaches.

Fortunately, the problems of the current agent-oriented approaches have been identified and teams of specialists, from both academia and industry, are working together on their elimination.

# Chapter 3

# Requirements on a MAS Modeling Language

**General quality criteria** In order to determine the quality of a modeling language explicitly, it is necessary to state its quality criteria. In the following we will define the general quality criteria of MAS modeling languages based on our analysis of the existing agent-oriented modeling languages (provided in Chapter 2), but also coming out of more than 10 years of our experience in the area of software modeling.

To qualify this more precisely, a MAS modeling language is intended to be:

☐ **theoretically sound**—integrates best practices from AOSE and OOSE[6] domains and is built on proven technical foundations,

☐ **well specified and documented**—provides detailed and comprehensive specification of its syntax, semantics, and use,

☐ **comprehensive**—is highly expressive and enables to create complex models of systems, capturing various aspects of the system modeled,

☐ **consistent**—is internally consistent from the conceptual, semantic and syntactic perspectives,

☐ **easy to use**—provides the modeling constructs which are easy to learn and apply,

☐ **extensible**—allows to specialize and extend the provided modeling means,

☐ **generic**—is independent of any particular theory, software development process or technology, and

☐ **automatable**—is easily supportable by CASE tools.

---

[6]  Object-Oriented Software Engineering.

To build a modeling language that would satisfy these quality criteria is a non-trivial and ambitious task, vindicated by the fact that none of the existing agent-oriented modeling languages are able to satisfy them completely.

**Application of the quality criteria** In order to achieve high level of AML's quality, it was necessary to take into account also the stated quality criteria. They represented the fundamental requirements which were used in the development of AML as the mandatory criteria that our solution had to unconditionally adhere.

However, the aforementioned quality criteria are specified generically enough, so they can be used as general rules for designing any other software (but not necessarily) modeling/specification language, or/and to be used as evaluation criteria to determine the quality of some of existing modeling/specification languages.

# Part II

# Solution Summary

This part describes the main concepts and design principles which guided us in the development of AML. We outline the fundamental AML concepts used to describe an abstract metamodel of MAS. The core AML modeling constructs are explained and demonstrated by examples. We also discuss results that go beyond satisfaction of the primary goals of this work, but relate to the introduction of AML and its underlying ideas into practice in terms of software development and standardization.

# Chapter 4

# The AML Approach

In this chapter we discuss the main motivational and technical aspects which influenced our design of AML, and we describe the overall language architecture and its extensibility mechanisms.

## 4.1 The Purpose of AML

The **Agent Modeling Language** (AML) is a semi-formal visual modeling language for specifying, modeling and documenting systems in terms of concepts drawn from MAS theory [18].

The primary application context of AML is to systems explicitly designed using software multi-agent system concepts. AML can, however, also be applied to other domains such as business systems, social systems, robotics, etc. In general, AML can be used whenever it is suitable or useful to build models that:

- ❏ consist of a number of autonomous, concurrent and/or asynchronous (possibly proactive) entities,
- ❏ comprise entities that are able to observe and/or interact with their environment,
- ❏ make use of complex interactions and aggregated services,
- ❏ employ social structures,
- ❏ capture mental characteristics of systems and/or their parts, etc.

## 4.2 The Scope of AML

AML is designed to support business modeling, requirements specification, analysis, and design of software systems that use MAS concepts and principles.

The current version of AML offers:

❑ Support for the human mental process of requirements specification and analysis of complex problems/systems, particularly:

- mental aspects, which can be used for modeling intentionality in business and use case models, goal-based requirements, problem decomposition, etc. (for details see section 6.7, and chapter 12), and

- contexts, which can be used for situation-based modeling (see sections 6.9, and 14.1).

❑ Support for the abstraction of architectural and behavioral concepts associated with multi-agent systems:

- MAS entities (see sections 6.2, 10.2, 10.3, and 10.4),

- social aspects (see sections 6.3, and 10.5),

- behavior abstraction and decomposition (see sections 6.5, 11.1, and 11.2),

- communicative interactions (see sections 6.6, and 11.3),

- services (see sections 6.6.3, and 11.4),

- observations and effecting interactions (see sections 6.6.4, and 11.5),

- mental aspects used for modeling mental attitudes of entities (see section 6.7, and chapter 12),

- MAS deployment (see sections 6.4, and 10.6),

- agent mobility (see sections 6.4, and 11.6), and

- ontologies (see section 6.8, and chapter 13).

**Outside the scope of AML** AML does not cover most operational semantics of the modeling elements, which is often dependent on a specific execution model given by an applied theory or deployment environment (e.g. agent platforms, reasoning engines, or other technologies used). However, the basic operational semantics is inherited from UML which is the underlying modeling language; for details see later in this chapter.

## 4.3 The Development of AML

In forming the main principles and the design of AML we applied a systematic approach based upon unification of significant, well defined, generally accepted and practically useful principles and concepts from the broadest possible set of existing multi-agent theories and abstract models, modeling and specification languages, methodologies, agent-based technologies and multi-agent driven applications.

Toward achieving the stated goals, we used the process that should be basically characterized by the following steps:

1. Identification and study the relevant sources.

2. Determination of the applicable concepts, modeling mechanisms and techniques from the selected sources.

3. Unification of the concepts and building the AML conceptual framework. This framework determines the scope of AML and modeling mechanisms used.

4. Identification of the additional requirements for building AML, which are aimed at improvement of the specified concepts to provide their richer models, or to support for modeling of MAS aspects still covered insufficiently, inappropriately or not at all, etc.

5. Transformation of the concepts and the additional requirements onto modeling elements. In the case where UML modeling is insufficient or inappropriate, we have defined specific AML modeling elements.

6. Assembling the AML modeling elements into a consistent framework specified by the AML metamodel (covering abstract syntax and semantics of the language) and notation (covering the concrete syntax).

7. Creation of the UML 2.0 and 1.5. profiles based on the AML metamodel.

The process could be characterized as iterative and incremental. Thus the above-mentioned procedure was repeated several times, once per iteration, and the language specification was built stepwise by successively adding new features.

## 4.4 AML Sources

Tab. 4-1 provides a summary of the most significant AML sources and their contribution to the language.

| Source | Used for |
|---|---|
| UML 1.5 [102], UML 2.0 [103,104] | the underlying foundation of AML, language definition principles (metamodel, semantics and notation), and extension mechanisms |
| OCL 2.0 [100] | the constraints language used in AML specification |

**Tab. 4-1** AML sources (1/2)

| Source | Used for |
|--------|----------|
| MESSAGE [40,86] | inspiration for the core AML modeling principles, partially also notation |
| AUML [7,8,9,10,92,93,94, 95,96,113,116] | inspiration for modeling of interactions, mobility and partially class diagrams |
| i* [4,163,164], GRL [51,80], TROPOS [12,143], KAOS [31,146], NFR [23,88], GBRAM [5], etc. | inspiration for and principles of goal-based requirements and modeling of intentionality |
| Gaia [161,168], ROADMAP [68], Styx [15], PASSI [25,26], Prometheus [111,112] MAS-ML [127,129,130], AOR [150,151], CAMLE [125], OPM/MAS [55,136], INGENIAS [52,59,114], MASSIVE [77], ADELFE [11], Cougaar Design Methodology [27], etc. | inspiration for modeling techniques, concepts, and constructs |
| OWL [110,132], DAML [30,43], OIL [41,43,97], etc. | inspiration for the specification and modeling of ontologies |
| FIPA standards [47] | principles of MAS architecture and communication |
| Web services [149], OWL-S [84] | inspiration for the specification of services |
| existing agent-oriented technologies, e.g. agent platforms | architectural principles |
| modal, deontic, temporal, dynamic, and epistemic logics [147,152] | formal approach to the specification of *distributed artificial intelligence* (*DAI*) systems, extensions of the constraint language |
| MAS theories and abstract models, e.g. DAI [152], BDI [119], CDL [155], SMART [35] | identification of problems to model and principles of formal system specification |

**Tab. 4-1** AML sources (2/2)

## 4.5 The Language Architecture

**UML 2.0 as a base** AML is based on the *UML 2.0 Superstructure* [104], augmenting it with several new modeling concepts appropriate for capturing typical features of multi-agent systems.

The main advantages of this approach are:

❑ Reuse of well-defined, well-founded, and commonly used concepts of UML.

❑ Use of existing mechanisms for specifying and extending UML-based languages (metamodel extensions and UML profiles).

❑ Ease of incorporation into existing UML-based CASE tools.

**Structure of AML** AML is defined at two distinct levels—*AML Metamodel and Notation* and *AML Profiles*. Fig. 4-1 depicts these two levels, their derivation from UML 2.0 and optional extensions based on UML 1.* and 2.0.

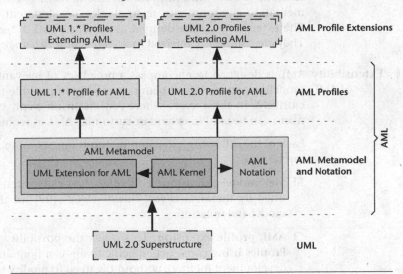

**Fig. 4-1** Levels of AML specification

With reference to Fig. 4-1, the *UML* level contains the UML 2.0 Superstructure which defines the abstract syntax, semantics and notation of UML. AML uses this level as the foundation upon which to define MAS-specific modeling constructs.

The *AML Metamodel and Notation* level defines the AML abstract syntax, semantics and notation. The *AML Metamodel* is further structured into two main packages: *AML Kernel* and *UML Extension for AML*.

The *AML Kernel* package is the core of AML where the AML specific modeling elements are defined. It is logically structured into several packages, each of which covers a specific aspect of MAS. The AML Kernel is a *conservative extension*[7] of UML 2.0

The *UML Extension for AML* package adds meta-properties and structural constraints to the standard UML elements. It is a non-conservative extension of UML, and thus is an optional part of the language. However, the extensions contained within are simple and can be easily implemented in most of the existing UML-based CASE tools and other technologies based on UML and *XML Metadata Interchange (XMI)* [106].

At the level of *AML Profiles*, two UML profiles built upon the AML Metamodel and Notation are provided: *UML 1.\* Profile for AML* (based on UML 1.\*) and *UML 2.0 Profile for AML* (based on UML 2.0). These profiles, inter alia, enable implementation of AML within UML 1.\* and UML 2.0 based CASE tools, respectively.

Based on AML Profiles, users are free to define their own language extensions to customize AML for specific modeling techniques, implementation environments, technologies, development processes, etc. The extensions can be defined as standard UML 1.\* or 2.0 profiles. They are commonly referred to as *AML Profile Extensions*.

**Extensibility of AML**  AML is designed to encompass a broad set of relevant theories and modeling approaches, it being essentially impossible to cover all inclusively. In those cases where AML is insufficient, several mechanisms can be used to extend or customize AML as required.

Each of the following extension methods (and combinations thereof) can be used:

❑ **Metamodel extension.** This offers first-class extensibility—as defined by the *Meta Object Facility (MOF)* [99]—of the AML metamodel and notation.

❑ **AML profile extension.** This offers the possibility to adapt AML Profiles using constructs specific to a given domain, platform, or development method, without the need to modify the underlying AML metamodel.

❑ **Concrete model extension.** This offers the means to employ alternative MAS modeling approaches as complementary specifications to the AML model.

---

[7]  A conservative extension of UML is a strict extension of UML which retains the standard UML semantics in unaltered form [144].

# Chapter 5

# Concepts of AML

In order to properly understand AML, it is necessary to understand its underlying concepts. This chapter provides the reader with a description of the fundamental concepts used to describe an abstract metamodel of a MAS, referred to as the *MAS metamodel* [44]. The intention is not to provide a comprehensive metamodel for all aspects and details of a MAS (such as detailed architectural design, system dynamics, or operational semantics), but rather to explain the concepts that were used as the underlying principles of AML and influenced the design of comprised modeling constructs. The presented conceptual MAS metamodel is used as a basis for the design of the AML metamodel described in Part III.

The conceptual MAS metamodel is described in the form of UML class diagrams, where each class represents a particular concept. UML relationships (generalizations and associations) are used in the metamodel with their standard semantics.

The conceptual MAS metamodel is described by several diagrams, each of which represents the portion capturing a particular MAS aspect. The following sections present the diagrams and brief descriptions of the defined concepts and their relationships.

**Note:** In the metamodel diagrams presented in the following sections, the filled (gray) classes represent the concepts defined within a particular diagram, and the outlined classes represent concepts defined within other diagrams.

## 5.1 Multi-Agent System

**Scope** This part of the conceptual MAS metamodel specifies the overall model of a multi-agent system.

**Metamodel**  Fig. 5-1 shows the metamodel of a multi-agent system.

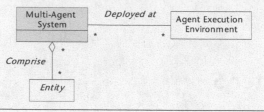

**Fig. 5-1** Conceptual metamodel of a multi-agent system

**Metaclasses**  Description of the defined concepts follows:

**Multi-agent system**
Is a system composed of several agents, capable of mutual interaction [156]. In the AML framework, a multi-agent system consists of, in addition to agents, other entity types, e.g. environments or resources (see section 5.2). In general we say that a multi-agent system comprises entities. Physically, such a system can be deployed on several agent execution environments (see section 5.5).

## 5.2  MAS Semi-entities and Entities

**Scope**  This part of the AML conceptual model of MAS deals with the modeling of constituents of a multi-agent system. MAS may consist of a set of interconnected entities of different types, namely agents, resources and environments. They are represented by concrete classes in the MAS conceptual metamodel. Furthermore, these entities are categorized, according to their specific characteristics, into several categories expressed in the conceptual metamodel by abstract classes used as superclasses to the concrete ones.

**Semi-entities**  In order to maximize reuse and comprehensibility of the concepts, AML defines several auxiliary abstract metamodeling concepts called semi-entities. *Semi-entity* is a modeling concept that defines certain features specific to a particular aspect or aspects of entities, but does not itself represent an entity. All entities inherit their features from semi-entities. Because semi-entities are abstractions, the metaclasses representing semi-entities in the MAS conceptual metamodel are abstract, and therefore they cannot be instantiated at a system's run time. The AML conceptual metamodel of MAS defines the following semi-entities:

**Structural semi-entity**
Represents the capability of an entity to have attributes, to be decomposed into other structural semi-entities, and to be linked to other structural semi-entities. For details see section 5.3.

**Socialized semi-entity**

Represents the capability of an entity to form societies and to participate in social relationships. See section 5.4 for details.

**Behaviored semi-entity**

Represents the ability of an entity to own capabilities, interact with other behaviored semi-entities, provide and use services, to observe and effect their environment by means of perceptors and effectors, and to be decomposed into behavior fragments. For details see section 5.6.

**Mental semi-entity**

Represents the capability of an entity to possess (or to be characterized in terms of) mental attitudes, for example, which information it believes in, what are its objectives, needs, motivations, desires, what goal(s) it is committed to, when and how a particular goal is to be achieved, or which plan to execute. For details see section 5.7.

**Metamodel**  Fig. 5-2 shows the metamodel of the MAS entities.

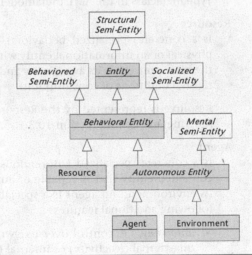

**Fig. 5-2** Conceptual metamodel of MAS entities

**Metaclasses**  Description of the defined concepts follows:

**Entity**

Is an abstract specialized structural semi-entity used to represent an object, which can exist in the system independently of other objects. An entity can be hosted by agent execution environments and can be mobile (see section 5.5).

Entity is represented by the EntityType metaclass in the AML metamodel, see section 10.1.1.

### Behavioral entity

Is an abstract specialized entity which represents entities having the features of behaviored semi-entities (see section 5.6) and socialized semi-entities (see section 5.4), and can play entity roles (see section 5.4).

Behavioral entity is represented by the BehavioralEntityType metaclass in the AML metamodel, see section 10.1.2.

### Autonomous entity

Is an abstract specialized behavioral entity and mental semi-entity (see section 5.7), used to represent self-contained entities that are capable of autonomous behavior in their environment, i.e. entities that have control of their own behavior, and act upon their environment according to the processing of (reasoning on) perceptions of that environment, interactions and/or their mental attitudes. Autonomous entity can be characterized in terms of its mental attitudes (see section 5.7).

Autonomous entity is represented by the AutonomousEntityType metaclass in the AML metamodel, see section 10.1.3.

### Resource

Is a concrete specialized behavioral entity used to represent a physical or an informational entity within the system, with which the main concern is its availability and usage (e.g. quantity, access rights, conditions of consumption).

Resource is represented by the ResourceType metaclass in the AML metamodel, see section 10.3.1.

### Agent

Is a concrete specialized autonomous entity representing a self-contained entity that is capable of autonomous behavior within its environment. An agent is a special object[8] having at least the following additional features:

- *autonomy*, i.e. control over its own state and behavior, based on external (reactivity) or internal (proactivity) stimuli, and

- *ability to interact*, i.e. the capability to interact with its environment, including perceptions, effecting actions, and speech act based interactions.

Other features such as *mobility, adaptability, learning*, etc., are optional in the AML framework.

Agent is represented by the AgentType metaclass in the AML metamodel, see section 10.2.1.

---

[8]  *Object* is defined in the object-oriented paradigm as an entity (in a broader sense) having identity, status and behavior. We do not narrow the concept of object to an object-oriented programming concept.

**Environment**

Is a concrete specialized autonomous entity representing the logical or physical surroundings of a collection of entities which provides conditions under which those entities exist and function. Environment defines a particular aspect or aspects of the world which entities inhabit, its structure and behavior. It can contain the space and all the other objects in the entity surroundings, and also those principles and processes (laws, rules, constraints, policies, services, roles, resources, etc.) which together constitute the circumstances under which entities act. One entity can appear in several environments at once, and one environment can comprise several entities.

Environments are not considered to be static. Their properties, structure, behavior, mental attitudes, participating entities and their features, etc. can change over time.

Environment is represented by the EnvironmentType metaclass in the AML metamodel, see section 10.4.1.

## 5.3 Structural Aspects

**Scope** Entities can be structured internally and externally. The *internal structure* of an entity is given by values of owned attributes and by nesting of entities. The *external structure* of an entity is specified by means of links to other entities.

Attribute represents a set of value-key pairs that are used to specify properties of its owner. Values of all attributes of an entity determine its state.

In order to model hierarchical structures, entities can be nested, i.e. one entity can contain other entities.

An entity can also be linked to other entities. A link represents a semantic relationship of two or more entities that know each other and can communicate.

**Metamodel** Fig. 5-3 shows the metamodel of structural aspects.

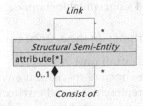

**Fig. 5-3** Conceptual metamodel of structural aspects

**Metaclasses** A description of the defined concepts follows:

**Structural semi-entity**
Is a semi-entity used to represent the capability of an entity to have attributes, to be decomposed into other structural semi-entities, and to be linked to other structural semi-entities.

The AML metamodel does not contain representation of the structural semi-entity explicitly, because the possibility to own attributes, to be decomposed and to be linked is inherited from the UML Class which is used as a common superclass to all semi-entity types defined in the AML metamodel.

## 5.4 Social Aspects

**Scope** Social aspects define the concepts used to model organizational structure of entities, their social relationships and the possibility to play (social) roles.

**Note:** A detailed discussion about the conceptual background and mechanisms of modeling social aspects of multi-agent systems in AML is provided in [20,21].

**Metamodel** Fig. 5-4 shows the metamodel of social aspects.

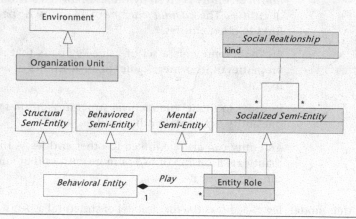

**Fig. 5-4** Conceptual metamodel of social aspects

**Metaclasses** A description of the defined concepts follows:

**Organization unit**
Is a concrete specialized environment type (see section 5.2) used to represent a social environment or its part. Organization units are usually used to model different kinds of societies, e.g. groups, organizations, and institutions.

From an *external perspective*, organization units represent co-herent autonomous entities which can have external structure (see section 5.3), perform behavior, interact with their environment, offer services (see section 5.6), possess mental attitudes (see section 5.7), play roles, etc. Properties and behavior of organization units are both:

- emergent properties and behavior of all their constituents, and

- the properties and behavior of organization units themselves.

From an *internal perspective*, organization units are types of environments that specify the social arrangements of entities in terms of structures, interactions, roles, constraints, norms, etc.

Organization unit is represented by the OrganizationUnitType metaclass in the AML metamodel, see section 10.5.1.

### Socialized semi-entity

Is a semi-entity used to represent the capability of an entity to form societies and to participate in social relationships with other socialized semi-entities.

Socialized semi-entity is represented by the SocializedSemiEntityType metaclass in the AML metamodel, see section 10.5.2.

### Social relationship

Is a particular type of connection between socialized semi-entities related to or having to deal with each other. A social relationship is characterized by its kind. AML predefines two generic kinds of social relationships: peer-to-peer and superordinate-to-subordinate. The set of supported social relationship kinds can be extended as required, e.g. by producer-consumer, competitors, or kinds of interpersonal relationships inspired by sociology, for instance, intimate relationships, sexual relationships, friendship, acquaintanceship, or brotherhood.

Social relationship is represented by the SocialProperty, SocialRoleKind, and SocialAssociation metaclasses in the AML metamodel, see sections 10.5.3, 10.5.4, and 10.5.5.

### Entity role[9]

Is a concrete specialized structural semi-entity (see section 5.3), behaviored semi-entity (see section 5.6), mental semi-entity (see section 5.7), and socialized semi-entity, and is used to represent either a usage of structural properties, execution of a behavior, participation in interactions, or possession of a certain mental

---

[9] AML uses the term 'entity role' rather than the commonly used 'role' [26,40,92,168] to differentiate agent-related roles from the roles defined by UML 2.0 Superstructure, i.e. roles used for collaborations, parts, and associations.

state by a behavioral entity in a particular context (e.g. interaction or social). We say that the behavioral entity, called *entity role player* (or simply *player*), *plays* a given entity role. One behavioral entity can play several entity roles at the same time and can change them dynamically. The entity role exists only while a behavioral entity plays it. Entity role is an abstraction of features required from the behavioral entities which can play it. Each entity role should be realized by a specific implementation possessed by its player. Thus an entity role can be used as an indirect reference to behavioral entities, and as such can be utilized for the definition of reusable patterns (usually defined at the level of types).

Entity role is represented by the EntityRoleType metaclass in the AML metamodel, see section 10.5.6. Playing of entity roles by behavioral entities is modeled by the RoleProperty and Play-Association metaclasses, see sections 10.5.7 and 10.5.8 respectively. The possibility to create new and dispose of existing entity roles dynamically is modeled by special AML actions represented by the CreateRoleAction and DisposeRoleAction metaclasses, see sections 10.5.9 and 10.5.10.

## 5.5 MAS Deployment and Mobility

Scope  MAS deployment specifies the set of concepts that are used to define the execution architecture of a MAS in terms of the deployment of MAS entities to a physical execution environment. The execution environment is modeled by one or more, possibly interconnected and nested, agent execution environments. The placement and operation of entities at agent execution environments is specified by the concept of hosting.

The AML deployment model also supports mobility, i.e. movement or cloning of entities among different agent execution environments, that is modeled by the dynamic reallocation of hostings. A moving entity changes its present hosting to a new one located at another agent execution environment. Cloned entity creates its copy (called *clone*) with a new hosting placed at the same or different agent execution environment.

**Metamodel**  Fig. 5-5 shows the metamodel of MAS deployment.

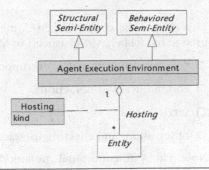

**Fig. 5-5** Conceptual metamodel of MAS deployment in AML

**Metaclasses**  A description of the defined concepts follows:

### Agent execution environment

Is a concrete specialized structural semi-entity (see section 5.3) and behaviored semi-entity (see section 5.6), used to represent an execution environment of a multi-agent system. Agent execution environment provides the physical infrastructure in which MAS entities can run. One entity can run in, at most, one agent execution environment at one time. An agent execution environment can run at one computational resource (computer) or can be distributed among several nodes possibly connected by a network. It can provide (use) a set of services that the deployed entities use (provide) at run time. Owned hostings specify entities hosted by (running at) the agent execution environment.

Agent execution environment is represented by the AgentExecutionEnvironment metaclass in the AML metamodel, see section 10.6.1.

### Hosting

Is a relationship between an entity and the agent execution environment where the entity runs. It can be characterized by the hosting kind, which is one of the following:

- *resident*—the entity is perpetually hosted by the agent execution environment, or

- *visitor*—the entity is temporarily hosted by the agent execution environment.

Hosting is represented by the HostingProperty, HostingKind, and HostingAssociation metaclasses in the AML metamodel, see sections 10.6.2, 10.6.3, and 10.6.4.

## 5.6 Behaviors

**Scope** This part of the conceptual MAS metamodel specifies the concepts used to model behavioral aspects of MAS entities, namely:

❑ behavior abstraction and decomposition,

❑ communicative interactions,

❑ services, and

❑ observations and effecting interactions.

**Note:** The AML conceptual metamodel of MAS is very brief in this part, because AML reuses many of the concepts from UML (concept of behavior, interactions, activities, state machines, etc.), and therefore they do not need to be explicitly mentioned in the AML conceptual metamodel. For principles about how AML utilizes behavioral aspects of UML see sections 6.5 to 6.6.4. The details are described in Chapter 11.

**Metamodel** Fig. 5-6 shows the metamodel of behaviors.

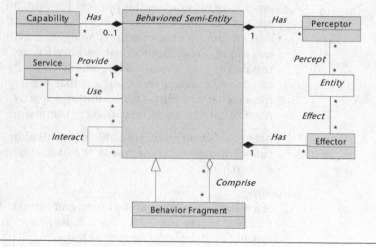

**Fig. 5-6** Conceptual metamodel of behavior abstraction and decomposition

**Metaclasses** A description of the defined concepts follows:

**Behaviored semi-entity**

Is a semi-entity used to represent the ability of an entity to have capabilities, to interact with other behaviored semi-entities, to provide and use services, to perceive and effect, and to be decomposed into behavior fragments.

Behaviored semi-entity is represented by the Behaviored-SemiEntityType metaclass in the AML metamodel, see section 11.1.1.

### Capability

Is used to model an abstract specification of a behavior that allows reasoning about and operations on that specification. Technically, a capability represents a unification of common specification properties of UML's behavioral features and behaviors expressed in terms of inputs outputs, pre- and post-conditions.

Capability is represented by the Capability metaclass in the AML metamodel, see section 11.1.2.

### Behavior fragment

Is a concrete specialized behaviored semi-entity used to represent a coherent reusable fragment of behavior. It is used to decompose a complex behavior into simpler and possibly concurrently executable fragments. A behavior fragment can be shared by several behaviored semi-entities and behavior of a behaviored semi-entity can be (possibly recursively) decomposed into several behavior fragments.

Behavior fragment is represented by the BehaviorFragment metaclass in the AML metamodel, see section 11.2.1.

### Service

Is a coherent block of functionality provided by a behaviored semi-entity, called *service provider*, that can be accessed by other behaviored semi-entities, called *service clients*.

Specification of a service is represented by the ServiceSpecification and ServiceProtocol metaclasses in the AML metamodel, see sections 11.4.1 and 11.4.2. The possibility to provide and use services is represented by the ServiceProvision and Service-Usage metaclasses, see sections 11.4.6 and 11.4.7 respectively.

### Perceptor[10]

Is a means to enable its owner, a behaviored semi-entity, to observe, i.e. perceive a state of and/or to receive a signal from its environment (surrounding entities).

Perceptor and its type is represented by the Perceptor, PerceptorType and PerceivingAct metaclasses in the AML metamodel, see section 11.5.3, 11.5.2, and 11.5.1. Perceiving action is modeled by the PerceptAction metaclass, see section 11.5.4, and the relationship between the perceiving behaviored semi-entity and perceived entity is represented by the Perceives metaclass, see section 11.5.5.

---

[10] Called also *sensor*.

**Effector[11]**

Is a means to enable its owner, a behaviored semi-entity, to bring about an effect on others, i.e. to directly manipulate with (or modify a state of) some other entities.

Effector and its type is represented by the Effector, EffectorType and EffectingAct metaclasses in the AML metamodel, see sections 11.5.8, 11.5.7, and 11.5.6. Effect action is modeled by the EffectAction metaclass, see section 11.5.9, and the relationship between the effecting behaviored semi-entity and effected entity is represented by the Effects metaclass, see section 11.5.10.

## 5.7 Mental Aspects

**Scope** Autonomous entities can be characterized by their mental attitudes (such as beliefs, goals, and plans), which represent their informational, motivational and deliberative states. This part of the conceptual MAS metamodel deals with modeling these aspects.

**Metamodel** Fig. 5-7 shows the metamodel of mental aspects.

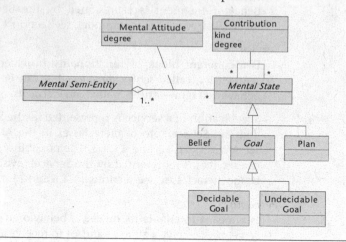

**Fig. 5-7** Conceptual metamodel of mental aspects

**Metaclasses** A description of the defined concepts follows:

**Mental semi-entity**

Is a semi-entity used to represent the capability of an entity to have mental attitudes.

Mental semi-entity is represented by the MentalSemiEntityType metaclass in the AML metamodel, see section 12.1.7.

---

[11] Called also *actuator*.

**Mental state**

Is an abstract concept serving as a common superclass to all the metaclasses which can be used to specify mental attitudes of mental semi-entities. Mental states can be related by contributions. Mental states referred to by several mental semi-entities simultaneously represent their common mental states, e.g. common beliefs or common goals.

Mental state is represented by the MentalState, MentalClass, and ConstrainedMentalClass metaclasses in the AML metamodel, see sections 12.1.1, 12.1.2, and 12.1.3.

**Mental attitude**

Is a relationship between a mental semi-entity and a mental state representing that the mental semi-entity possesses the mental state as its mental attitude, i.e. it believes a belief, is committed to a goal, or is intended to perform a plan. Mental attitude is characterized by the degree attribute of which the semantics may vary with the concrete type of the linked mental state. It represents either the subjective reliability or confidence of the linked mental semi-entity in the information specified by belief, relative importance of a goal, or preference of a plan.

Mental attitude is represented by the MentalProperty and MentalAssociation metaclasses in the AML metamodel, see sections 12.1.8 and 12.1.9.

**Belief**

Is a concrete specialized mental state used to model information which mental semi-entities have (believe) about themselves or their environment, and which does not need to be objectively true.

Belief is represented by the Belief metaclass in the AML metamodel, see section 12.2.1.

**Goal**

Is an abstract specialized mental state used to model conditions of states of affairs, the achievement or maintenance of which is controlled by an owning (committed) mental semi-entity. Goals are thus used to represent objectives, needs, motivations, desires, etc. of mental semi-entities.

Goal is represented by the Goal metaclass in the AML metamodel, see section 12.3.1.

**Decidable goal**

Is a concrete specialized goal used to model goals for which there are clear-cut criteria according to which the mental semi-entity controlling the goal can decide whether the goal has been achieved or not.

Decidable goal is represented by the DecidableGoal metaclass in the AML metamodel, see section 12.3.2.

**Undecidable goal**

Is a concrete specialized goal used to model goals for which there are no clear-cut criteria according to which the mental semi-entity controlling the goal can decide whether the goal has been achieved or not.

Undecidable goal is represented by the UndecidableGoal meta-class in the AML metamodel, see section 12.3.3.

**Plan**

Is a concrete specialized mental state used to represent an activity (expressed e.g. by a series of steps) that a mental semi-entity is intended to perform.

Plan is represented by the Plan metaclass in the AML meta-model, see section 12.4.1.

**Contribution**

Represents a logical relationship between mental states. Contribution specifies the manner in which the *contributor* (a mental state which contributes) influences its *beneficiary* (a mental state which is contributed to). Contribution refers to the conditions which characterize related mental states (e.g. pre-conditions, post-conditions, and invariants) and specifies their logical relationship in terms of logical implication. AML thus defines three kinds of contribution: necessary, sufficient, and equivalent. Contribution's degree can be used to specify the extent to which the contributor influences the beneficiary.

Contribution is represented by the Contribution metaclass in the AML metamodel, see section 12.5.1.

## 5.8 Ontologies

Scope The basic means for modeling ontologies in AML are ontology classes and instances, their relationships, and ontology utilities. Ontologies are structured by means of the ontology packages. This model is relatively simple, but general enough and flexible.

**Metamodel**  Fig. 5-8 shows the metamodel of ontologies.

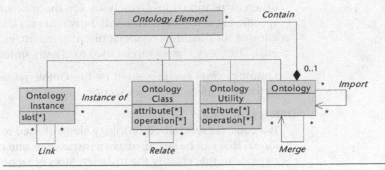

**Fig. 5-8** Conceptual metamodel of ontologies

**Metaclasses**  A description of the defined concepts follows:

**Ontology element**

Is an abstract concept representing any element which is a part of an ontology.

There is no equivalent of the ontology element in the AML metamodel, because the association Contain (which is the main purpose of existence of the ontology element) from the conceptual MAS metamodel, is already expressed in the UML metamodel and inherited by AML metaclasses[12].

**Ontology**

Is a concrete specialized ontology element used to specify a single ontology. Ontology can contain a set of ontology elements, including other ontologies. Ontology can import elements from other ontologies and can also merge several other ontologies. The mechanism of ontology import is identical to the UML package import, and the mechanism of ontology merge is analogous to the UML package merge. See [104] for details.

Ontology is represented by the Ontology metaclass in the AML metamodel, see section 13.1.1.

**Ontology class**

Is a concrete specialized ontology element used to represent an ontology class defined as the specification of a group of individuals that belong together because they share some properties [110]. An ontology class can be characterized by attributes and operations. Attributes state relationships between individuals or from individuals to data values. Operations represent the invocation of

---

[12] AML metaclass Ontology specialize UML Package and AML metaclasses OntologyClass and OntologyUtility both specialize UML metaclass Class. Because a UML class, as specialized named element, can be member of a package, which is specialized namespace, also AML ontology classes and utilities can therefore be members of ontologies.

related behavior. Ontology classes can be related to each other by different relationships, which are for the sake of simplicity not specified in detail here, and AML fully relies on UML relationships allowed for classifiers (associations, dependencies, generalization, etc.). Ontology classes can be used to classify ontology instances.

Ontology class is represented by the OntologyClass metaclass in the AML metamodel, see section 13.1.2.

### Ontology instance

Is a concrete specialized ontology element used to define an individual that can be specified as an instance of one or several ontology classes that classify the instance. Slots of an ontology instance refer to the values that characterize status of the instance. Slots correspond to the properties defined for classifying ontology classes, if specified. Ontology instances can be linked to each other to represent their acquaintance and interactions.

To model ontology instances, AML reuses the mechanism of instance specifications from UML. Therefore the AML metamodel does not contain any explicit representation of the ontology instance.

### Ontology utility

Is a concrete specialized ontology element used to cluster global *ontology constants*, *ontology variables*, and *ontology functions/actions/predicates* modeled as owned attributes and operations. Properties of a ontology utility can be used by (referred to by) other ontology elements within the owning and importing ontologies.

Ontology utility is represented by the OntologyUtility metaclass in the AML metamodel, see section 13.1.3.

# Chapter 6

# AML Modeling Mechanisms

This chapter describes the principles of modeling systems by AML. Formation of the AML modeling mechanisms, expressed by the language's metamodel and notation, comes out of the concepts from the AML conceptual MAS metamodel expressed by means of the (extended and customized) modeling constructs of UML. Therefore the main, immediate sources for designing AML language were firstly, its conceptual model (see Chapter 5) and secondly, the UML 2.0 Superstructure [104].

Our intention is to discuss in this chapter the selected modeling principles that differentiate AML from other modeling approaches and those that significantly influence the character of modeling systems with AML. For a detailed description of all particular modeling elements, including their notation which is not explained in this chapter, we refer to Part III. For details about the AML architecture and the way in which it extends the UML 2.0 Superstructure see Fig. 4-1 in Chapter 4.

**Used example** Throughout this chapter we will demonstrate the explained AML modeling mechanisms on examples taken from a simplified case study of the software soccer simulator. The system:

1. Enables two teams of simulated autonomous players to play a soccer match and visualizes it for the user. This part of the system is similar e.g. to the *RoboCup Soccer Simulator* [122], *Java RoboCup Simulator* [62], or the *MiS20 - Robotic Soccer* simulator [87].

2. Simulates some activities of a soccer league related to its organization and operation. The focus is on social constitution and interactions of soccer associations organizing leagues, clubs, players, referees, etc.

**Note:** The presented modeling examples use the AML notation described in Part III, not in this chapter. However, we believe that the textual descriptions explaining the examples are sufficient to understand the presented models without frequent consultation of Part III.

## 6.1  Generic Modeling Mechanisms

This section describes the generic AML modeling mechanisms applied in the design of several modeling constructs.

### 6.1.1  Class and Instance Levels

All kinds of the AML semi-entities, and inherently also entities, are modeled as *types* (AgentType, EnvironmentType, EntityRoleType, etc.). All types are specialized UML classes. This principle, in accordance with the four-layer metamodeling specification model defined by MOF, allows the modeling of (semi-)entities either at the class level, or by exploiting the UML instantiation mechanism, at the instance level, or at both levels.

The *class level* specifies the types of (semi-)entities, their properties and relationships. This level of abstraction allows the explicit specification of the principal features of entities without needing to specify particular individuals. The class level model is specified as a UML class model, with the specification of classes, other classifiers (Agent-Type, ResourceType, EnvironmentType, EntityRoleType, etc.) and their relationships (associations, dependencies, generalizations, etc.).

The *instance level* models allow, by means of instances, the representation of snapshots of the running system. The instances represent (semi-)entities with the specification of values of their structural features and the concrete links among them. The instance level is modeled by means of the UML instance specification. There is the possibility to explicitly refer to the class level modeling elements which have been instantiated into the modeled instance level elements by the mechanism of instance classification.

UML, and therefore also AML, allows the specification of multiple and dynamic classification [8,10,94]. *Multiple classification* allows one instance to be classified by several classifiers[13] to determine that the instance is an instance of all its classifiers. In this case the instance can possess values to all the properties specified by all its classifiers. Multiple classification is used to combine the classifiers and their features into entities at the instance level. This is an important mechanism which allows flexibility in application types and their features in the instance specification.

*Dynamic classification* means that the set of classifiers of one instance can change over time. This mechanism allows dynamic reclassification of instances in the system and therefore also dynamic change of

---

[13] Class is a specialized (i.e. inherits from) Classifier in the UML metamodel. Therefore also AML (semi-)entities are classifiers and can be used to classify instances.

their owned features and behaviors (not values of their slots, but the set of slots as such). Because UML 2.0 provides a special action ReclassifyObjectAction to change instance's classification, the dynamic change of classifiers can be modeled in the context of activity diagrams and can be incorporated into an entity's behavior. Entities can change their own classification or classification of other entities, depending on the level of autonomy.

## 6.1.2 Utilization of Structural Features

The modeling of (semi-)entity types as specialized UML classes allows AML to make use of UML structural features[14] to model specific characteristics of the (semi-)entity types corresponding to specific MAS aspects. In addition to the traditional usage of structural features as owned attributes or ports, AML exploits them to also model:

◻ social relationships of specific kinds among socialized semi-entities,

◻ possibility to play entity roles of a given type under specific conditions,

◻ hosting and running entities at the agent execution environments,

◻ provision and usage of services, and

◻ possessing mental attitudes.

Technically, this is realized by specialization of the UML Property[15] metaclass into several specific properties, each of which corresponds to one of the aforementioned purposes.

In general, the AML-specific properties are used to represent relationship, see Fig. 6-1 (a), between their owning (semi-)entities and their types (also (semi-)entities). A property can be owned either as an owned attribute or as a navigable end of a connected association.

An owned attribute represents a unidirectional relationship of its owner to its type. The (semi-)entity type referred to by the property's type is not aware of the relationship. See Fig. 6-1 (b).

To allow modeling of bidirectional relationships where one (semi-)entity type is aware of other(s) and vice versa, associations connecting several (two or more) properties can be utilized. A navigable end

---

[14] A structural feature is an abstract typed feature of a classifier that specify the structure of instances of the classifier [104]. It is in the UML 2.0 Superstructure represented by the StructuralFeature metaclass. Its concrete subclasses are Property and Port.

[15] In UML metamodel, the metaclass Property is a subclass of the metaclass StructuralFeature.

of a connected association represents a relationship of its owner to the opposite end type (the type of corresponding property). See Fig. 6-1 (c).

The kind of represented relationship varies for different property kinds. The following specialized AML properties are defined:

❏ social property (for details see section 6.3.1),

❏ role property (for details see section 6.3.1),

❏ hosting property (for details see section 6.4),

❏ service property (for details see section 6.6.3), and

❏ mental property (for details see section 6.7).

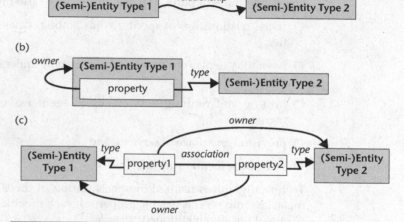

**Fig. 6-1** Representation of relationships by owned properties: (a) relationship in principle, (b) one-directional relationship modeled as an owned attribute, and (c) possibly bi-directional relationship represented by association.

Exploiting UML structural features for representing specialized MAS aspects gives us another advantage which resides in convenient and straightforward definition of dynamic changes of their values (modeled by means of UML state machines), and also incorporation of their changes and reasoning about their values into the system's algorithms (modeled by means of UML activities). For this purpose a special UML event ChangeEvent (which may also occur when some values of structural features and/or links change) can be used in state machines to trigger transitions or actions based on changing MAS-specific properties. UML also specifies a rich set of actions for manipulating the structural feature values and links (AddStructuralFeature-ValueAction, ClearStructuralFeatureAction, CreateLinkAction, Create-LinkObjectAction, ReadStructuralFeatureAction, RemoveStructuralFeatureValueAction etc.), which can be used to model accessing the MAS-specific properties within activities.

In addition, by combining these actions with other UML actions (e.g. used to create or destroy objects), AML also defines higher-level actions for structural changes (CreateRoleAction, DisposeRoleAction, CommitGoalAction, CloneAction, etc.) that cumulate more commonly used operation sequences into single actions thus simplifying activity models.

## 6.2 Modeling Entity Types

**All entity types as specialized classes**  As discussed in section 6.1.1, all AML semi-entities and entities are modeled as specialized UML classes. Consequently, (semi-)entity types inherit, and therefore can make use of, a rich set of the modeling possibilities allowed for UML classes. They can:

- ❑ be placed into packages,
- ❑ be named and commented,
- ❑ own attributes,
- ❑ own operations and receptions,
- ❑ define nested classes (including other entity types),
- ❑ be specialized and redefined by inheritance,
- ❑ be connected by associations, dependencies,
- ❑ be decomposed into parts, ports, and their connectors,
- ❑ be used as type for attributes, parts, operations, parameters, etc.,
- ❑ own behaviors (activities, state machines, use cases, etc.),
- ❑ characterize associations as the association classes,
- ❑ provide and/or realize interfaces,
- ❑ define tagged values, etc.

For details on the aforementioned features see UML 2.0 Superstructure [104].

Because all of these features are inherited from UML, the AML metamodel does not need to define them explicitly, even if the entity types can exploit them. Such a simplified AML metamodel and quite rich set of modeling features was the primary motivation to designate the UML Class metaclass as a common superclass to all AML semi-entity type metaclasses (i.e. SocializedSemiEntityType, Behaviored-SemiEntityType, and MentalSemiEntityType).

Some other agent-oriented modeling languages based on UML (AUML, MAS-ML, etc.) define their metamodels of MAS entities (agents, groups, environments, etc.) based on an abstract UML meta-class Classifier. If such a language intends to provide a subset of the modeling features taken e.g. from the UML Class, its metamodel must define semantically similar (or the same) meta-elements as in the UML metamodel. We consider this approach as cumbersome, which can lead to inconsistencies between UML and the modeling language based upon UML. Furthermore, it would be difficult to define the implementable UML profile for such a language, because the stereotypes should be based on concrete UML modeling element types (i.e. concrete metaclasses in UML), not on abstract ones.

**Abstract entity types**  In order to maximize reuse and comprehensibility of the metamodel, AML defines an abstract entity type for each of the abstract entities defined in section 5.2. The AML metamodel, therefore, defines the following metaclasses: entity type, behavioral entity type, and autonomous entity type.

**Entity type** (metaclass EntityType) is an abstract specialized UML metaclass Type used to represent types of entities of a multi-agent system.

**Behavioral entity type** (metaclass BehavioralEntityType) is an abstract specialized entity type, behaviored semi-entity type (see section 6.5), and socialized semi-entity type (see section 6.3.1) used to represent types of behavioral entities. In addition to the modeling features inherited from these semi-entity types, and indirectly also from UML class, a behavioral entity type can also specify playing of entity roles modeled as owned role properties, see section 6.3.1 for details.

**Autonomous entity type** (metaclass AutonomousEntityType) is an abstract specialized behavioral entity type and mental semi-entity type (see section 6.7) used to model types of autonomous entities.

The aforementioned AML metaclasses representing the abstract entity types are used within the metamodel to specify common characteristics and features inherited by other (abstract or concrete) metaclasses.

**Concrete entity types**  AML defines three modeling constructs used to model types of fundamental MAS entities: agents, environments, and resources.

**Agent type** (metaclass AgentType) is a specialized autonomous entity type used to model the type of agents.

**Resource type** (metaclass ResourceType) is a specialized behavioral entity type used to model the type of resources within the system[16].

---

[16] A resource positioned outside a system is modeled as a UML actor.

**Environment type** (metaclass EnvironmentType) is a specialized autonomous entity type used to model the type of a system's inner environment[17].

To model the internal structure of enclosed entities and objects, environment types usually utilize the possibilities inherited from UML structured classifier and model them by means of contained parts, ports and connectors. Aggregation and composition associations are also used.

**Modeling autonomy**
Because autonomy is one of the fundamental characteristics of MASs, it is worth mentioning how it is modeled within the framework of AML.

Autonomy cannot be modeled as a single element or as a declaration that a given entity is autonomous or not. Autonomy is a relatively vague concept that can be obtained only by analysis of the entity's behavior, structural features, and how they can be accessed by other entities.

In real situations absolute autonomy rarely exists, if at all. Entities are usually autonomous only to some extent or only in some aspects of their behavior. One entity can expose full autonomy over some part of its behavior, while only partial or non autonomy over another one.

By providing specific autonomous entity types, AML can model autonomous entities. But it must be clarified that not every entity classified as an autonomous entity (e.g. an agent) must be really autonomous (even agents can be with certain respects or with certain situations fully dependent). AML autonomous entity type does not automatically guarantee autonomy; it just enables entities to be modeled at different levels of autonomy.

Autonomy is technically realized by the combination of the following modeling elements and their properties:

❏ **Visibility of features.**
   The public or protected features of an entity that are accessible from other entities can be used for the direct manipulation of an entity's state (by accessing attributes) or for the direct invocation of an entity's behavior (by calling operations) that decreases its autonomy. Private features increase autonomy.

❏ **Ownership of receptions.**
   If an entity owns receptions, it is obliged to provide a certain behavior for processing a corresponding signal from its environment. The behavior is executed each time the signal occurs, and possibly certain conditions (modeled as reception's pre-condi-

---

[17] *Inner environment* is that part of an entity's environment that is contained within the boundaries of the system.

tions) are fulfilled, independently from an entity's current intentions. Declaring receptions decrease an entity's autonomy, because it can be directly influenced from environment.

❏ **Performing actions on other entities.**
Several kinds of UML actions can directly change the status of other entities (AddStructuralFeatureValueAction, RemoveStructuralFeatureValueAction, etc.), call their operations (CallOperationAction), send signals (SendSignalAction), execute their behavior (CallBehaviorAction), etc. Their use in activities can decrease the level of autonomy.

❏ **Using triggers based on changes of other entities.**
If a trigger, used within a state machine owned by an entity, is based on changes of other entities (i.e. it uses the UML change event), it may decrease autonomy of its owning entity, because its state and/or executed actions may depend on the state of the watched entities.

❏ **Effecting other entities.**
An entity being effected by other entities is less autonomous, because its state can be affected or its behavior can be triggered by the effecting entities.

❏ **Dependent owned mental states.**
If mental states (beliefs, goals, and plans) of an entity depend on mental states of other entities, it looses its autonomy. Autonomous entities eliminate influences of other entities on their own mental attitudes.

Based on these properties, *fully autonomous entities* are characterized as entities with no public and protected features, no receptions, no owned behavior called from external behaviors, no triggers in their state machines based on changes of other entities, no effects by other entities, and no owned mental states depending on the mental states of other entities. *Partially autonomous entities* can break any of these rules. *Non-autonomous entities* either break all the rules, or have the respective modeling properties unspecified (do not own attributes, operations, behaviors, etc.).

**Example 1:** Fig. 6-2 shows a model of MAS entity types, classes, and their relationships used to model constituents of a physical environment for a soccer game. An abstract class 3DObject represents spatial objects, characterized by shape and position, existing inside a containing space. An abstract environment type 3DSpace represents a three dimensional space. This is a special 3DObject and as such can contain other spatial objects. Three concrete 3DObjects are defined: an agent type Person, a resource type Ball and a class Goal. 3DSpace is furthermore specialized into a concrete environment type Pitch representing a soccer pitch containing two goals, one ball, and several persons participating in the game.

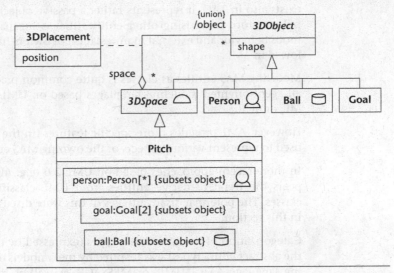

**Fig. 6-2** Example of MAS entity types

**Example 2:** Fig. 6-3 shows the specification of the agent type Person. It has the attribute name, and possesses parts referring to the behavior fragments Reasoning, Sight and Mobility, which provide the person with corresponding sets of capabilities; for details see section 6.5. The agent type Person interacts with its environment by means of the perceptor eyes, and effectors hands and legs; for details see section 6.6.4. The owned perceptors and effectors require corresponding services, namely Localization, Manipulation and Motion, provided by the person's environment.

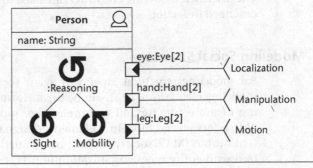

**Fig. 6-3** Example of an agent type

**Comparison to other approaches** Because MAS entities are the fundamental concepts of multi-agent systems, they appear as modeling elements in all existing agent-oriented modeling languages. Agents are represented in each modeling language, resources appear relatively rarely (for example, in Prometheus, Tropos, or MESSAGE), but the concept of environments as autonomous entities is unique. Even if the notion of environment exists also in TAO, it represents rather a passive object with an internal structure comprising other entities that is incapable of autonomous behavior and external manifestation of own behavior, as it is allowed in AML.

Modeling MAS entities as classes is quite common practice in almost all agent-oriented modeling languages based on UML 1.*, e.g. MAS-ML, or AOR.

However, AML provides more specific features (in the sense of UML) used to represent various aspects of the owning MAS entities.

In more recent approaches based on UML 2.0 (e.g. AUML) there appears the trend to derive entities from UML classifiers instead of classes. The potential disadvantages of this were discussed previously in this section.

Categorization of the AML entity types (expressed by the structure of the abstract entity types) was inspired by metamodels of other modeling languages, e.g. AUML, or MESSAGE, as well as theoretical MAS metamodels, e.g. SMART.

## 6.3  Modeling Social Aspects

This section presents mechanisms of AML to model social aspects of multi-agent systems. The modeling of structural as well as behavioral aspects of multi-agent systems from the social perspective is discussed and demonstrated by examples.

The discussed modeling constructs are used to represent the concepts described in section 5.4.

### 6.3.1  Modeling Social Structure

For modeling structural aspects of agent societies, to some extent, modeling elements of UML can be used. However, to allow the building of more concise and comprehensive models of MAS societies, AML offers several modeling elements designated to explicitly represent various (MAS) society abstractions. In particular these are: socialized semi-entity types, organization unit types, entity role types, social relationships, role properties and play associations.

**Modeling social entities** **Organization unit type** (metaclass OrganizationUnitType) is a specialized environment type, and thus inherits features of behaviored, socialized and mental semi-entity types, as well as of UML class. It is used to model the type of organization units, i.e. societies (groups, organizations, institutions, etc.) that can evolve within the system from both the external as well as internal perspectives, as described in section 5.4.

For modeling organization unit types from the external perspective, in addition to the features defined for UML classes (structural and behavioral features, owned behaviors, relationships, etc.), all the features of behaviored, socialized, and mental semi-entity types can also be utilized.

To model the internal perspective of organization unit types, they usually utilize the possibilities inherited from UML structured classifier, and model their internal structure by contained parts and connectors, in combination with entity role types used as types of the parts.

**Socialized semi-entity type** (metaclass SocializedSemiEntityType) is a specialized UML class used to model the type of socialized semi-entities. Possible participation of socialized semi-entities of a given type in social relationships is modeled by means of owned social properties.

Socialized semi-entity types represent modeling elements, which would most likely participate in communicative interactions, and therefore they can specify related properties, particularly: a set of agent communication languages, a set of content languages, a set of message content encodings, and a set of ontologies they support.

**Modeling social relationships** Apart from other general-purpose UML relationships applicable in social models (generalization, aggregation, association, etc.), AML defines a special kind of UML property, called social property, and a special kind of UML association, called social association, used to model social relationships.

The **social property** (metaclass SocialProperty) is a specialized UML property used to represent a social relationship of the property's owner, a social semi-entity type, to the social semi-entity type referred to by the property's type. In addition to UML property, social property allows the specification of the relationship's social role kind. AML supports two predefined kinds of social relationships, peer-to-peer and superordinate-to-subordinate, and the analogous social role kinds: peer, superordinate, and subordinate. The set of supported social role kinds can be extended as required (e.g. to model producer-consumer, competitive, or cooperative relationships). Social property can be used either in the form of an owned social attribute or as the end of a social association.

**Social association** (metaclass SocialAssociation) connects two or more social properties in order to model bi-directional social relationships. In addition to social attributes, the social associations also provide an alternative way of modeling social relationships in the form of UML relationships.

**Example 1:** Fig. 6-4 shows a simplified model of a soccer league. A league is represented by the organization unit type SoccerLeague. It is organized by (subordinated to) some entity or entities modeled as an abstract organization unit type LeagueOrganizer. SoccerLeague comprises many registered referees (modeled by the entity role type Referee) and soccer teams (represented by entity role type SocerTeams). Soccer teams compete with each other. Each soccer team has many players (modeled by entity role type TeamPlayer) who play for the team. Soccer team is superordinated to each team player. The diagram also depicts players who are not in teams but are their potential members. Such players are modeled by the entity role type FreePlayer. Common properties of TeamPlayer and FreePlayer are extracted to their common superclass, an abstract entity role type Player.

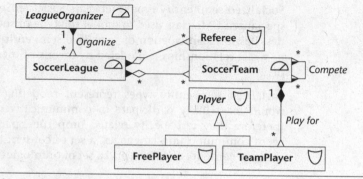

**Fig. 6-4** Example of a soccer league organization structure

**Example 2:** Fig. 6-5 depicts a simplified model of the organization structure of a soccer match.

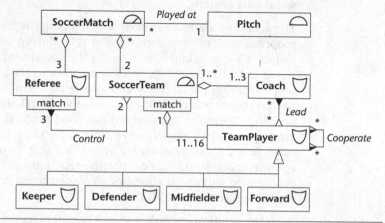

**Fig. 6-5** Example of a soccer match organization structure

The top-most organization unit type SoccerMatch represents a soccer match itself. It is played at a pitch (modeled as an environment type

Pitch) and comprises three referees and two soccer teams. Entity role type Referee models referees of a soccer match who control the two soccer teams within a given soccer match. Organization unit type SoccerTeam represents participating soccer teams. Each consists of one to three coaches and eleven to sixteen players. The entity role type Coach models coaches of a soccer team who supervise (are super-ordinated to) the players in a team (modeled by social association Lead). Abstract entity role type TeamPlayer models soccer players of a team who cooperate with each other (modeled by social association Cooperate). The TeamPlayer is specialized into several concrete entity role types representing specific roles of players in a team, in particular Keeper, Defender, Midfielder and Forward.

**Modeling entity roles** Entity roles are used to define a normative behavioral repertoire of entities and thus provide the basic building blocks of MAS societies. For modeling entity roles, AML provides **entity role type** (metaclass EntityRoleType), a specialized behaviored semi-entity type (see section 6.5), socialized semi-entity type (see section 6.3.1), and mental semi-entity type (see section 6.7). It is used to model a coherent set of features, behaviors, relationships, participation in interactions, observations, and services offered or required by entities participating in a particular context. Each entity role type, being an abstraction of a set of capabilities, should be realized by a specific implementation possessed by a behavioral entity type that can play that entity role type.

Entity roles types can thus be effectively used to specify (1) social structures, (2) positions[18], and also (3) required structural, behavioral and attitudinal features of their constituents.

The AML approach provides the possibility to model social roles at both the class level—where the required types of features and behavior are defined, and the instance level—where the concrete property values and behavior realization of a particular role playing can be specified explicitly.

**Example 3:** Fig. 6-6 shows a simplified example of the entity role type Player representing the type of a soccer player and its specialization TeamPlayer representing a player as a member of a soccer team. The Player specifies attribute active to determine whether the player is in the field or on the bench and association Possess to model the situation if a player has a ball in possession. In addition to Player, the entity role type TeamPlayer has an attribute number to identify him in his team.

---

[18] A *position* is a set of roles typically played by one agent [4]. Positions are in AML explicitly modeled by means of composed entity roles types.

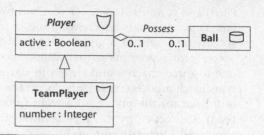

**Fig. 6-6** Example of an entity role type

**Entity role playing** The possibility of playing an entity role by a behavioral entity is modeled by the role property and the play association.

**Role property** (metaclass RoleProperty) is a specialized UML property used to specify that an instance of its owner (a behavioral entity type) can play one or several entity roles of the entity role type specified as the property's type.

An instance of a role property's owner represents the entity role player (or simply player). An instance of the role property's type represents the played entity role. The role property can be used either in the form of a role attribute or as the member end of a play association.

One entity can at each time play several entity roles. These entity roles can be of the same as well as of different types. The multiplicity defined for a role property constraints the number of entity roles of a given type that the particular entity can play concurrently. Additional constraints which govern playing of entity roles can be specified by UML constraints.

The AML approach to model role playing allows:

❑ Specification of the possibility to play particular entity roles by entities expressed at the class level, and the actual playing of entity roles by instances expressed at the instance level.

❑ Separation of an entity's own features and behaviors from the features and behaviors required for playing an entity role in a particular situation.

❑ Separation of a specification of the features, behavior, and attitudes required (or expected) from a potential player of that entity role from their actual realization by actual players.

❑ Specification of the behavior related to role playing, for instance, role playing dynamics, life cycle of roles, or reasoning about roles (for more details see section 6.3.2)

**Play association** (metaclass PlayAssociation) is a specialized UML association used to specify a role property in the form of an association end.

**Example 4:** Fig. 6-7 models that an agent of type Person can play entity roles of type FreePlayer, TeamPlayer, Coach, and Referee. The possibility of playing entity roles of a particular type is modeled by play associations. A person cannot be a free player and a team player at the same time, that is expressed by a constraint on corresponding play associations.

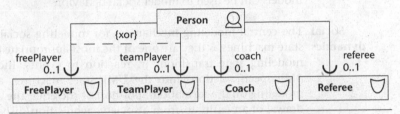

**Fig. 6-7** Example of role properties specified as play association ends

**Comparison to other approaches** Social ability of agents is one of their most fundamental properties and therefore of central concern for the majority of the MAS modeling approaches.

Modeling of organization units, usually known as organizations, groups or institutional agents, is contained in most of the socially aware modeling languages, e.g. MESSAGE, AUML, and MAS-ML.

Explicit modeling of social relationships similar to AML social association, known as acquaintance relationships (Gaia, MESSAGE, Prometheus, etc.) or plain associations in UML-based modeling languages (AUML, PASSI, etc.), appear in some modeling languages. However, classification of the social relationship kind (peer-to-peer or superordinate-subordinate) is new for AML. Notion of the social property is new as well.

Also, the modeling of roles is quite an obvious feature available in Gaia, AUML, PASSI, MESSAGE, MAS-ML, etc. Nevertheless, the AML approach to model entity roles as complex semi-entities with social, behavioral, and mental properties is unique. Similarly, the AML interpretation of entity roles (i.e. instances) do not appear in other approaches. Therefore, AML mechanism of modeling entity roles at the level of classes and instances is considered to be a very interesting and useful feature.

Modeling the entity role playing by utilizing structural features is also a very effective and useful mechanism introduced by AML, which allows the expression of static and dynamic aspects of the role playing. This does not appear in other modeling languages.

## 6.3.2 Modeling Social Behavior

Social behavior is the behavior of a social entity (behavior of a single social entity, or emergent behavior of a society) which influences or is influenced by the state (social features, attitudes, etc.) or behavior of other social entities (members of the society or the society itself). Social behavior thus covers social dynamics, social interactions, and social activities.

This section briefly describes how AML extensions to UML behavioral models can be used to model social behavior.

**Social dynamics** The central modeling mechanism for modeling social dynamics are state machines as they are one of the most appropriate techniques for modeling state transitions in reaction to events. Incorporation of AML specific actions into the UML state machines allows explicit modeling of: the formation/abolition of societies, the entrance/withdrawal of an entity to/from a society, acquisition/disposal/change of a role by an entity, etc.

**Social interactions** To model social interactions, AML defines specialized modeling constructs for modeling speech act based interactions (see section 6.6 for details), observations and effecting interactions (see section 6.6.4 for details).

**Social activities** For modeling social activities UML activities can be used. However, to allow development of more concise and comprehensive models, AML offers several additional modeling concepts and mechanisms.

To allow modeling of modification of social features (i.e. social relationships, roles played, social attitudes), they are modeled as structural features of entities. This allows the use of all UML actions for manipulation with structural features (AddStructuralFeatureValueAction, ClearStructuralFeatureAction, CreateLinkAction, CreateLinkObjectAction, ReadStructuralFeatureAction, RemoveStructuralFeatureValueAction, etc.) to model modification of social structures, reasoning about played entity roles, access and reason about social attitudes, execute social behavior, etc.

Furthermore, to allow explicit manipulation of entity roles in UML activities and state machines, AML defines two actions for entity role creation and disposal, namely **create role action** (metaclass CreateRoleAction) and **dispose role action** (metaclass DisposeRoleAction).

**Example:** Fig. 6-8 shows an example of the activity describing the scenario of recruitment of a new free soccer player into a team.

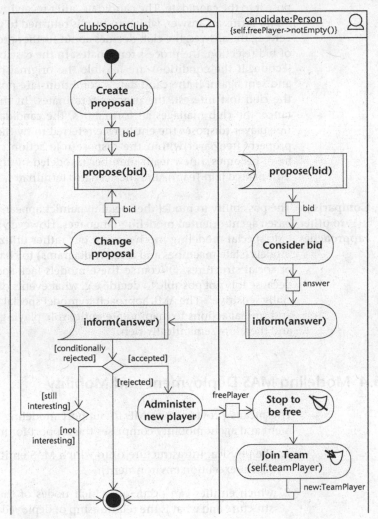

**Fig. 6-8** Example of role manipulation actions

The activity comprises two activity partitions: an organization unit club representing a SportClub which recruits a new player and an agent candidate representing the recruited free player (candidate's role property freePlayer is set and therefore the candidate plays an entity role of the type FreePlayer, see Fig. 6-7). The presented scenario is simplified and does neither comprise some actions nor involve some concerned entities (e.g. the player's agent) as it is in reality. However, it is sufficient to demonstrate the discussed modeling mechanisms.

The club, after previous selection of a potential candidate, creates a proposal for the contract (modeled as an object named bid), and propose it to the candidate. The candidate, after receiving a bid, considers it and forms an answer, which in turn is returned to the club. After receiving the answer, the club decides about further process. In the case of bid rejection, the process terminates. In the case of conditional rejection, if the conditions are feasible the original offer is modified and sent again. If the candidate's conditions are not feasible and/or the club lost interest, the process terminates. In the case of acceptance, the club manages all formalities, the candidate stops being a free player (disposes the entity role referred to by the partition's role property freePlayer within the dispose role action called Stop to be free), becomes a new team member (modeled by the create role action named Join Team), and the scenario terminates.

**Comparison to other approaches** The possibility to model the social dynamics appears mostly in UML-based agent-oriented modeling languages. However, they do not provide special modeling mechanisms, but rather utilize standard UML models (state machines and activity diagrams) to change role playing or social structures. Of course these models lack specific semantics, because it is not possible to decide e.g. what events or actions are "socially sensitive". The AML approach to model special social properties and special actions to manipulate entity role playing is more explicit and therefore semantically rich.

## 6.4 Modeling MAS Deployment and Mobility

The means provided by AML to support modeling of MAS deployment and agent mobility comprises the support for modeling:

1. the physical infrastructure onto which MAS entities are deployed (agent execution environment),

2. which entities can occur on which nodes of the physical infrastructure and what is the relationship of deployed entities to those nodes (hosting property),

3. how entities can get to a particular node of the physical infrastructure (move and clone dependencies), and

4. what can cause the entity's movement or cloning throughout the physical infrastructure (move and clone actions).

**MAS deployment** **Agent execution environment** (metaclass AgentExecutionEnvironment) is a specialized UML execution environment used to model types of execution environments within which MAS entities can run. While it is a behaviored semi-entity type, it can specify e.g. a set of services that the deployed entities can use or should provide at run time.

Agent execution environment can also own hosting properties, which are used to classify the entities which can be hosted by that agent execution environment.

**Hosting property** (metaclass HostingProperty) is used to specify what entity type, referred to by the property's type, can be hosted by an agent execution environment, an owner of the hosting property. The property can also specify the type of hosting which specifies the relationship of the referred entity type to the owning agent execution environment. It is either *resident* (an entity of the given type is perpetually hosted by the agent execution environment), or *visitor* (an entity of the given type can be temporarily hosted by the agent execution environment, i.e. it can be temporarily moved or cloned to the specified agent execution environment).

**Hosting association** (metaclass HostingAssociation) is a specialized UML association used to specify hosting property in the form of an association end.

**MAS mobility**  AML also supports modeling of mobility, which is understood as moving or cloning the deployed entities between different hosting properties. To model these moving/cloning paths in the class diagrams explicitly, AML defines two relationships: move and clone.

**Move** (metaclass Move) is a specialized UML dependency between two hosting properties, used to specify that the entities represented by the source hosting property can be moved to the instances of the agent execution environment owning the destination hosting property.

**Clone** (metaclass Clone), a specialized UML dependency between two hosting properties, is used to specify that the entities represented by the source hosting property can be cloned to the instances of the agent execution environment owning the destination hosting property.

AML does not specify the type and other details of moving or cloning, which may be technology dependent.

**MAS deployment-related behavior**  For modeling deployment-related activities (action of placement and displacement of entities into agent execution environments, reasoning about the place of entity's deployment, etc.), standard UML actions for manipulation structural features can be used. The reason is that the deployment of MAS entities into agent execution environments is modeled by means of the hosting properties, which are specialized structural features.

**Mobility-** AML provides two additional actions to explicitly model acts of mov-
**related** ing and cloning, namely **move action** (metaclass MoveAction) and
**behavior** **clone action** (metaclass CloneAction).

Move and clone actions are specialized UML add structural feature actions used to model actions that cause movement or cloning of an entity from one agent execution environment to another one. Both the
actions thus specify:

1. which entity is being moved or cloned,

2. the destination agent execution environment instance where the
   entity is being moved or cloned, and

3. the hosting property where the moved or cloned entity is being
   placed.

**Example:** Fig. 6-9 shows the example of a MAS deployment model.

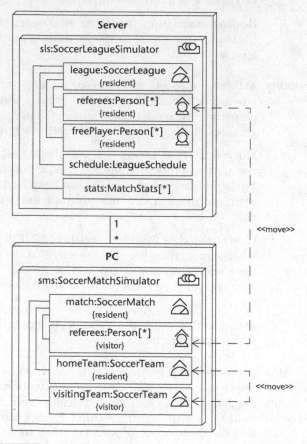

**Fig. 6-9** Example of a MAS deployment and mobility model

The diagram depicts a part of the soccer league simulator's physical deployment model. A node Server runs an agent execution environment SoccerLeagueSimulator used to run the soccer league simulator. It comprises one organization unit SoccerLeague (referred to by the hosting property league), a pool of referees (agents of type Person playing the entity role referee, see Fig. 6-7) registered in the league, free players (agents of type Person playing entity role freePlayer, see Fig. 6-7), league schedule (part schedule), and statistics of the soccer matches and their results (part stats). The Server is connected to several PC nodes, each of which runs an agent execution environment SoccerMatchSimulator. The SoccerMatchSimulator enables the performance of a simulated soccer match of the homeTeam against the visitingTeam under supervision of referees. The agents referred to by the referees hosting property move to a SoccerMatchSimulator from a pool of registered referees within the SoccerLeagueSimulator. A SoccerTeam referred to by the visitingTeam hosting property moves from another PC. After a match the referees and the visitingTeam move back to their resident hosting places.

**Comparison to other approaches** Only a few agent-oriented modeling languages deal with modeling of mobility explicitly. *m-GAIA* [137], an extension of GAIA towards mobility, provides concepts similar to AML (place types, movement and travelling paths) but with less comprehensive modeling language. Furthermore it does not provide the mobility-related dynamics and behavior.

The second approach that is able to model mobility is the extension of AUML presented in [116]. This approach extends the UML 2.0 deployment diagrams, in a similar way as AML does. The used modeling constructs allow the modeling of the deployment only at the instance level of nodes and components, and the used notation is relatively confusing. In reality, the deployment diagrams become easily unreadable, because this approach enforces the use of many relationships (*reside*, *acquaintance*, etc.). Similar to m-GAIA, the authors do not provide any mechanisms for the mobility-related dynamics and behavior.

Compared to the existing modeling approaches, AML allows the modeling of mobility more complexly, and covers the static deployment structure, as well as the mobility dynamics and behavior.

## 6.5 Modeling Capabilities and Behavior Decomposition

AML extends the capacity of UML to abstract and decompose behavior by two other modeling elements: capability and behavior fragment.

**Modeling behaviored semi-entities** To better understand AML behavioral models, we first explain the modeling concept of behaviored semi-entity type, which is commonly used in the AML metamodel to represent the possibility of an entity type to make use of AML-specific extensions of the UML behavior modeling.

**Behaviored semi-entity type** (metaclass BehavioredSemiEntityType) is a specialized UML class and serviced element used to model the type of behaviored semi-entities. Technically, it can own capabilities, be decomposed into behavior fragments, provide and use services (see section 6.6.3), and own perceptors and effectors (see section 6.6.4).

**Modeling capabilities** **Capability** (metaclass Capability) is an abstract specification of a behavior which allows reasoning about and operations on that specification. Technically, a capability represents a unification of the common specification properties of UML's behavioral features and behaviors, expressed in terms of their inputs, outputs, pre-conditions, and post-conditions.

**Example:** Fig. 6-10 (b) shows some of the capabilities of a soccer player modeled as operations of behavior fragments. Furthermore, the explicit pre- and post-conditions are specified for the capability BallManipulation::shoot().

**Modeling behavior decomposition** **Behavior fragment** (metaclass BehaviorFragment) is a specialized behaviored semi-entity type used to model a coherent reusable fragment of behavior and related structural and behavioral features. It enables the (possibly recursive) decomposition of a complex behavior into simpler and (possibly) concurrently executable fragments, as well as the dynamic modification of an entity behavior at run time. The decomposition of a behavior of an entity is modeled by owned aggregate attributes of the corresponding behavior fragment type.

**Example:** Fig. 6-10 (a) shows the decomposition of an entity role type's behavior into behavior fragments. The behavior of the entity role type Player is decomposed into three behavior fragments: SoccerPlayerThinking, Teamwork, and BallManipulation. Fig. 6-10 (b) shows the definition of the used behavior fragments. SoccerPlayerThinking comprises different strategies and ad-hoc behaviors of a soccer player. Strategy allows the execution of a certain strategy which influences the global long-term behavior of a player. AdHocReaction allows short-term behaviors triggered by a particular situation, e.g. certain pre-learned tricks. Teamwork comprises social capabilities of a soccer player within his team. BallManipulation is used to manipulate the ball.

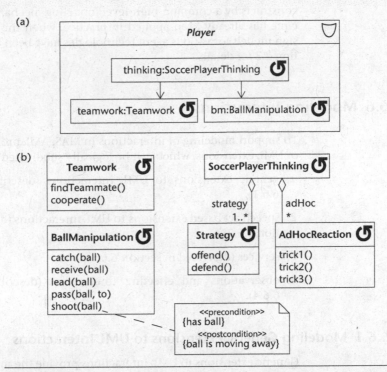

**Fig. 6-10** Example of behavior fragments: (a)   decomposition   of   a behavior of an entity role, (b) definition of used behavior fragments.

**Comparison to other approaches** An agent's capabilities are explicitly modeled in very few agent-oriented modeling languages. The notion 'capability' is used rather informally and other terms are used instead, for example, service (in Gaia), task (in PASSI), or plan (in TROPOS). These approaches understand capabilities as the concepts similar to the UML behavior, which is a quite restrictive view. In addition, most of them do not provide meta-information used to specify the capability characteristics (i.e. inputs, outputs, pre- and post-conditions) as in AML.

The AML approach was inspired mainly by the *Capability Description Language (CDL)* [155], providing a formal basis for specification and reasoning about capabilities of agents in a MAS. We transformed the CDL concepts into the context of UML modeling and, by unification of behavioral features and behaviors, we provided a unique approach to model capabilities.

Explicit modeling of behavior fragments, as reusable libraries of capabilities, does not appear in any other modeling language. The AML concept of behavior fragment was inspired by several agent-based technologies, e.g. *message handlers* or *fragments* in LS/TS [81], *capabilities* in Lars [89], or *plugins* in Cougaar [27]. Therefore, due to AML behavior fragments, it is possible to represent these technology-specific constructs by a common high-level modeling mechanism. This principle has already been applied in practice, when the AML-based design models for various agent technologies have been created, see section 7.3 for details.

## 6.6 Modeling Interactions

To support modeling of interactions in MAS, AML provides a number of UML extensions, which can be logically subdivided into:

1. generic extensions to UML interactions (described in section 6.6.1),

2. speech act based extensions to UML interactions (described in section 6.6.2),

3. services (described in section 6.6.3), and

4. observations and effecting interactions (described in section 6.6.4).

### 6.6.1 Modeling Generic Extensions to UML Interactions

Generic extensions to UML interactions provide the means to model:

1. interactions between groups of entities (multi-lifeline and multi-message),

2. dynamic change of an object's attribute values to express changes in state, internal structure, relationships, played entity roles, etc. of entities induced by interactions (attribute change),

3. messages and signals not explicitly associated with the invocation of corresponding methods and receptions (decoupled message),

4. mechanisms for modification of interaction roles of entities (not necessary entity roles) induced by interactions (subset and join dependencies), and

5. actions of dispatch and reception of decoupled messages in activities (send and decoupled message actions, and associated triggers).

**Multi-lifeline** (metaclass MultiLifeline) is a specialized UML lifeline used to represent (unlike UML lifeline) multiple participants in interactions.

**Multi-message** (metaclass MultiMessage) is a specialized UML message which is used to model particular communication between (unlike UML message) multiple participants, i.e. multiple senders and/or multiple receivers.

**Decoupled message** (metaclass DecoupledMessage) is a specialized multi-message used to model asynchronous dispatch and reception of a message payload without (unlike UML message) explicit specification of the behavior invoked on the side of the receiver. The decision of which behavior should be invoked when the decoupled message is received is up to the receiver what allows the preservation of its autonomy in processing messages.

**Attribute change** (metaclass AttributeChange) is a specialized UML interaction fragment used to model the change of attribute values (state) of interacting entities induced by the interaction. Attribute change thus enables the expression of addition, removal, or modification of attribute values, as well as the expression of the added attribute values by sub-lifelines. The most likely utilization of attribute change is in the modeling of dynamic change of entity roles played by behavioral entities represented by lifelines in interactions and in the modeling of entity interactions with respect to the played entity roles (i.e. each sub-lifeline representing a played entity role can be used to model interaction of its player with respect to this entity role).

**Subset** (metaclass Subset) is a specialized UML dependency between event occurrences owned by two distinct (superset and subset) lifelines. It is used to specify that, since the event occurrence on the superset lifeline, some of the instances it represents (specified by the corresponding selector) are also represented by another, the subset lifeline.

Similarly, **join** (metaclass Join) dependency is also a specialized UML dependency between two event occurrences on lifelines (subset and union ones). It is used to specify that a subset of instances, which have been until the subset event occurrence represented by the subset lifeline, is, after the union event occurrence, represented by the union lifeline. Thus after the union event occurrence, the union lifeline represents the union of the instances it has previously represented and the instances specified by the join dependency.

**Send decoupled message action** (metaclass SendDecoupledMessage-Action) is a specialized UML send object action used to model the action of dispatch of a decoupled message, and **accept decoupled message action** (metaclass AcceptDecoupledMessageAction) is a specialized UML accept event action used to model reception of a decoupled message action that meets the conditions specified by the associated decoupled message trigger.

**Example:** Fig. 6-11 shows an example of the communicative interaction in which the attribute change elements are used to model changes of entity roles played by agents. The diagram realizes the scenario of the change of a captain which takes place when the original captain is substituted.

At the beginning of the scenario the agent player2 is a captain (modeled by its role property captain). During the substitution, the main coach gives the player2 order to hand the captainship over (handCaptainshipOver() message) and the player1 the order to become the captain (becomeCaptain() message). After receiving these messages, player2 stops playing the entity role captain (and starts playing the entity role of ordinary player) and player1 changes from ordinary player to captain.

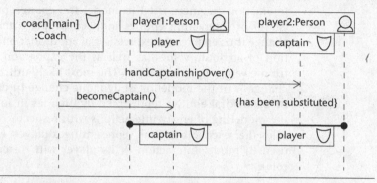

Fig. 6-11 Example of a social interaction with entity role changes

**Comparison to other approaches** Interactions, as the primary mechanism used in agents' communication, are covered by almost all agent-based modeling languages. For this purpose, most of the UML-based modeling languages use standard UML interaction diagrams without modifications. However, this approach is insufficient, because agents do not treat messages in the traditional object-oriented approach, where messages represent the direct invocation of the respective methods. Rather, an agent, after receiving a message, (autonomously) decides which method (capability or behavior) to invoke, if any.

Only AUML and MAS-ML extend the UML interaction model. Both provide several specific modeling mechanisms to allow modeling advanced interactions which occur in MAS. However, AUML does not address all related problems and does not provide technical solutions for decoupling a message reception from the execution of receiver's method, discriminating receivers of multi-messages, effective modeling of role changing, and so on. MAS-ML provides only mechanisms related to the social dynamics, namely lifecycle of playing roles and occurrence within organizations and environments. Therefore it has relatively limited scope.

AML provides a consistent framework for modeling advanced interactions which solves all the aforementioned problems. Furthermore, all the aforementioned AML extensions to the UML 2.0 interaction modeling represent innovations (or any semantically equivalent modeling constructs) which do not appear in other UML-based agent-oriented modeling languages.

It is also worth mentioning that AML, as the only UML-based agent-oriented modeling language, also provides notational equivalents to all its UML interaction model extensions for the communication diagrams.

## 6.6.2 Modeling Speech Act Specific Extensions to UML Interactions

Speech act specific extensions to UML interactions comprise modeling of:

1. speech acts (communication message),

2. speech act based interactions (communicative interactions),

3. patterns of interactions (interaction protocols), and

4. actions of dispatch and reception of speech act based messages in activities (send and accept communicative message actions and associated triggers).

**Communication message** (metaclass CommunicationMessage) is a specialized decoupled message used to model communicative acts of speech act based communication within communicative interactions with the possibility of explicit specification of the message performative and payload.

**Communicative interaction** (metaclass CommunicativeInteraction) is a a specialized UML interaction used to represent a speech act based interaction.

Both the communication message and communicative interaction can also specify used agent communication and content languages, ontology and payload encoding.

**Interaction protocol** (metaclass InteractionProtocol) is a parameterized communicative interaction template used to model reusable templates of communicative interactions.

**Send communication message action** (metaclass SendCommunicationMessageAction) is a specialized UML send object action used to model the action of dispatching a communication message, and **accept communication message action** (metaclass AcceptCommunicationMessageAction) is a specialized UML accept event action used to model reception of a communication message action that meets the conditions specified by the associated communication message trigger.

**Example:** A simplified interaction between entities taking part in a player substitution is depicted in Fig. 6-12. Once the main coach decides which players are to be substituted (p1 to be substituted and p2 to be the substitute), he first notifies player p2 to get ready and then asks the main referee for permission to make the substitution. The main referee in turn replies by an answer. If the answer is "accepted", the substitution process waits until the game is interrupted. If so, the coach instructs player p1 to exit and p2 to enter. Player p1 then leaves the pitch and joins the group of inactive players, and p2 joins the pitch and, thus, the group of active players.

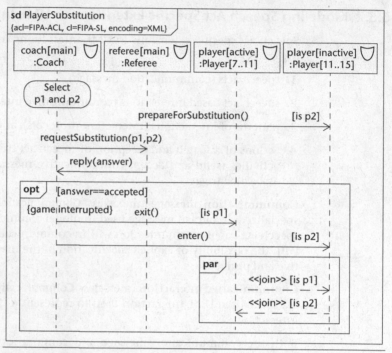

Fig. 6-12 Example of a communicative interaction

**Comparison to other approaches** Despite the quite common incorporation of interaction modeling into existing MAS modeling languages, most of them do not provide sufficient means to model speech act based interactions explicitly. For instance UML-based languages (AUML, MAS-ML, etc.) model the speech acts implicitly, i.e. as plain UML messages. It is then difficult to decide at the level of model semantics what is UML message and what is speech act based message. Furthermore, none of the examined agent-oriented modeling languages provides explicit modeling of the speech act characteristics (like communication language, content language, ontology, etc.).

AML differentiates between speech act messages and the traditional UML messages. This allows the combination of both interaction approaches mentioned above.

Modeling of interaction protocols can also be found in other agent-oriented modeling languages (Gaia, AUML, MAS-ML, PASSI, etc.), but they mostly use less comprehensive modeling elements. For instance

AUML uses stereotyped UML note to express the formal protocol parameters, instead of the more natural template parameters as in AML.

In some modeling languages the interaction protocols are specified at an insufficient level of detail. For instance, Gaia describes protocols textually in terms of their purposes, initiators, responders, inputs, outputs, and descriptions of processing; instead of by a detailed specification of exchanged messages. On one hand this kind of specification provides a high level abstraction, but on the other hand it is insufficient to describe actual communication and therefore cannot be straightforwardly used for designing interactions.

Another deficiency is that even if the interaction protocols can be modeled, the existing modeling languages do not provide mechanisms for binding the formal protocol parameters to actual values and therefore do not enable the specification of concrete interactions in this way. The only endeavor to solve this problem can be found in an older version of AUML, which has already been deprecated by FIPA.

AML can solve all of the aforementioned problems.

### 6.6.3 Modeling Services

A *service* is a coherent block of functionality provided by a behaviored semi-entity, called *service provider*, that can be accessed by other behaviored semi-entities (which can be either external or internal parts of the service provider), called *service clients*.

The AML support for modeling services includes:

1. the means for the specification of the functionality of a service and the way a service can be accessed (service specification and service protocol),

2. the means for the specification of what entities provide/use services (service provision, service usage, and serviced property), and

3. the means for the specification of the distinct interaction points for provision and use of services (serviced port).

**Service specification** (metaclass ServiceSpecification) is used to specify a service by means of owned service protocols. A service specification can also contain structural features to model additional structural characteristics of the service, e.g. attributes can be used to model the service parameters. A service specification can, in addition to the service protocols, also own other behaviors describing additional behavioral aspects of the service; for instance, interaction overview diagrams used to describe the overall algorithm (also called the process) of invoking particular service protocols, etc.

**Service protocol** (metaclass ServiceSpecification) is a specialized interaction protocols extended with the ability to specify two mandatory,
disjoint and non-empty sets of (not bound) parameters, particularly:
provider and client template parameters.

The **provider template parameters** of all contained service protocols
specify the set of the template parameters that must be bound by the
service providers, and the **client template parameters** of all contained service protocols specify the set of template parameters that
must be bound by the service clients. Binding of these complementary template parameters specifies the features of the particular service provision/usage which are dependent on its providers and clients. Binding of all these complementary template parameters results
in the specification of the communicative interactions between the
service providers and the service clients.

**Service provision** (metaclass ServiceProvision) and **service usage**
(metaclass ServiceUsage) are specialized UML dependencies used, in
combination with the binding of template parameters that are declared to be bound by service providers/clients, to model provi-
sion/use of a service by particular entities.

Technically, the services can be provided and/or used only by behaviored semi-entity types, serviced properties, and serviced ports, commonly called *serviced elements*.

**Serviced property** (metaclass ServicedProperty) is a specialized UML
property used to model attributes that can provide or use services.

Analogously, **serviced port** (metaclass ServicedPort) is a specialized
UML property used to model ports that can provide or use services.

**Example 1:** Fig. 6-13 shows a specification of the Motion service defined as a collection of three service protocols. The CanMove service
protocol is based on the standard FIPA protocol FIPA-Query-Protocol
[46] and binds the proposition parameter (the content of a query-if
message) to the capability canMove(what, to) of a service provider.
The participant parameter of the FIPA-Query-Protocol is mapped to a
service provider and the initiator parameter to a service client. The
CanMove service protocol is used by the service client to ask if an object referred by the what parameter can be moved to the position referred by the to parameter. The remaining service protocols MoveFor-
ward and Turn are based on the FIPA-Request-Protocol [46] (see also
Fig. 11-48 and Fig. 11-49) and are used to change the position or direction of a spatial object.

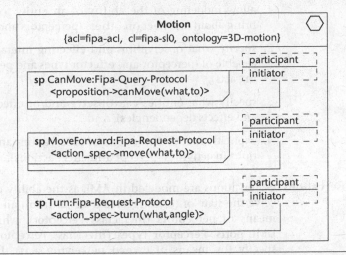

**Fig. 6-13** Example of service specification

**Example 2:** Binding of the Motion service specification to the provider 3DSpace and the client Person is depicted in Fig. 6-14.

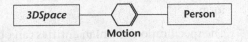

**Fig. 6-14** Example of service provision and usage

**Comparison to other approaches** Explicit specification of services as patterns of interactions, together with obligations of the service provider and user is a unique approach and does not appear in other agent-oriented modeling languages.

## 6.6.4 Modeling Observations and Effecting Interactions

To extend the repertoire of supported interaction mechanisms by providing high-level abstractions of information exchange, AML enables modeling of observations and effecting interactions.

*Observation* is the act of perceiving the environment, or its part, with the purpose of obtaining information about its state or changes of its state. In observation, the observed entity does not need to be aware of observing, and therefore observations are not considered to be interactions.

*Effecting interaction* is the act of directly manipulating the state of another entity. The affected entity does not need to be aware that it is being changed, and also it cannot avoid the subsequent execution of its own behavior caused by an effecting interaction after it happens.

AML provides several mechanisms for modeling observations and effecting interactions in order to:

1. allow modeling of the ability of an entity to observe and/or to bring about an effect on others (perceptors and effectors),

2. specify what observation and effecting interactions the entity is capable of (perceptor and effector types and perceiving and effecting acts),

3. specify what entities can observe and/or effect others (perceives and effects dependencies), and

4. explicitly model the actions of observations and effecting interactions in activities (percept and effect actions).

**Observations**  Observations are modeled in AML as the ability of an entity to perceive the state of (or to receive a signal from) an observed object by means of **perceptors** (metaclass Perceptor), which are specialized UML ports. **Perceptor types** (metaclass PerceptorType) are used to specify (by means of owned perceiving acts) the observations an owner of a perceptor of that type can make.

**Perceiving acts** (metaclass PerceivingAct) are specialized UML operations which can be owned by perceptor types and thus used to specify what perceptions their owners, or perceptors of given type, can perform.

The specification of which entities can observe others is modeled by a **perceives** (metaclass Perceives) dependency. For modeling behavioral aspects of observations, AML provides a specialized **percept action** (metaclass PerceptAction) used to specify invocation of a perceiving act from within activities.

**Effecting**  Different aspects of effecting interactions are modeled analogously, **interactions**  by means of **effectors** (metaclass Effector), **effector types** (metaclass EffectorType), **effecting acts** (metaclass EffectingAct), **effects** dependencies (metaclass Effects), and **effect actions** (metaclass EffectAction).

**Example 1:** Fig. 6-15 shows a specification of the perceptor type Eye, which is used to provide information about status of the environment where the Player, described in Fig. 6-17, is placed. The Eye provides two perceiving acts (look and localize), which return information about surrounding objects and their positions, and can process the signal newObjectAppeared, which is raised when a new object appears in a view angle.

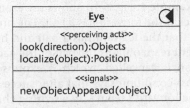

**Fig. 6-15** Example of perceptor type

**Example 2:** Fig. 6-16 shows a specification of the effector type Leg, which is used to move in the environment of the Player, described in Fig. 6-17. The Leg provides several effecting acts: step used to move a player one step in the specified direction, walk to enable a player to walk to the specified position, run to enable a player to run to the specified position, kick to perform kicking of a player to the specified object, and soccer-specific leadBall to combine running with leading a ball.

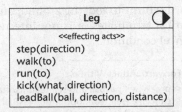

**Fig. 6-16** Example of effector type

**Example 3:** Fig. 6-17 shows an entity role type Player having two eyes—perceptors named eye of type Eye, and two legs—effectors named leg of type Leg. Eyes are used to see other players, the pitch and the ball. Legs are used to change the player's position within the pitch (modeled by changing of internal state implying that no effects dependency need be placed in the diagram), and to manipulate the ball.

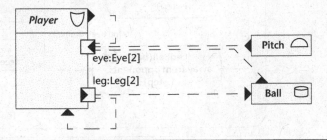

**Fig. 6-17** Example of perceives and effects dependencies

**Example 4:** Fig. 6-18 shows an example of the forward's plan to attack if the forward has a ball. The precondition for executing the plan is that the forward has a ball and his team is attacking. If the opponent team obtains the ball or the game is interrupted, the plan execution is cancelled, which is expressed in the cancel condition. The post-condition says that after successful accomplishment of the plan the forward's team is in a scoring chance or one of the teammates has the ball. The plan starts with obtaining information about the surroundings of the player as the result of an execution of the percept action look. If the opponent's goal is near the team reached the scoring chance, the plan terminates successfully. In the other case, the forward either leads the ball towards the opponent's goal (if no opponent is near), or tries to find a free teammate to whom to pass the ball. This is expressed by the leadBall effect action and Find free teammate action, respectively. If a free teammate is found, the forward passes him the ball (kickBall effect action). Otherwise, the forward tries to avoid attacks of opponents by leading the ball away from them. After leading the ball one step in the desired direction, the forward returns to looking around, and the whole algorithm is repeated until it terminates or is not interrupted by satisfaction of the plan's cancel condition.

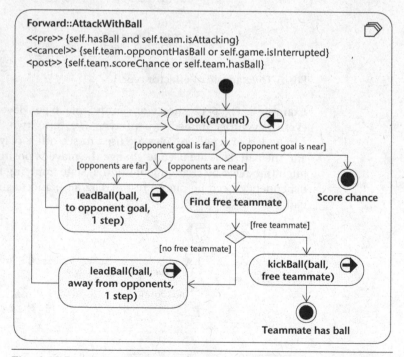

**Fig. 6-18** Example of percept actions and effect actions used in plan

Comparison   Very simple and semantically weak modeling of observations and ef-
to other   fecting interactions appears in Prometheus. Agents can declare what
approaches   percepts they can receive and what actions they can do in order to effect their environment.

Complex modeling of non-communicative interactions and effecting
acts, as well as explicit modeling of perceptors and effectors in AML is
a unique approach that does not appear in other agent-oriented modeling languages to this extent.

## 6.7 Modeling Mental Aspects

Mental semi-entities can be characterized in terms of their mental attitudes, i.e. motivations, needs, wishes, intentions, goals, beliefs,
commitments, etc. To allow modeling all the above, AML provides:
goals, beliefs, plans, contribution relationships, mental properties
and associations, mental constraints, and commit/cancel goal actions.

Modeling   **Mental semi-entity type** (metaclass MentalSemiEntityType) is a spe-
mental semi-   cialized UML class used to model the type of mental semi-entities.
entities
Possible mental attitudes of mental semi-entity types are modeled by
means of a special type of UML property called mental property. **Mental property** (metaclass MentalProperty) is used to specify that instances of its owner, i.e. mental semi-entities, have control over instances of the mental classes (see section 12.1.2) referred to by property's type, for example, can decide whether to believe or not (and to
what extent) in a belief, or whether and when to commit to a goal.

Mental property can be used either in the form of an owned mental
attribute or as the end of a mental association.

In general, two kinds of mental attitudes can be recognized:

1. mental attitudes shared by several entities within a society, such
   as common beliefs, goals, and plans which include collaboration
   of several entities, etc. By shared mental attitudes we can express
   the kinds of cooperation between mental semi-entities, and in
   this way refine their social relationships (implicit, or modeled explicitly). For instance cooperative entities share their goals, trust-
   ed entities share their beliefs, superordinate entities dictate their
   goals or form goals of subordinate entities, competitive entities
   have goals in contradiction, etc., and

2. mental attitudes of individual entities toward anything of a social
   value, for example, commitments to perform social actions, or beliefs in some facts about other entities.

Both cases can be modeled by AML.

**Mental states**  **Belief** (metaclass Belief) is a specialized UML class used to model a state of affairs, proposition or other information relevant to the system and its mental model.

**Goal** (metaclass Goal) is an abstract specialized UML class used to model types of goals, i.e. conditions or states of affairs with which the main concern is their achievement or maintenance. Goals can thus be used to represent objectives, needs, motivations, desires, etc.

AML defines two special kinds of goals:

**Decidable goal (metaclass DecidableGoal)**
A goal for which there are clear-cut criteria according to which the *goal-holder*[19] can decide whether the decidable goal (particularly its post-condition) has been achieved or not.

**Undecidable goal (metaclass UndecidableGoal)**
A goal for which there are no clear-cut criteria according to which the goal-holder can decide whether the post-condition of the undecidable goal is achieved or not.

Beliefs and goals are modeled as specialized UML classes which allows their modeling at both class and instance levels. The belief and goal classes can therefore be used as the types of mental properties. The attitude of a mental semi-entity to a concrete belief (e.g. 'Player Ronaldo in 8th minute of the match recognized a scoring chance.') or commitment to a concrete goal (e.g. 'Player Ronaldo decided to score a goal.') is modeled by the belief or the goal instance being held in a slot of the corresponding mental property.

**Plan** (metaclass Plan) is a specialized UML activity used to model predefined plans or fragments of behavior from which the plans can be composed.

All the mentioned mental states can be characterized by various kinds of conditions (pre-conditions, post-conditions, commit conditions, cancel conditions and invariants) that are technically specified by means of mental constraints.

**Mental constraint** (metaclass MentalConstraint) is a specialized UML constraint used to specify properties of owning beliefs, goals and plans which can be used within the reasoning processes of mental semi-entities.

**Mental**  **Contribution** (metaclass Contribution) is a specialized UML directed
**relationships** relationship used to model logical relationships between goals, beliefs, plans and their mental constraints. The manner in which the specified mental constraint (e.g. post-condition) of the contributor

---

[19] *Goal-holder* is the stakeholder or mental semi-entity which has control over a goal. Stakeholder is an individual who is affected by the system or by the system modeling process.

influences the specified mental constraint kind of the beneficiary (e.g. pre-condition) as well as the degree of the contribution can also be specified.

**Responsibility** (metaclass Responsibility) is a specialized UML realization used to model a relation between a belief, goal or plan (called *responsibility object*) and an element (called *responsibility subject*) which is obligated to accomplish (or to contribute to the accomplishment of) this belief, goal, or plan (e.g. modification of the belief, achievement or maintenance of the goal, or realization of the plan).

**Mental actions** AML provides two special actions to explicitly model commitments to and de-commitments from goals within activities.

**Commit goal action** (metaclass CommitGoalAction) is a specialized UML create object action and add structural feature value action, used to model the action of commitment to a goal by instantiating the goal (type) and adding the created instance as a value to a mental property of the committing mental semi-entity.

**Cancel goal action** (metaclass CancelGoalAction) is a specialized UML destroy object action used to model de-commitment from goals by destruction of the corresponding goal instances.

Even though these actions can be used in any activities, they are usually used in plans.

**Example 1:** Fig. 6-19 shows the detail of a decidable goal named ObtainBall which represents a desire of a soccer player to obtain the ball. Keyword 'self' from the owned mental constraints is therefore used to refer to the player (an entity playing an entity role of type TeamPlayer, see Fig. 6-5). The goal is committed to whenever the player's team looses the ball. In order to commit to the goal, the player must be free (no opponent is blocking the player). If its team (some teammate) obtains the ball or the game is interrupted, the player abandons this goal. The goal is successfully accomplished when the soccer player obtains the ball. The default degree of committing to this goal is 0.5; however it can be overridden by any goal instance owner.

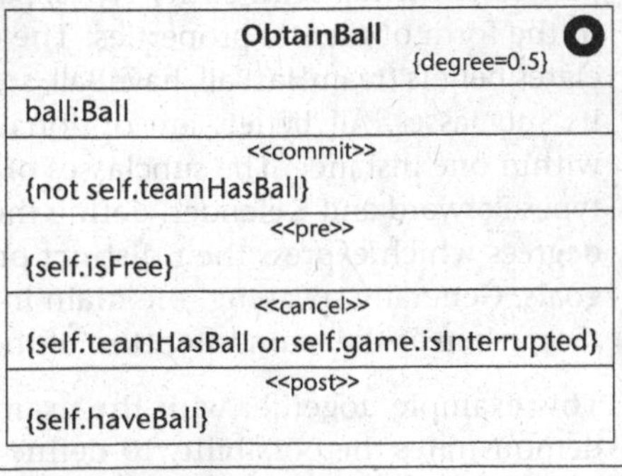

| ObtainBall ○ {degree=0.5} |
| --- |
| ball:Ball |
| <<commit>> |
| {not self.teamHasBall} |
| <<pre>> |
| {self.isFree} |
| <<cancel>> |
| {self.teamHasBall or self.game.isInterrupted} |
| <<post>> |
| {self.haveBall} |

Fig. 6-19 Example of decidable goal

**Example 2:** Fig. 6-18 shows an example of the plan.

**Example 3:** Fig. 6-20 shows the class-level mental model of the soccer player's basic tactics by means of beliefs, decidable goals and their mutual contributions. The semantics of the model is as follows: The player is either attacking or defending, depending on which team keeps the ball. During attacking the player can create the scoring chance, score goal (if he has the ball and possibly there occurs a scoring chance), or block opponents (if a teammate has the ball). During defending the player blocks opponents and tries to obtain ball. If during defence a teammate obtains the ball, the player switches to attacking.

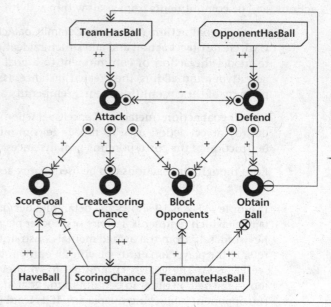

**Fig. 6-20** Example of mental model

**Example 4:** Fig. 6-21 shows an example of usage of the previously defined mental classes (see Fig. 6-20) to express the mental model of particular mental semi-entity types, particularly the entity role types, in the form of mental properties. The entity role type TeamPlayer declares beliefs (teamHasBall, haveBall, scoringChance, etc.) shared by all its subclasses. All beliefs are optional and can occur at most once within one instance. The subclasses of the TeamPlayer, the entity role types Forward and Defender, define the same goals but with different degrees which express their distinct preferences for achievement the goals. Generally speaking, the main intention of the Forward is to attack; whereas the main intention of the Defender is to defend.

This example, together with the example depicted in Fig. 6-20, also demonstrates the possibility to define mental states at the class level once in the model and then to reuse them as types of mental properties of different mental semi-entities.

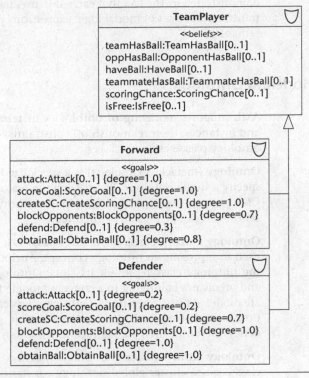

Fig. 6-21 Example of mental properties

**Comparison to other approaches** Modeling beliefs, goals and plans of agents (or other autonomous entities) also appear in several other modeling languages, for instance TROPOS, MAS-ML, Prometheus, etc. However, these languages particularly do not provide sufficient explicit specification of mental states in terms of pre-conditions, post-conditions, commit conditions, cancel conditions and invariants, allowed in AML.

The ability to model mental states at both class and instance levels, as well as the ability to express the attitudinal characteristics of mental entities by means of specific owned attributes, is unique for AML.

Some other modeling languages (mainly goal-driven approaches, such as i*, GRL, NFR, or TROPOS) allow the structuring of mental models by special relationships of different types, for example, means-ends relationship, decomposition relationship, contribution relationship, satisficing link, dependency link, and justification-for-selection. AML tries to avoid possible ambiguities in interpretation of these different relationships and therefore it introduces the concept of contribution, which serves the purpose of a universal mental relationship with the semantics derived from formal logics.

In contrast to other agent-oriented modeling languages, AML specifies precise semantics for all mental elements. This assertion can be demonstrated by the fact that each AML mental model can be directly transferred to a set of modal logic expressions with formally specified semantics.

## 6.8 Modeling Ontologies

AML supports modeling of ontologies in terms of ontology classes and instances, their relationships, constraints, ontology utilities, and ontology packages.

**Ontology** (metaclass Ontology) is a specialized UML package used to specify a single ontology. By utilizing the features inherited from the UML package (package nesting, element import, package merge, etc.), ontologies can be logically structured.

**Ontology class** (metaclass OntologyClass) is a specialized UML class used to represent an ontology concept. Attributes and operations of the ontology class represent its slots. Ontology functions, actions, and predicates belonging to a concept modeled by the ontology class are modeled by its operations. Ontology class can use all types of relationships allowed for UML class (association, generalization, dependency, etc.) with their standard UML semantics.

**Ontology utility** (metaclass OntologyUtility) is a specialized UML class used to cluster global ontology constants, variables, functions, actions, and predicates, which are modeled as its features. These features can be used by (referred to) other elements within the owning ontology. One ontology package can contain several ontology utilities allowing logical clustering of the features.

**Example:** The diagram in Fig. 6-22 depicts a simplified version of a SoccerMatch ontology. Rectangles with the icon "C" placed in a rounded square represent ontology classes that model concepts from the domain. Their relationships are modeled by standard UML relationships with standard semantics.

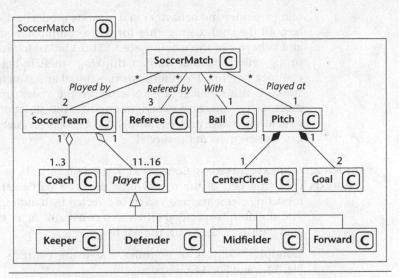

**Fig. 6-22** Example of ontology

**Comparison to other approaches** AML provides relatively simple but generic mechanisms for modeling ontologies by extending the UML class diagrams. There are also other agent-oriented modeling languages used to model ontologies by specialized UML class diagrams, but usually they provide more specific ontology modeling constructs. For instance PASSI defines *concepts*, *actions*, and *predicates* instead of a generic AML ontology class. On one hand specific ontology elements allow the building of more precise models, but on the other hand, they restrict a set of ontology categories (element types).

Instead, AML defines the basic concepts more generically. The provided extension mechanisms can then be used to specialize these concepts into more specific ontology element types, possibly mapped to the constructs of a particular ontology specification language (OWL, DAML, OIL, etc.).

## 6.9 Modeling Contexts

**Situation-based modeling** Multi-agent systems are usually aimed at solving complex, non-trivial problems, and many times are also the systems having complex behavior and architecture difficult to model. To cope with the complexity of the problem to be solved or the system to be specified, we have developed a specific approach called *situation-based modeling*. In this approach a system is examined from the perspective of possible situations that can occur during a system's lifetime and influence behavior of the system or some of its parts. The developer identifies such situations and for each of them models the relevant part of the system (structure and behavior) in a separate model package, called *context*. All the contexts together form the complete model of structure and behavior of the whole system. This kind of logical model structuring reflects natural human thinking when trying to cope with complex systems. Together with functional and structural decomposition, it is a useful means to structure the system model. Furthermore, as our practical experience shows, the situation-based model structuring makes understanding of MAS models easier, mainly in the case of new users of the model.

**Modeling contexts** Context (metaclass Context) is a specialized UML package used to contain a part of the model relevant for a particular situation, i.e. modeling elements involved in of affected by handling the situation. The situation is specified either as a constraint or an explicitly modeled state associated with the context.

**Example:** Examples of defining and using contexts are shown in Fig. 14-5 and Fig. 14-6 respectively.

**Comparison to other approaches** Mechanisms of contexts is a unique modeling approach that does not appear in any other agent-oriented modeling language. The situation-based modeling approach has been brought into existence by AML.

# Chapter 7

# Related Work

In addition to the work aimed directly at fulfilling the stated goals, i.e. to develop an agent-oriented modeling language, we also made an effort to bring AML into practice and to disseminate our ideas in the community of software developers and engineers. Practically, we were engaged in the following activities:

❑ To implement AML in CASE tools.

❑ To support AML by a methodology.

❑ To apply AML in real-world projects.

❑ To involve AML into the related standardization processes.

This chapter provides a summary of these activities.

## 7.1 CASE Tool Support

**Importance of language automation** An important factor of the practical applicability of a software modeling language is its implementation in CASE tools supporting the software development process. Having such tools enables automating or assisting in the creation of the model, checking and validating the model, generation and/or reverse engineering the code to/from supported development platforms, producing the model documentation, storage and providing the model to several cooperating software developers, etc. By the use of appropriate supporting tools, we can significantly improve the effectiveness of the software development process.

**Implementation of the AML profiles** Thanks to the UML profiles defined for AML (see [18] for details), the language's incorporation into existing UML-based CASE tool is possible, and furthermore also relatively easy. To provide analysts and other users of AML with the AML-based modeling tools, we have implemented the AML profiles in three CASE tools:

1. Enterprise Architect (EA) [38]—a commercial UML 2.0 modeling tool,

2. StarUML [135]—a free UML 2.0 modeling tool, and

3. IBM Rational Rose [57]—a commercial UML 1.5 modeling tool.

All three tools provide the customizing mechanisms for defining and applying UML profiles in the application models, and therefore implementation of UML profiles for AML is very straightforward.

Fig. 7-1 shows screenshots of three CASE tools extended by AML.

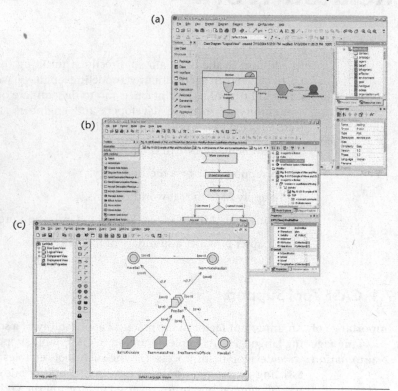

**Fig. 7-1** AML Add-ins. (a) UML 2.0 Profile for AML implemented in Enterprise Architect, (b) UML 2.0 Profile for AML implemented in StarUML, and (c) UML 1.5 Profile for AML implemented in IBM Rational Rose.

**LS/TS Modeler** In addition to the general-purpose modeling tools, we have also designed (and a team of programmers from Whitestein Technologies under our supervision also implemented) an AML-based tool for modeling and forward engineering implementation-specific applications. The tool, *LS/TS Modeler,* is integrated into Whitestein's commercial agent-based software development and runtime suite *Living Systems Technology Suite (LS/TS)* [81].

LS/TS Modeler is based on implementation of the UML 2.0 Profile for AML in EA and augments it with several LS/TS-specific modeling extensions in the form of new stereotypes and tagged values. By incorporation it into EA, the Modeler inherits without further implementation efforts important modeling features such as: comprehensive support for UML 2.0, flexible documentation generation, forward and reverse code engineering (for Java, C++, C#, Delphi, PHP, Visual Basic, and VB.NET), support for testing, support for model maintenance, import/export into XMI, multi-user capabilities, etc.

The LS/TS Modeler therefore serves as a tool for:

❑ **General-purpose AML modeling.**
Creation of general-purpose, platform independent models of multi-agent systems by means of AML and UML modeling constructs and diagrams.

❑ **Modeling LS/TS applications.**
Creation of the LS/TS-specific design models, enabled by adding the specific modeling constructs into AML, and also defining the specific modeling guidelines. For convenient manipulation with the LS/TS-specific modeling constructs the LS/TS Modeler also provides some GUI elements (dialogs, pop-up menus, etc.).

❑ **Checking consistency of the LS/TS application models.**
Checking the AML models against the modeling guidelines specified for the LS/TS application models, constraints specified for the AML profile, and also UML consistency constraints which are not checked by EA itself, but, nevertheless, are important for code generation.

❑ **Generation of the LS/TS code.**
Automatic analysis of the model, transformation of the AML modeling constructs to the LS/TS architectural constructs according to the specified pattern-based rules, and transformation of the results to the LS/TS Developer (a programming tool within LS/TS).

The integration of the LS/TS Modeler within LS/TS is depicted in Fig. 7-2.

**Architecture** The LS/TS Modeler consists of two components:

1. UML 2.0 Profile for AML, and

2. the LS/TS Modeler Add-in.

The *UML 2.0 Profile for AML* is the implementation of the standard UML 2.0 profile for AML (see [18] for details) extended by LS/TS-specific modeling elements. It can be used either as generic-purpose or LS/TS-specific modeling tools based on AML.

The *LS/TS Modeler Add-in* is an EA add-in[20] implementing the specific GUI functionality, the model checker and the LS/TS code generator.

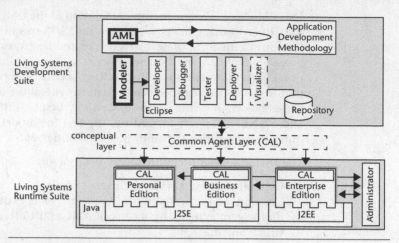

**Fig. 7-2** Architecture of LS/TS

The overall architecture of the LS/TS Modeler is shown in Fig. 7-3. The boxes represent particular components, and the arrows represent flows of data and mutual interconnection of components.

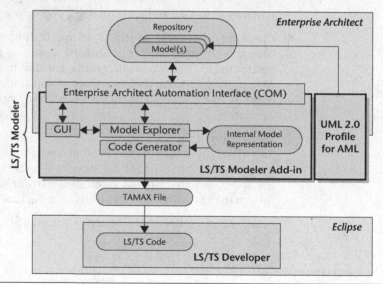

**Fig. 7-3** Architecture of the LS/TS Modeler

The LS/TS Modeler Add-in consists of the following components:

**Model Explorer**

By means of the EA Automation Interface it browses the model, visits particular elements, recognizes the element patterns, and

---

[20] EA add-in is an ActiveX COM component used to extend EA by additional functionality.

creates an internal model representation. The Model Explorer also implements checking of the model according to the AML constraints, LS/TS modeling guidelines, and selected UML constraints.

**Code Generator**

Based on the internal model representation, it generates a TAMAX[21] file.

**GUI**

Creates the Modeler-specific menus, implements Modeler's GUI, processes events from EA, starts the Model Explorer, and displays the model checking and code generation progress in the EA's output window.

**Mapping of AML to LS/TS** A crucial part of analysis and design of the LS/TS code generator was the creation of the mapping from the AML modeling constructs to the LS/TS architectonic constructs. For each LS/TS construct we identified a corresponding pattern of the AML modeling elements which can be used for its modeling. On the contrary, for each AML element or patterns of elements, we identified a pattern of the LS/TS constructs used to implement them. Some mappings were straightforward (e.g. class and activity diagrams), but some were very complicated (e.g. state machines and sequence diagrams). The AML to LS/TS mapping was consequently used to describe the LS/TS application modeling guidelines. By following these guidelines in the modeling process, the code generator's features can be utilized to their maximum extent, which allows the transformation of as large as possible portions of models to the LS/TS code.

In addition to the relatively common generation of a code from the static structure diagrams (implemented by most UML code generators), a very important aspect of the LS/TS code generator is its support for the UML behavioral models, i.e. activities, state machines, and interactions. The code used to implement the application's business logic can therefore be generated (to a relatively high extent) directly from the UML behavior diagrams.

In order to make the code generation easier, we have developed a unified metamodel of the mentioned UML 2.0 behavior models. We perceive this as a very important achievement also from the theoretical point of view. We practically proved that it is possible to create a common metamodel of UML 2.0 activities, state machines, and interactions, unifying their operational semantics. It is therefore possible

---

[21] *TAMAX* is an XML-based interchange format used to represent LS/TS models in the form independent form the LS/TS application programming interface (API). By means of TAMAX we can increase the independence of the Code Generator from other LS/TS tools which directly use the LS/TS API.

to transform a model of any of these kinds to a model of another kind, without altering its semantics.

Based on the unified behavior and static structure metamodels, we designed an internal AML model representation format. The representation format specifies semantics that is extracted from the internal model and UML diagrams in EA. This format is reflected by the internal representation of AML model within the LS/TS Modeler Add-in, as well as by the XML-based interchange format TAMAX used between the LS/TS Modeler and the LS/TS Developer. Because TAMAX shares the same concepts as the internal representation of AML models, the transformation of a model from the internal format to TAMAX is very straightforward.

**Design and implementation pitfalls** Unfortunately most of the existing CASE tools, including the selected ones, support the UML specification just partially, as for instance they provide a limited set of modeling elements, incomplete UML notation, restricted implementation of the UML extensibility features, etc. We had, therefore, to tailor the UML profile for AML and the code generator's implementation to adapt them to these specific constraints. The following list enumerates some of the problems we faced in design and implementation of the LS/TS Modeler:

❑ **Impossibility of specifying constraints in the UML profile specification.**
In general, the constraints specified for a UML profile help to create semantically consistent models. Because EA does not provide sufficient generic tools for specifying such constraints, the EA Automation Interface had to be used to implement the constraint checking within the implemented model checker.

❑ **Restricted set of UML elements.**
EA does not provide all modeling elements specified by the UML 2.0 Superstructure. Because some of the missing element types were used for the specification of the UML profile for AML, we either removed them from the profile's implementation (Subset, Join, AttributeChange, etc.) or we defined modeling workarounds that enabled us to model the same semantics but with other types of underlying modeling elements (ProviderParameters and ClientParameters modeled as a stereotyped note, etc.).

❑ **Stereotypes cannot be specified for all modeling element types.**
EA, as most of the existing CASE tools, provides the possibility to define stereotypes just for a restricted set of modeling element types it supports. If AML implementation required the use of stereotypes for unsupported element types, we identified "similar" (from the semantics and/or notation point of view) types and defined stereotypes for them.

☐ **Restricted automation API.**
The AML model checker and the LS/TS code generator were built upon the EA Automation Interface, a CASE tool automation interface which does not sufficiently allow access to and manipulation of the stored UML model. The only possible way was therefore to extract the required model semantics from the topology of UML diagrams. For instance a partial ordering of the messages in a sequence diagram is obtained from their vertical positions in the diagram. On one hand this kind of model processing decreases flexibility of implementation, but on the other hand it allows extracting and processing of the required semantics which extends the implemented functionality.

With successful solutions to these problems we were finally able to realize the implementation which, to the maximum possible extent, provides users with the modeling elements, their notation and the dynamic semantics as originally specified by the UML 1.*/2.0 Profiles for AML.

**Summary** Implementations of AML in Enterprise Architect, StarUML, and IBM Rational Rose have proved that AML can be automated by means of a quite easy integration into UML 1.* and 2.0 based CASE tools. AML implementation can effectively extend the functionality of existing UML-based CASE tools by the possibility of modeling MAS applications. These facts indirectly point out the appropriateness and usefulness of the AML language architecture, the provided extension mechanisms, as well as the CASE tool support.

# 7.2 Methodological Support

**Purpose of a** The full potential of a software modeling language can usually be un-
**methodology** derstood only if it is practically used. Organized approach to software development requires a controlled process, driven by explicitly specified software development methods. Since the software development process also includes the creation and usage of models of the system being developed, it is necessary for the given method to also include procedures and techniques specifying how to apply the particular modeling language.

On that account, we have defined a methodology to define the process of applying AML and to incorporate the MAS modeling activities into a framework of a complete software development process.

**ADEM** The **Agent-Oriented Development Methodology (ADEM)** [19] is a comprehensive agent-based system development methodology with a special focus on modeling aspects. ADEM provides guidelines for the use of AML in the context of a MAS development process, by extending and making use of the best practices of AOSE.

**Goals**  ADEM was developed to be a methodology that:

☐ completely covers at least all models and modeling techniques defined in AML,

☐ is applicable in as many software development process *disciplines* (see and [105] and [56]) as possible,

☐ is applicable for any system application domain, technology, or specific circumstances of the *development case* (see [56]) to the maximum possible extent,

☐ is built on proven theoretical and technical foundations,

☐ integrates the best practices from AOSE and OOSE domains,

☐ is comprehensive, well specified and documented,

☐ is consistent, methodically complete and methodically minimal (see [134]),

☐ is effectively maintainable and easy to extend, and

☐ can be supported by CAME[22] tools.

**The scope of ADEM**  ADEM is a general-purpose development methodology that consists of method fragments, techniques, artifacts and guidelines for creating and evolving MAS models. Guidelines on how to transform generic ADEM into a concrete situational software development method are also provided.

The current version of ADEM is designed to support several disciplines including Business Modeling, Requirements, and Analysis & Design (see [56] for details).

**Outside the scope of ADEM**  Defining a concrete, detailed software development method applicable to a particular project environment with detailed descriptions of concrete workflow, worker roles, artifacts, guidelines of application of concrete automation tools, etc. (called a situational method), is outside the scope of ADEM. However, ADEM provides an adequate framework for defining such concrete development methods.

**Context of ADEM**  As already mentioned, the primary intention of ADEM is to cover the modeling aspects of the MAS development process. Even though modeling is a substantial part of the technical activities performed within disciplines such as Business Modeling, Requirements, and Analysis & Design, it is less applicable in other areas of the software development process, e.g. Implementation, Test, Deployment, Con-

---

[22] Computer-Aided Method Engineering.

figuration & Change Management, Project Management, and Environment (for details see [56]) which are not specifically covered by the current version of ADEM.

To provide a methodology covering the whole software development process, ADEM extends *Rational Unified Process* (*RUP*) [56]. ADEM defines solely the MAS-specific parts of the process, while RUP defines everything else. In combination this produces a complete methodology, with ADEM providing guidelines that describe the specific combination process. Furthermore, the ADEM specification can be used to define a MAS extension of RUP in the form of a RUP plug-in.

Fig. 7-4 depicts the relationships between AML, UML, ADEM, and RUP.

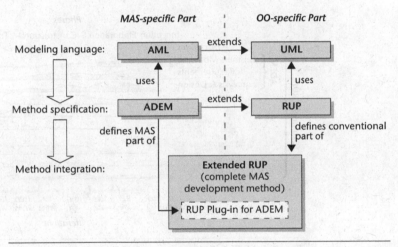

**Fig. 7-4** Context of ADEM

AML is the primary modeling language used in ADEM-specific model artifacts. ADEM extends RUP and defines MAS-specific aspects of the software development process. RUP makes use of UML and provides the conventional object-oriented parts of the process. *Extended RUP* is the result of combining ADEM with RUP. It represents a complete methodology for the MAS development process.

**Application of situational method engineering** In order to build a flexible methodology, the *Situational Method Engineering* (*SME*) approach has been adopted as the reference paradigm (see [13], [29], [90], [123], [124], [134], [139], and [157]). The key idea behind SME is the conviction that system development is unique and different each time. This is the opposite of universal applicability of methods. For every project, variations occur in factors (such as expertise of the development team and customers, complexity of the system, experience with technology, etc.) that force developers to place different emphasis on aspects of the systems development process. In this context the concrete *situational method*[23] is constructed by selecting and assembling coherent pieces of the process. To simplify the process of selecting and assembling parts of the process into situational methods, the methodology provides the system of predefined method fragments called the method base.

**ADEM process framework**  The basic ADEM process framework is adopted from RUP [56]. Fig. 7-5 shows its two orthogonal dimensions and how the effort emphasis over time.

- ❑ The *horizontal dimension* shows the dynamic aspect of the process in terms of phases, iterations, and milestones.

- ❑ The *vertical dimension* shows disciplines which logically group activities, workflows, artifacts, roles, and guidances.

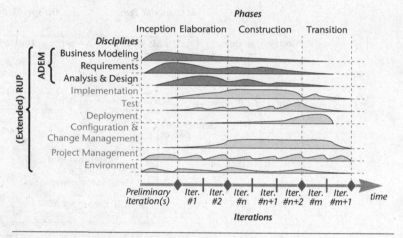

**Fig. 7-5** ADEM (RUP) process framework

**Lifecycle**  The *Software Process Engineering Metamodel Specification* (*SPEM*) [105] defines a process **lifecycle** as a sequence of phases that achieve a specific goal. It defines the behavior of a complete process to be enacted in a given project. The ADEM lifecycle is characterized as *iterative*—consisting of several iterations repeated in time, and *incremental*—the system is built by adding more and more functionality at each iteration.

The lifecycle of ADEM is structured as the lifecycle in RUP [56], see Fig. 7-6.

---

23 Called *development case* in RUP.

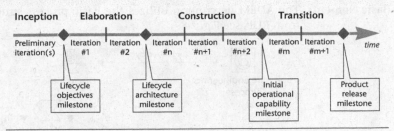

**Fig. 7-6** ADEM lifecycle

The software lifecycle of ADEM is decomposed over time into four sequential phases: Inception, Elaboration, Construction, and Transition. A **phase** is the span of time between two major project milestones of a development process, during which a set of objectives is accomplished and artifacts are produced or refined.

Each phase concludes by a **major milestone** at which management makes crucial go/no-go decisions and decides on schedule, budget, and requirements on the project.

Each phase is further divided into several **iterations**, distinct sequences of activities conducted according to devoted iteration plans and evaluation criteria that result in releases (internal or external).

One pass through the four phases resulting in a generation of the software product, is a **development cycle**, see Fig. 7-7. The subsequent product generations are produced by repeating the development cycle, but each time with a different emphasis on the various phases. These subsequent cycles are called **evolution cycles**.

For further information about the lifecycle see RUP [56].

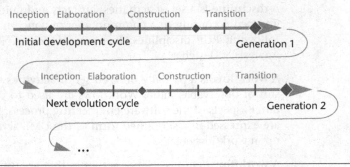

**Fig. 7-7** Development cycles

**Basic elements** The ADEM description utilizes the basic process structure elements from RUP, see Fig. 7-8.

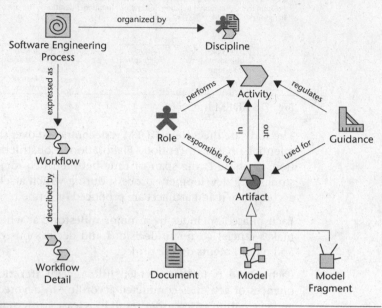

**Fig. 7-8** Basic Elements of ADEM (RUP)

The **software engineering process** is an organized set of activities, artifacts and guidances intended to develop or enhance a software product. In RUP (and therefore also in ADEM) the process is organized into a set of disciplines that further define the workflows and other process elements.

A **discipline** is a set of activities, artifacts and guidances of a process grouped according to a common area of concern. ADEM covers the following RUP disciplines: Business Modeling, Requirements, and Analysis & Design.

A **workflow** is a partially ordered set of activities that produces a result of observable value. Workflows are used to describe the procedural aspects of the software engineering process. In RUP, workflows are expressed in a simplified form of the UML activity diagram built upon workflow details.

A **workflow detail** is a set of activities that are usually performed together, the roles that perform those activities, and the resulting artifacts.

An **activity** is a unit of work that provides a meaningful result in the context of the project. It has a clear purpose, which usually involves creating or updating artifacts. Every activity is assigned to a specific role. Activities may be repeated several times, especially when executed in different iterations.

A **role** defines the behavior and responsibilities of an individual, or a team, within the organization of a software engineering process. ADEM, rather than defining its own roles, reuses roles from RUP and extends their responsibilities.

An **artifact** is a physical or information entity that is produced, modified or used during the execution of the process. Examples of artifacts include documents, models, model fragments, model elements, source files, binary executable files, databases, etc. ADEM makes use of three special artifacts: document, model, and model fragment.

A **document** is a special artifact capturing the information in a textual form regardless of its physical representation.

A **model** is an artifact representing an abstraction of a system.

A **model fragment** is a part of the model, usually modeling a particular aspect of the system.

A **guidance** provides more detailed information to practitioners about the associated element. Possible types of guidance are for example: guidelines, techniques, measurements, examples, UML profiles, tool mentors, checklist, templates, etc.

For further information about the basic process elements see RUP [56] and SPEM [105].

**Method fragments**  The software engineering process specified in ADEM is defined as a system of well-defined method fragments used to compose situational methods in an effective way.

A **method fragment**[24] is a coherent portion of the process specification that may be used with other method fragments to assemble a complete method.

Method fragments are defined at different levels of granularity. Lower-level fragments are combined into higher-level fragments to from the hierarchical (tree) structure of a **method base**—a repository of method fragments. This structuring allows flexible and effective specification and maintenance of the fragments. We differentiate two kinds of method fragments:

**Atomic method fragment**
  A method fragment which comprises no other method fragments. An atomic method fragment usually represents a portion of the process at the level of RUP or SPEM activities.

---

[24] Called also *method component*, see [157].

**Composite method fragment**
A method fragment composed of other (atomic or composite) method fragments. It is used to group related method fragments that together represent a well-defined portion of the process with clearly specified purpose and interfaces.

The concepts used in the ADEM method base are depicted in Fig. 7-9.

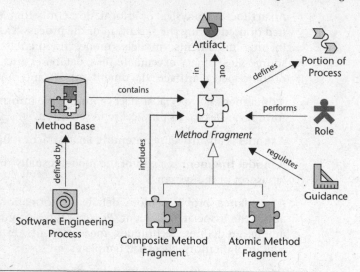

**Fig. 7-9** ADEM Method Fragments

ADEM method fragments are specified in terms of:

**Type**
The type of the method fragment. It can be either *atomic* or *composite*.

**Purpose**
Textual description of the purpose and goals of the method fragment.

**Enclosing fragment**
Name of the method fragment which encloses the specified fragment.

**Inputs (only for atomic method fragment)**
A list of artifacts which serve as a source of information for the method fragment.

**Common inputs (only for composite method fragment)**
A list of artifacts which serve as a source of information for each of the enclosed method fragments.

**Outputs (only for atomic method fragment)**
A list of artifacts produced by the method fragment.

**Aggregated outputs (only for composite method fragment)**
A list of artifacts produced by all enclosed fragments. It is not necessary to also list the model fragments if their models are specified.

**Role (only for atomic method fragment)**
A role responsible for performing the method fragment.

**Steps (only for atomic method fragment)**
List of atomic elements specifying the actions preformed by the method fragment to transform inputs to outputs. In this document we use simple steps, but the UML activity diagrams can be used to describe the portion of the process more precisely. Each step is specified as to whether it is added to RUP or modifies an existing RUP step (if the name of the modified RUP step is not explicitly stated, it is identical to ADEM step).

**Enclosed fragments (only for composite method fragment)**
A list of enclosed method fragments that together form the specified method fragment.

**RUP application**
An explanation of how the method fragment is incorporated into RUP to obtain the complete software engineering method.

**Rationale**
A brief explanation of the reasons why a given method fragment is defined within ADEM.

**SPEM compatibility** Concepts used in ADEM are compatible with SPEM. Even if ADEM primarily uses the terminology of RUP, the concepts used in the methodology specification are identical or can be directly mapped to the concepts defined by SPEM. The mapping is depicted in Tab. 7-1.

| ADEM/RUP concept | SPEM concept |
| --- | --- |
| Role | ProcessRole |
| Workflow, Workflow Detail | WorkDefinition |
| Activity | Activity |
| Step | Step |
| Artifact, Document, Model, Model Fragment | WorkProduct |
| Discipline | Discipline |
| Process | Lifecycle |
| Phase | Phase |
| Iteration | Iteration |
| Guidelines, ToolMentors, Templates | Guidance |

**Tab. 7-1** Mapping of ADEM to SPEM concepts (1/2)

| ADEM/RUP concept | SPEM concept |
|---|---|
| Method Base | Set of ProcessComponents |
| Method Fragment | ProcessComponent |
| Situational Method | Process |

**Tab. 7-1** Mapping of ADEM to SPEM concepts (2/2)

**Method base**  Fig. 7-10 shows a hierarchy of all ADEM method fragments. Names of the composite method fragments are depicted in bold. Detailed description of the ADEM method base can be found in [19].

**Artifacts**  ADEM artifacts reflect the AML diagram types and the corresponding model aspects. One AML diagram type (or a model aspect) can be used for several ADEM artifacts (usually produced in different method fragments) expressing different concepts but technically modeled by the same modeling constructs, e.g. AML Society Diagram can be used to model ADEM Business Organization Structure Model as well as Social Model.

Several ADEM artifacts correspond to some RUP artifacts. The main purpose is:

❑ either to provide *more appropriate models*, e.g. RUP Glossary (a "flat" textual document) is in ADEM replaced by the Domain Ontology Model (the system domain concepts modeled in the form of AML ontology), or

❑ to enrich them by *additional semantics* expressed by means of the AML modeling constructs, e.g. RUP Business Use Case Model is extended in the ADEM Extended Business Use Case Model by mental modeling concepts of agentified business actors and explicitly modeled responsibilities of business use cases for realization particular actor's mental states and goal-based requirements.

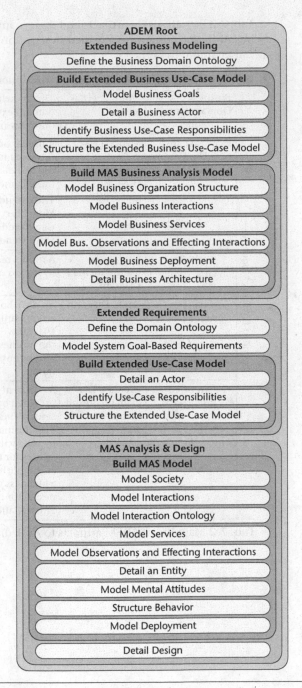

**Fig. 7-10** Hierarchy of the ADEM method fragments

Tab. 7-2 lists all ADEM artifacts and their mapping to the corresponding AML diagram types. Detailed description of the ADEM artifacts can be found in [19].

| | ADEM artifact | AML diagrams | Description |
|---|---|---|---|
| Extended Business Modeling | Business Domain Ontology Model | Ontology Diagram | The knowledge of the business domain expressed in terms of AML ontology modeling concepts. |
| | Extended Business Use-Case Model | Mental Diagram, Entity Diagram, and Use-Case Diagram (RUP) | A model of the business goals and intended functions, which extends the RUP Business Use-Case Model by AML mental modeling concepts. The Extended Business Use-Case Model is composed of the Business Goals Model, Business Actor Detail, and Extended Business Use-Case. |
| | Business Goals Model | Goal-Based Requirements Diagram | A model of business goals captured by means of AML Mental Diagrams. |
| | Business Actor Detail | Entity Diagram | An AML Entity Diagram, possibly accompanied with the AML Mental Diagrams, capturing the details of the business actor as an AML autonomous entity, mainly its mental model. |
| | Extended Business Use-Case | Use-Case Diagram (RUP) and Mental Diagram | A coherent unit of functionality provided by a business to business actors. The expressiveness of the RUP Business Use-Case is enhanced by the facility to express responsibilities for (contributions to) the accomplishment (maintenance) of a business goal or a goal of an business actor in terms of AML responsibility relationship. |

**Tab. 7-2** Mapping of ADEM artifacts to AML diagram types (1/5)

| ADEM artifact | AML diagrams | Description |
|---|---|---|
| Extended Business Analysis Model | All kinds of UML and AML diagrams. | An extension of the RUP Business Analysis Model. The Extended Business Analysis Model is composed of the Extended Business Use-Case Realization, Business Organization Structure Model, Extended Business Worker, Extended Business Entity, Business Organization Unit Type, and Business Deployment Model. |
| Extended Business Use-Case Realization | UML and AML interaction diagrams, AML service diagrams, and Activity Diagram (UML) | Describes how business workers, business entities, and business events collaborate to perform a particular Business Use-Case. The extension to the RUP Business Use-Case Realization involves several AML modeling concepts, such as: communicative interactions, interaction protocols, observations and effecting interactions, services, and AML extensions to activities. |
| Business Organization Structure Model | Society Diagram | Used to capture the business organization structure in terms of AML Society Diagrams containing mainly: (extended) business workers, (extended) Business Entities, AML entity roles, AML organization units, and all kinds of relationships. |
| Extended Business Worker | Entity Diagram | A RUP Business Worker enriched by the features of AML autonomous entity. |
| Extended Business Entity | Entity Diagram | A RUP Business Entity extended by the features of the AML behavioral entity. |
| Business Organization Unit Type | Entity Diagram | A specialized AML OrganizationUnitType used to model a type of unit of a business organizational structure. |
| Business Deployment Model | Deployment Diagram (UML) | A model of the physical deployment of the business organization structure (possibly capturing its geographical distribution, physical interconnections, mobility of deployed entities, etc.) specified by means of the AML modeling concepts for deployment and mobility. |

*The leftmost vertical label spanning the table rows reads: Extended Business Modeling*

**Tab. 7-2** Mapping of ADEM artifacts to AML diagram types (2/5)

| | ADEM artifact | AML diagrams | Description |
|---|---|---|---|
| **Extended Requirements** | Domain Ontology Model | Ontology Diagram | The knowledge of the business domain expressed in terms of AML ontology modeling concepts.<br><br>The system domain concepts expressed in terms of AML ontology modeling mechanisms. |
| | System Goal-Based Requirements Model | Goal-Based Requirements Diagram | A model of functional and non-functional requirements which utilizes AML goals as the central means of their specification. |
| | Extended Use-Case Model | Mental Diagram, Entity Diagram, and Use-Case Diagram (RUP) | A model of the system's intended functions and its environment, which extends the RUP Use-Case Model by AML mental modeling concepts, particularly: agentified actors, and responsibility relationships for explicit modeling of responsibilities (contributions) of Use-Cases for (to) fulfillment or maintenance of goal-based requirements and goals of actors.<br><br>The System Goal-Based Requirements Model is composed of the Actor Detail, and Extended Use-Case. |
| | Actor Detail | Entity Diagram | An AML Entity Diagram, possibly accompanied with the AML Mental Diagrams, capturing the details of the actor as an AML autonomous entity, mainly its mental model. |
| | Extended Use-Case | Use-Case Diagram (RUP), and Mental Diagram | A coherent unit of functionality provided by a system to actors. The expressiveness of the RUP Use-Case is enhanced by the facility to express responsibilities for (contributions to) the accomplishment (maintenance) of goal-based requirements or goals of actors in terms of AML responsibility relationship. |

**Tab. 7-2** Mapping of ADEM artifacts to AML diagram types (3/5)

| ADEM artifact | AML diagrams | Description |
|---|---|---|
| MAS Model | All kinds of UML and AML diagrams. | A model describing the system in terms of concepts drawn from MAS theory.<br>The MAS Model is composed of the Social Model, Interaction Model, Interaction Ontology Model, Service Model, Entity Detail, Behavior Decomposition Model, Mental Model, Perceptor/Effector Model, and MAS Deployment Model. |
| Social Model | Society Diagram | A model of the system architecture developed in terms of AML Society Diagrams. |
| Interaction Model | UML and AML interaction diagrams and AML service diagrams | A model of interactions and interaction patterns that can occur between entities of the system, or between entities and actors. For this purpose the concepts of AML communicative interactions and interaction protocols are used. |
| Interaction Ontology Model | Ontology Diagram | AML Ontology Diagrams which capture the ontology used within the communicative interactions and services. |
| Service Model | Service Diagram and Service Protocol Sequence (Communication) Diagram | AML Service Diagrams specifying the services offered and used by the entities and actors. |
| Entity Detail | Entity Diagram | An AML Entity Diagram specifying the details of the internal structure of an AML entity in terms of its owned features and behaviors. |
| Behavior Decomposition Model | Behavior Decomposition Diagram | A set of AML Behavior Decomposition Diagrams specifying AML behavior fragments and their mutual relationships. |
| Mental Model | Mental Diagram | A model of mental attitudes of AML mental semi-entities describing their goals, plans, beliefs, and relationships thereof. It is composed of a set of AML Mental Diagrams. |

*(Row group label, vertical:* MAS Analysis & Design*)*

**Tab. 7-2** Mapping of ADEM artifacts to AML diagram types (4/5)

| | ADEM artifact | AML diagrams | Description |
|---|---|---|---|
| MAS Analysis & Design | Percep-tor/Effector Model | (Composite) Structure Dia-gram (UML) | A model of AML perceptor and effector types. |
| | MAS Deploy-ment Model | Deployment Diagram (UML) | A RUP Deployment Model enriched by AML MAS deployment and mobility facilities. |
| | Detailed Design Model | All kinds of UML and AML diagrams. | A design model specifying the implementation and runtime char-acteristics of the system. It serves as an abstraction of the implementa-tion model and its source code. |

**Tab. 7-2** Mapping of ADEM artifacts to AML diagram types (5/5)

**Methodology maintenance** An organization which wants to adopt ADEM should establish spe-cific business processes to customize, maintain and effectively apply the methodology to software development projects. The fundamental adoption, application and maintenance process comes from the prin-ciples of SME. This process is outlined in Fig. 7-11.

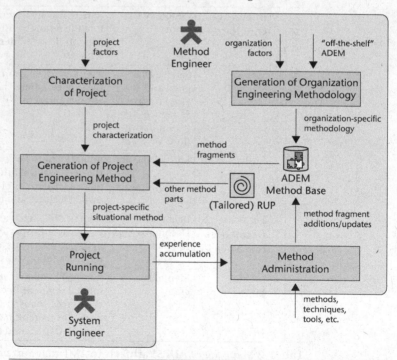

**Fig. 7-11** The process of ADEM adoption, application and mainte-nance

**Note:** Even if not shown in the diagram, each activity can also provide feedback to the activities performed earlier on, for instance, *Characterization of Project* reports back to the project management problems with the project setup, or *Project Running* requests a method engineer to perform the *Generation of Project Engineering Method* to deliver further method adaptations.

**Generation of Organization Engineering Methodology.** Prior to its application in concrete projects, a generic "off-the-shelf" ADEM specification is customized to reflect the specific environment and conditions of the organization. Factors specific to the organization (laws, regulations, standards, specific application domains, available technologies, etc.) must be taken into account to customize the methodology and to increase efficiency of its application in concrete projects.

This activity comprises:

❏ Customizing the method base by:

- adding new method fragments to enrich the method with new activities,

- changing specifications of existing method fragments to customize them to local conditions, and

- removing method fragments which are not expected to be used.

❏ Changing the set of artifacts.

❏ Defining new, changing existing or removing redundant roles.

❏ Adding or updating existing guidances. Usually, local regulations, standards, guidelines, tool mentors, artifact templates, etc. are expressed in a compatible form and are included in the localized ADEM. Redundant guidances may be removed.

❏ Customizing the ADEM generic process workflow or defining a new one.

❏ Customizing the tools to provide specific features required by ADEM and AML.

**Characterization of Project.** If a new software development project begins, its characterization will identify contextual and contingency factors derived from the project. The produced project environment characterization is important for supporting the selection of the appropriate method fragments from the method base and their assembly.

The contingency factors are determined during project characterization as a result of interviews, brain-storming sessions, questionnaires or other knowledge acquisition techniques.

The following contingency factors are usually evaluated (see [148] for details):

- ❑ management commitment for the project,
- ❑ importance of the project,
- ❑ impact of the project,
- ❑ resistance and conflict (to what extent stakeholders have different or conflicting interests),
- ❑ time pressure,
- ❑ shortage of human resources,
- ❑ shortage of means,
- ❑ formality (of the project procedures),
- ❑ knowledge and experience of the project team,
- ❑ required and acquired skills,
- ❑ project size,
- ❑ relationships to other systems,
- ❑ dependency of the project to external factors,
- ❑ clarity of the project goals, objectives, etc.,
- ❑ stability of the project goals and requirements, and
- ❑ level of innovation.

**Generation of Project Engineering Method.** Based on the available method fragments, the project-specific situated method is constructed at this stage. The construction is supported by rules to assemble fragments and constraints to be satisfied by the constructed method. The method construction based on ADEM consists of: (1) selection of appropriate method fragments, (2) assembly of selected fragments, (3) incorporation of the fragments with (possibly already tailored) RUP, and (4) defining specific process workflow.

The selection process is driven by the project characterization and should result in a complete but minimal configuration of the method fragments. According to Spit, Lieberherr, and Brinkkemper [134], these fragments should be:

- ❑ *situationally complete*—completely fulfilling the needs of the situation in which they are applied, and
- ❑ *situationally minimal*—no superfluous artifacts should be produced.

Once the method engineer has decided which ADEM method fragments she/he wants to use, integration to form a MAS method can take place. After preparing this complete ADEM-based MAS method, it should also be optionally integrated with (already tailored) RUP to obtain the complete software engineering method.

If required, either a new process workflow can be defined, or the generic workflow can be tailored to the project situation and possibly also detailed. In some cases the ADEM generic workflow can be used without customization.

The resulting situational method should be [134]:

❏ *consistent*—the various method fragments should not contradict each other,

❏ *methodically complete*—containing all method elements (roles, artifacts, guidances, etc.) referred to by the fragments of which it is constructed, and

❏ *methodically minimal*—all parts are necessary to derive the products of the method.

**Project Running.** Once a project-specific situational method is prepared, it can be applied to the project. During the project execution, the method engineer supervises the process, identifies problems, and collects different inputs applicable to method or methodology improvement.

**Method Administration.** Evaluations during and after project execution may yield new knowledge about situated method development, which is captured in the method base. Existing method fragments can be modified, or new method fragments can be added to the repository for future use.

Apart from project running, method engineers can also obtain further know-how from external sources. This know-how can also be used to improve the adopted methodology.

**Summary** ADEM is a coherent and extensible methodology based on RUP, which utilizes concepts drawn from MAS theory as specified by AML. The methodology follows the SME approach in order to provide flexibility in defining concrete methods customized to specific conditions of particular system development projects.

In particular, the basic underlying concepts, the methodology metamodel, the initial set of method fragments forming the ADEM method base, the artifacts used as inputs and outputs of the method fragments, and the generic process workflow are specified. Beyond that, the principles of the adoption, application and maintenance are outlined.

We feel confident that ADEM is a useful methodological framework for software engineers to build systems based on, or exhibiting characteristics of, multi-agent technology. In this respect we anticipate that ADEM may form a significant contribution to the effort of bringing about widespread adoption of intelligent agents across varied commercial marketplaces.

## 7.3 Practical Application of AML

**Projects** Driven by the project demands for documenting the requirements and the solution, as well as by our need to test AML in solving practical problems, AML has been applied as a language for modeling requirements, analysis and design of applications in several research and commercial software development projects at Whitestein Technologies. The applications were built in the following domains:

❑ **Planning/scheduling.**
Advanced planning and scheduling of intra-hospital coordination in the areas of surgical operations and preparation, personnel, equipment and materials, patient treatment, patients stay, tests, and therapy.

❑ **Simulations.**
Real-time simulation and visualization of group behavior in a game. Each member of a group (represented by an agent) changes its position in space in accordance with observed and communicated position changes of the other group members.

❑ **Network management.**
Efficient and flexible Service Level Agreement (SLA) Management in telecommunication networks. This includes a number of aspects like the negotiation and the conclusions of new SLAs, the provisioning and monitoring of the requested Quality of Service (QoS) level of a service, automatic reporting to the customer, an optimal deployment of network resources and a statistical analysis of customer requirements and system load (e.g. to help the provider to decide about new commercial offers) to mention the most important ones. The processes are controlled by corresponding policies. The top-level policy (Domain policy) from which all the lower-level policies are derived, is specified by the network provider. [70]

**Lessons learned** Application of AML in these projects gave it a chance to be tested under real-world conditions.

The relatively large scope of AML allowed the building of various models of the developed MAS applications. This enabled us to create complex models covering various MAS aspects, and in this way to better understand, analyze, and document the applications.

Another important applicability aspect is the ability of a software modeling language to express technology-specific application design.

Even more complications can appear when there are requirements to cover several various technologies, as it was in the case of the aforementioned projects.

For this purpose we had to practically examine the AML extensibility mechanisms and to create technology-specific language extensions. In order to capture specific architectonic constructs of the target implementation environment (we used the agent platforms Cougaar [27], Lars [89] and LS/TS [81]) in the design model of a created application, we extended AML by the modeling constructs able to represent the specific implementation constructs. For instance in the case of using Cougaar platform, we added to AML elements representing the Cougaar concepts of *task, task allocation, task aggregation, task expansion, task asset transfer*, etc., because the platform is specialized in building applications in the distributed planning domain. Similar extensions were provided also for the other technologies used.

All the technology-specific AML extensions were also implemented in the CASE tools used for designing applications in particular projects.

**Summary** These projects tested AML under real-world conditions and proved that it is a useful tool for modeling and documenting complex, concurrent, distributed and intelligent systems. Furthermore, the AML extensibility mechanisms allowed to customize the language for designing applications deployed at various target implementation technologies.

## 7.4 Standardization Activities

**Standardization in AOSE** Building standards in the area of MAS is seen as one possible way to bring order into this highly heterogeneous area with many diverse approaches. Not only to facilitate the interworking of agents and agent systems across multiple vendor platforms (aimed e.g. primarily by FIPA), but also unifying the used development techniques, methodologies, and tools is the mission of the current AOSE standardization. The standardization activities related to AOSE, since its beginning, have been focused on standardization of agent-oriented modeling languages and agent-based methodologies. See for instance efforts of FIPA Modeling Technical Committee [45], FIPA Methodology Technical Committee [44], AgentLink Agent-Oriented Software Engineering Technical Forum Group [2], and OMG Agents Special Interest Group [107].

**Contribution of AML** We believe that AML, and its underlying concepts, can also significantly contribute to formation of future standards in the area of agent-oriented modeling. Therefore, in order to:

1. utilize the modeling features offered by AML in building future standards,

2. disseminate our ideas into a broad community of the (agent-oriented) software engineering specialists, and

3. influence future industrial standards,

we were actively involved in the world-wide standardization activities. Thanks to Whitestein Technologies, we had a chance to take part in establishing, and consequently also becoming members, of the aforementioned FIPA and AgentLink working groups. In addition, we also contributed to the OMG Agents Special Interest Group by submitting AML as a response to the *Request for Information (RFI) on Modeling Agent-based Systems* [108].

**Summary**   Ongoing standardization activities in the area of AOSE are important means for its dissemination and acceptance by the industry. Particularly for agent-oriented modeling languages, it can be observed that their considerable large amount and diversity of approaches discourage software engineers from their extensive use in software development. It is believed that the current situation could be, at least partially, overcome by creating a standardized unified agent-oriented modeling language that would be accepted by industry.

# Part III

# AML Specification

This part contains a detailed technical specification of the AML meta-model, notation and demonstrates the defined modeling elements using examples.

**Note:** This part is intended to serve as a language specification and reference manual. Comprehension of the details and nuances of AML requires a deep understanding of UML 2.0 Superstructure [104].

# Chapter 8

# Extensions to Standard UML Notation

This chapter specifies presentation options for some UML elements in order to provide more intuitive and comprehensive notation. This alternative notation is then commonly used in next chapters to describe specific modeling elements of AML.

## 8.1 Stereotyped Classifier

The stereotype of a Classifier can, additionally to the stereotype keyword, be expressed also by an iconic notation. The possible notational variations are shown in the example of an AgentType, Fig. 8-1.

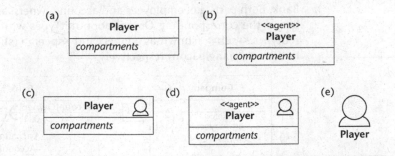

Fig. 8-1 Alternative notation for stereotyped Classifier. The stereotype is: (a) hidden, (b) shown as a label, (c) shown as an iconic decoration, (d) shown as a label and iconic decoration, (e) shown as a large icon.

## 8.2 ConnectableElement with a Stereotyped Type

The fundamental type[25] of a ConnectableElement's type can be visually expressed by its iconic notation, if defined. The possible notation variations are (see Fig. 8-2):

☐ a small stereotype icon shown in the upper right corner of the ConnectableElement's rectangle (so called iconic decoration), or

☐ a large stereotype icon used instead of ConnectableElement's rectangle.

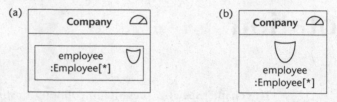

**Fig. 8-2** Alternative notation for a ConnectableElement with stereotyped type. The type's stereotype is shown as: (a) an iconic decoration, (b) a large icon.

The stereotype of the ConnectableElement itself (if defined) can be specified as a label or a small icon located in front of the ConnectableElement's name.

Fig. 8-3 shows an example of an OrganizationUnitType Company, that consists of employees which are subordinates. The other OrganizationUnitType Bank consists of accountOwners which are peers to the Bank. Both parts, i.e. employees and accountOwners, are SocialProperties of the corresponding OrganizationUnitTypes with their own stereotypes <<sub>> (shown as a label) and <<peer>> (shown as a small half-black triangle icon) respectively.

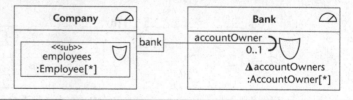

**Fig. 8-3** Example of stereotyped parts having also stereotyped types

---

[25] By *fundamental type* of a modeling element we understand the metaclass of which this element is an instance.

## 8.3 Connector with a Stereotyped Type

AML defines a few specialized Associations and Properties having own notation (see sections 10.5.5, 10.5.3, etc.).

In addition to standard UML notation, AML allows the depiction of Connectors with the notation of the fundamental types of their types, and ConnectorEnds with the notation of the fundamental types of the referred Properties.

Fig. 8-4 shows an example of two Connectors (typed by SocialAssociations) and their ends (referring SocialProperties) depicted by iconic notation.

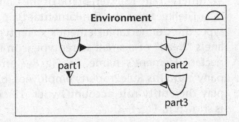

**Fig. 8-4.** Alternative notation for Connectors having SocialAssociation as a fundamental type of their types

## 8.4 Lifeline with a Stereotyped Type

To depict the fundamental type of the type of a ConnectableElement represented by a Lifeline, AML allows the placement of the stereotype small icon of that fundamental type into the Lifeline's "head", or to replace the Lifeline's "head" by the iconic notation of the fundamental type of the ConnectableElement's type. For an example see Fig. 8-5.

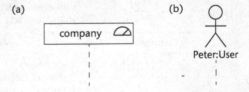

**Fig. 8-5** Alternative notation for Lifeline. The fundamental type of represented element is shown as: (a) an icon decoration, (b) a large icon.

The same notation can be applied also for a Lifeline representing an inner ConnectableElement (see Fig. 8-6 for an example). The corresponding class diagram is shown in Fig. 10-8.

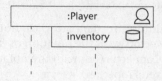

**Fig. 8-6** Stereotype specified for the Lifeline representing an inner ConnectableElement

To differentiate the stereotype of the ConnectableElement represented by a Lifeline from the fundamental type of the ConnectableElement's type, the ConnectableElement's stereotype label is placed in the Lifeline's "head" or a small stereotype icon is placed in front of the ConnectableElement's name. In Fig. 8-7 an OrganizationUnitType Company contains RoleProperty employees, but it can also simultaneously play the entity role accountOwner. The corresponding class diagram is shown in Fig. 8-3.

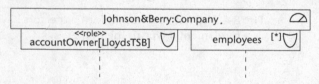

**Fig. 8-7** Stereotype specified for the Lifeline representing an entity role

Extending the Lifeline's "head" by a stereotype of the fundamental type of the represented ConnectableElement's type can be applied also for Lifelines in Communication Diagrams. See example in Fig. 8-8.

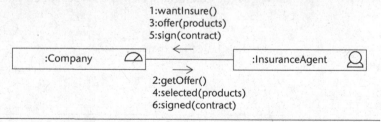

**Fig. 8-8** Alternative notation for Lifeline in Communication Diagrams

## 8.5 Composed Lifelines in Communication Diagrams

Lifelines that represent owned attributes of a StructuredClassifier can be nested within the Lifeline representing their owner. Parts are depicted as rectangles with solid outlines, and properties specifying instances that are not owned by composition are shown as rectangles with dashed outlines. Ports can be depicted as well. See example in Fig. 8-9.

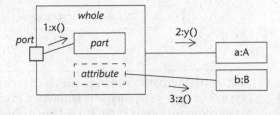

**Fig. 8-9** Alternative notation for composite Lifelines in Communication Diagrams

## 8.6 ObjectNode with a Stereotyped Type

The presentation option described in the following text applies for all concrete subclasses of the ObjectNode metaclass.

The fundamental type of an ObjectNode's type can be visually expressed by its iconic notation, if defined. The possible notation variations are (see Fig. 8-10):

☐ a small stereotype icon placed in the upper right corner of an ObjectNode's rectangle shown in a standalone style, or

☐ a large stereotype icon used instead of a standalone ObjectNode's rectangle, or

☐ a small stereotype icon placed in the middle of a pin style ObjectNode rectangle.

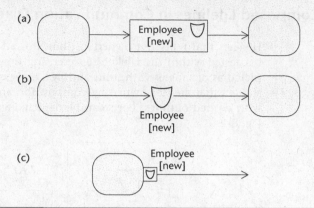

**Fig. 8-10** Alternative notation for an ObjectNode with a stereotyped type. The type's stereotype is shown as: (a) an iconic decoration in a standalone notation style, (b) a large icon in a standalone notation style, (c) a small icon in a pin notation style.

The stereotype of the ObjectNode itself (if defined) can be specified as a label or a small icon located in front of the ObjectNode's name.

Fig. 8-11 shows a fragment of an Activity named EliminateIntruder, having an ActivityParameterNode intruder with its own stereotype <<byref>>, while the stereotype of its type is depicted as an iconic decoration.

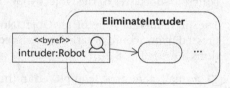

**Fig. 8-11** Example of a stereotyped ObjectNode having also stereotyped type

## 8.7 Bi-directional Dependencies

If two opposite Dependencies of the same kind connect two Named-Elements they can be alternatively drawn as one dashed line with arrows at the both ends, see Fig. 8-12.

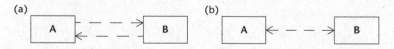

**Fig. 8-12** Alternative notation for binary Dependency: (a) UML notation, (b) simplified notation.

Analogous mechanism applies also for n-ary dependencies, see Fig. 8-13. In this case each connected NamedElement depends on all other connected NamedElements.

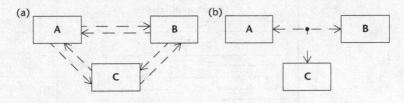

**Fig. 8-13** Alternative notation for n-ary Dependency: (a) UML notation, (b) simplified notation.

## 8.8 Internal Structure of ConnectableElements

To offer a more comprehensive notation for hierarchical structures expressed in terms of UML StructuredClassifiers, it is possible to depict the internal structure of their owned ConnectableElements. If the type of a ConnectableElement[26] is a StructuredClassifier, the ConnectableElement can depict a part of the internal structure of its type (expressed in terms of Parts, Ports, Variables and Connectors) relevant for the given ConnectableElement. ConnectableElements can be nested to any level.

Analogously to the notation of a StructuredClassifier, the additional compartment containing the internal structure is added below the name compartment of a ConnectableElement, see Fig. 8-14. The compartment may depict only a subset of the ConnectableElements and Connectors specified for the ConnectableElement's type.

A structured ConnectableElement without explicitly defined type, implicitly specifies a Class owned by the same element as the ConnectableElement, and having the identical internal structure as specified for the ConnectableElement. This Class is virtually used as the type of the structured ConnectableElement. Such a semantic workaround is introduced to enable specifying structured ConnectableElements without specified types, but still be consistent with the UML Superstructure metamodel.

This mechanism is usually used to describe internal structure of Parts, but can be applied also for Ports and Variables.

---

[26] Even if the ConnectableElement metaclass does not define its type, each concrete subclass of the ConnectableElement is a specialized TypedElement and therefore defines the type meta attribute.

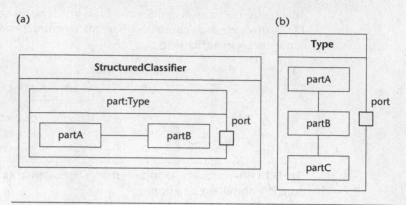

**Fig. 8-14** Notation for internal structure of Parts: (a)   Part   depicting internal structure of its type, and (b) definition of the Part's type.

# Chapter 9

# Organization of the AML Specification

## 9.1 Overall AML Package Structure

The overall package structure of the AML metamodel is depicted in Fig. 9-1.

The AML Metamodel is logically structured according to the various aspects of MAS abstractions. All packages and their content are described in the following chapters.

## 9.2 Specification Structure

Although this part is intended for advanced readers, we have tried to organize it in a way that it can be easily understood. In order to improve the readability and comprehension of the specification, it is organized according to a hierarchy of packages which group either further (sub)packages or metaclasses that logically fit together. All the AML metaclasses are defined only within the packages on the lowest level of the package hierarchy, i.e. within packages that do not contain further subpackages. For details on the package structure of AML see section 9.1.

**Package specification** Each metamodel package, described in a separate section, is specified in terms of Overview and either Abstract syntax (for the lowest level packages) or Package structure (for non-lowest level packages). The sections describing the lowest level packages also contain subsections for all comprised metaclasses.

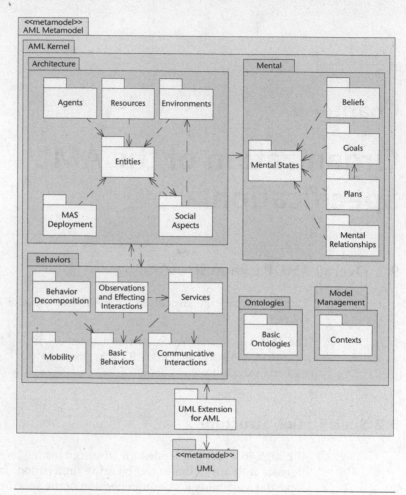

**Fig. 9-1** Overall package structure of the AML metamodel

Package specification sections are structured as follows:

### Overview (mandatory)
Natural language introduction to the content of the package.

### Abstract syntax (mandatory for lowest level packages)
AML metamodel class diagrams (i.e. the metaclasses and their relationships) contained within the package.

### Package structure (mandatory for non lowest level packages)
The package diagram of (sub)packages contained within the package together with their mutual dependencies.

**Class specification** Each AML metaclass is specified in a separate subsection of a package section. Class specification sections contain all the mandatory and some (possibly zero) of the optional subsections described in what follows:

**Semantics (mandatory)**
A summary of semantics and an informal definition of the metaclass specifying the AML modeling element.

**Attributes (optional)**
All owned meta-attributes of the metaclass are specified in terms of:

- name,

- type,

- multiplicity,

- natural language explanation of semantics, and

- if applicable, descriptions of additional property values that apply to the meta-attribute (ordered, union, etc.).

The structure of the meta-attribute specification is as follows:

| | |
|---|---|
| *name*: *type*[*multiplicity*] | *Description of semantics.* |

**Associations (optional)**
The owned (navigable) ends of meta-associations are described in the same way as the meta-attributes.

**Constraints (optional)**
Set of invariants for the metaclass, which must be satisfied by all instances of that metaclass for the model to be meaningful. The rules thus specify constraints over meta-attributes and meta-associations defined in the metamodel. Specification of how the derived meta-attributes and meta-associations are derived are also included. All the invariants are defined by the *Object Constraint Language* (*OCL*) [100] expressions accompanied with an informal (natural language) explanation.

**Notation (mandatory for all but enumerations)**
In this section the notation of the modeling element is presented.

**Enumeration values (mandatory for enumerations)**
The values of the enumeration metaclass are described in terms of:

- value,

- keyword, and

- semantics.

**Presentation options (optional)**

If applicable, alternative ways of depicting the modeling element are presented.

**Style (optional)**

An informal convention of how to present (a part of) a modeling element.

**Examples (optional)**

Examples of how the modeling element is to be used.

**Rationale (mandatory)**

A brief explanation of the reasons why a given metaclass is defined within AML.

# Chapter 10

# Architecture

**Overview** The *Architecture* package defines the metaclasses used to model architectural aspects of multi-agent systems.

**Package structure** The package diagram of the Architecture package is depicted in Fig. 10-1.

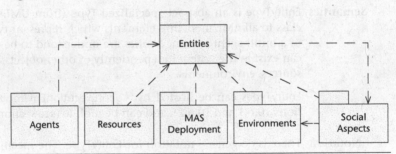

**Fig. 10-1** Architecture—package structure

## 10.1 Entities

**Overview** The *Entities* package defines a hierarchy of abstract metaclasses that represent different kinds of AML entities. Entities are used to further categorize concrete AML metaclasses and to define their characteristic features.

**Abstract**  The diagram of the Entities package is shown in Fig. 10-2.
**syntax**

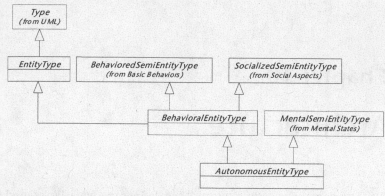

**Fig. 10-2** Entities—hierarchy of entities

## 10.1.1 EntityType

**Semantics**  EntityType is an abstract specialized Type (from UML). It is a super-class to all AML modeling elements which represent types of entities of a multi-agent system. *Entities* are understood to be objects, which can exist in the system independently of other objects, e.g. agents, resources, environments.

EntityTypes can be hosted by AgentExecutionEnvironments (see sections 10.6.1 and 10.6.2), and can be mobile (see section 11.6.3).

**Notation**  There is no general notation for EntityType. The specific subclasses of EntityType define their own notation.

**Rationale**  EntityType is introduced to allow explicit modeling of entities in the system, and to define the features common to all its subclasses.

## 10.1.2 BehavioralEntityType

**Semantics**  BehavioralEntityType is an abstract specialized EntitiyType used to represent types of entities which have the features of BehavioredSemiEntityType and SocializedSemiEntityType, and can play entity roles (see sections 10.5.7 and 10.5.6).

Instances of BehavioralEntityTypes are referred to as *behavioral entities*.

Associations

| /roleAttribute: RoleProperty[*] | A set of all RoleProperties owned by the BehavioralEntityType. It determines the EntityRoleTypes that may be played by the owning BehavioralEntityType. This association is ordered and derived. Subsets UML Class::ownedAttribute. |
|---|---|

Constraints 1. The roleAttribute meta-association refers to all ownedAttributes of the kind RoleProperty:

roleAttribute = self.ownedAttribute-> select(oclIsKindOf(RoleProperty))

Notation BehavioralEntityType is generally depicted as UML Class, but the specific subclasses of BehavioralEntityType define their own notation.

Rationale BehavioralEntityType is introduced to define the features common to all its subclasses.

## 10.1.3 AutonomousEntityType

Semantics AutonomousEntityType is an abstract specialized BehavioralEntityType and MentalSemiEntityType used to model types of self-contained entities that are capable of autonomous behavior in their environment, i.e. entities that have control of their own behavior, and act upon their environment according to the processing of (reasoning on) perceptions of that environment, interactions and/or their mental attitudes. There are no other entities that directly control the behavior of autonomous entities.

AutonomousEntityType, being a MentalSemiEntityType, can be characterized in terms if its mental attitudes, i.e. it can own MentalProperties.

Instances of AutonomousEntityTypes are referred to as *autonomous entities*.

Notation AutonomousEntityType is generally depicted as a UML Class, but the specific subclasses of AutonomousEntityType define their own notation.

Rationale AutonomousEntityType is introduced to allow explicit modeling of autonomous entities in the system, and to define the features common to all its subclasses.

## 10.2  Agents

Overview   The *Agents* package defines the metaclasses used to model agents in
           multi-agent systems.

Abstract   The diagram of the Agents package is shown in Fig. 10-3.
syntax

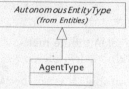

**Fig. 10-3** Agents—agent type

## 10.2.1  AgentType

Semantics   AgentType is a specialized AutonomousEntityType used to model a
            type of *agents*, i.e. self-contained entities that are capable of autono-
            mous behavior within their environment. An agent (instance of an
            AgentType) is a special object (which the object-oriented paradigm
            defines as an entity having identity, status and behavior; not nar-
            rowed to an object-oriented programming concept) having at least
            the following additional features[27]:

□ *Autonomy*, i.e. control over its own state and behavior, based on
  external (reactivity) or internal (proactivity) stimuli, and

□ *Ability to interact*, i.e. the capability to interact with its environment, including perceptions and effecting actions, speech act
  based interactions, etc.

AgentType can use all types of relationships allowed for UML Class,
for instance, associations, generalizations, or dependencies, with
their standard semantics (see [104]), as well as inherited AML-specific
relationships described in further sections.

**Note 1:** An agent in AML represents an architectonic concept, that
does not need to be necessarily implemented by a software or a physical agent. The implementation of AML agents can differ depending
on the implementation environment (which does not necessary need
to be an agent platform, or even a computer system).

**Note 2:** If required, potential AML extensions can define further subclasses of the AgentType metaclass in order to explicitly differentiate
special types of agents. For instance: biological agent, human agent
(specialized biological agent), artificial agent, software agent (special-

---

[27] Other features such as *mobility, adaptability, learning*, etc., are optional in
the AML framework.

ized artificial agent), robot (specialized artificial agent), embedded system (specialized artificial agent), etc.

**Notation**  AgentType is depicted as a UML Class with the stereotype <<agent>> and/or a special icon, see Fig. 10-4. All standard UML class compartments, user-defined compartments, internal structure of parts, ports, connectors, etc. (see UML StructuredClassifier), supported interfaces, provided and required services, owned behaviors, and a structure of the owned named elements can be specified as well. Their notation is described in further document sections or in UML 2.0 Superstructure [104].

**Fig. 10-4** Notation of AgentType

**Examples**  Fig. 10-5 shows an example of the agent type named AgentSmith, having Capabilities findIntruder and convertToSmith, the internal structure composed of connected BehaviorFragments, Perceptors eyes, and Effectors hands and legs.

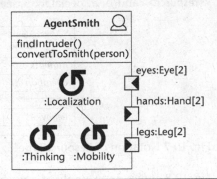

**Fig. 10-5** Example of an AgentType

**Rationale**  AgentType is introduced to model types of agents in multi-agent systems.

## 10.3 Resources

Overview   The *Resources* package defines the metaclasses used to model resources in multi-agent systems.

Abstract   The diagram of the Resource package is shown in Fig. 10-6.
syntax

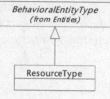

Fig. 10-6 Resources—resource type

### 10.3.1 ResourceType

Semantics   ResourceType is a specialized BehavioralEntityType used to model types of resources contained within the system[28]. A *resource* is a physical or an informational entity, with which the main concern is its availability and usage (e.g. quantity, access rights, conditions of consumption).

Notation   ResourceType is depicted as a UML Class with the stereotype <<resource>> and/or a special icon, see Fig. 10-7.

Fig. 10-7 Notation of ResourceType

Examples   Fig. 10-8 shows an example of a usage of a ResourceType. An Agent-Type RPG_Player, representing a player of an RPG (Role Playing Game), owns a read-write resource inventory of the Inventory type. An Inventory has specified capacity and contains a set of items.

Rationale   ResourceType is introduced to model types of resources in multi-agent systems.

---

[28] A resource positioned outside a system is modeled as a UML Actor (or any subtype of an Actor).

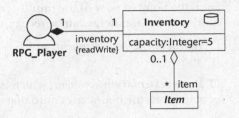

**Fig. 10-8** Example of ResourceType

# 10.4 Environments

**Overview** The *Environments* package defines the metaclasses used to model system internal environments (for definition see section 10.4.1) of multi-agent systems.

**Abstract syntax** The diagram of the Environments package is shown in Fig. 10-9.

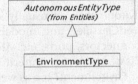

**Fig. 10-9** Environments—environment type

## 10.4.1 EnvironmentType

**Semantics** EnvironmentType is a specialized AutonomousEntityType used to model types of *environments*, i.e. the logical and physical surroundings of entities which provide conditions under which those entities exist and function. EnvironmentType thus can be used to define particular aspects of the world which entities inhabit, its structure and behavior. It can contain the space and all the other objects in the entity surroundings, and also those principles and processes (laws, rules, constraints, policies, services, roles, resources, etc.) which together constitute the circumstances under which entities act.

As environments are usually complex entities, different Environment-Types are usually used to model different aspects of an environment.

From the point of view of the (multi-agent) system modeled, two categories of environments can be recognized:

❑ *system internal environment*, which is a part of the system modeled, and

❑ *system external environment*, which is outside the system modeled and forms the boundaries onto that system.

The EnvironmentType is used to model system internal environments, whereas system external environments are modeled by Actors (from UML).

An instance of the EnvironmentType is called *environment*.

One entity can appear in several environments at once and this set can dynamically change in time.

If required, the EnvironmentType can be extended by properties (tagged values) which can provide explicit classification of environments. For example, determinism, volatility, continuity, accessibility, etc. Definition of such properties depends on specific needs and therefore is not part of the AML specification.

The EnvironmentType usually uses the possibilities inherited from StructuredClassifier, and models its internal structure by contained parts, connectors, ports, etc. All other relationship types defined for UML Class, and other inherited AML-specific relationships can be used for EnvironmentType as well.

**Notation** EnvironmentType is depicted as a UML Class with the stereotype <<environment>> and/or a special icon, see Fig. 10-10.

**Fig. 10-10** Notation of EnvironmentType

**Examples** Fig. 10-11 shows a definition of an abstract Class 3DObject that represents spatial objects, characterized by shape and positions within containing spaces. An abstract EnvironmentType 3DSpace represents a three dimensional space. This is a special 3DObject and as such can contain other spatial objects.

Three concrete 3DObjects are defined: an AgentType Person, a ResourceType Ball and a Class named Goal. 3DSpace is furthermore specialized into a concrete EnvironmentType Pitch representing a soccer pitch containing two goals and a ball.

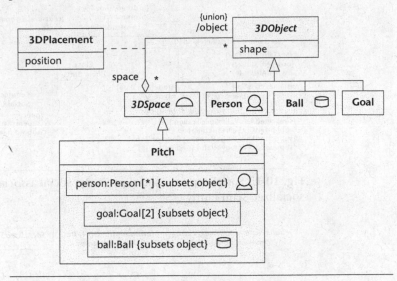

**Fig. 10-11** Example of EnvironmentType

**Rationale** EnvironmentType is introduced to model particular aspects of the system internal environment.

## 10.5 Social Aspects

**Overview** The *Social Aspects* package defines metaclasses used to model abstractions of social aspects of multi-agent systems, including structural characteristics of socialized entities and certain aspects of their social behavior.

**Abstract syntax** The diagrams of the Social Aspects package are shown in figures Fig. 10-12 to Fig. 10-17.

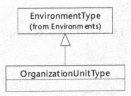

**Fig. 10-12** Social Aspects—organization unit type

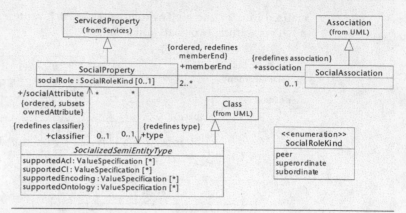

**Fig. 10-13** Social Aspects—social property, social association, and socialized semi-entity type

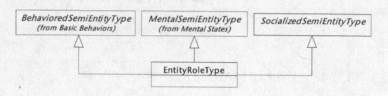

**Fig. 10-14** Social Aspects—entity role type

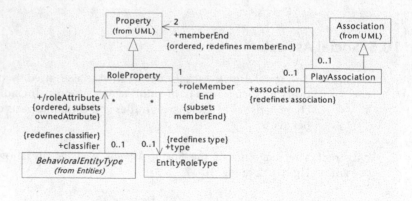

**Fig. 10-15** Social Aspects—role property and play association

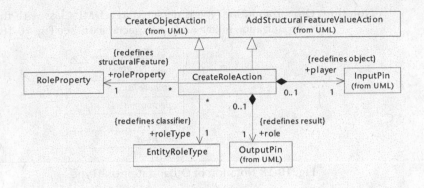

**Fig. 10-16** Social Aspects—create role action

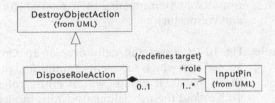

**Fig. 10-17** Social Aspects—dispose role action

## 10.5.1 OrganizationUnitType

**Semantics** OrganizationUnitType is a specialized EnvironmentType used to model types of organization units, i.e. types of social environments or their parts.

An instance of the OrganizationUnitType is called *organization unit*.

From an *external perspective*, organization units represent coherent autonomous entities which can have goals, perform behavior, interact with their environment, offer services, play roles, etc. Properties and behavior of organization units are both:

❑ emergent properties and behavior of all their constituents, their mutual relationships, observations and interactions, and

❑ the features and behavior of organization units themselves.

From an *internal perspective*, organization units are types of environments that specify the social arrangements of entities in terms of structures, interactions, roles, constraints, norms, etc.

Notation  OrganizationUnitType is depicted as a UML Class with the stereotype
&lt;&lt;organization unit&gt;&gt; and/or a special icon, see Fig. 10-18.

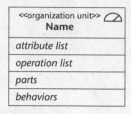

Fig. 10-18 Notation of OrganizationUnitType

Style  An OrganizationUnitType is usually depicted in the form of a UML
StructuredClassifier, and the contained entities (entity roles, agents,
resources, environments, their relationships, etc.) as its parts, ports
and connectors.

Examples  Fig. 10-19 shows the definition of an OrganizationUnitType called
SoccerTeam which represents a simplified model of a soccer team during a match. It groups several entity roles (for details see section
10.5.6) and their social relationships modeled by connectors of special types (for details see section 10.5.5).

A soccer team contains seven to eleven playing players and one to
three coaches. The coaches lead the players and the players cooperate
with each other.

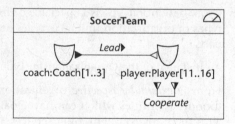

Fig. 10-19 Example of OrganizationUnitType's internal structure

OrganizationUnitType is used to model organization structures.
Fig. 10-20 shows a class diagram depicting a generic organization
structure of software development project. Types of project roles,
teams, and their social associations are shown.

The types defined in the previous organization diagram are used to
model the internal structure of the SoftwareDevelopmentProject, see
Fig. 10-21. Additionally, this OrganizationUnitType offers two external
services (see section 11.4).

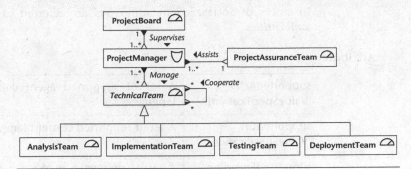

**Fig. 10-20** Organization structure example—definition of types

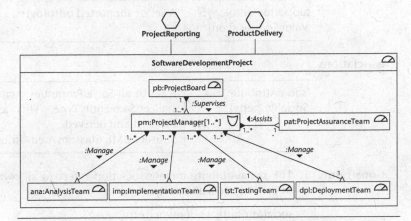

**Fig. 10-21** Organization structure example—internal class structure

**Rationale** OrganizationUnitType is introduced to model types of organization units in multi-agent systems.

## 10.5.2 SocializedSemiEntityType

**Semantics** SocializedSemiEntityType is an abstract specialized Class (from UML), a superclass to all metaclasses which can participate in SocialAssociatons and can own SocialProperties. There are two direct subclasses of the SocializedSemiEntityType: BehavioralEntityType and EntityRoleType.

SocializedSemiEntityTypes represent modeling elements, which would most likely participate in CommunicativeInteractions. Therefore they can specify meta-attributes related to the CommunicativeInteractions, particularly: a set of agent communication languages (supportedAcl), a set of content languages (supportedCl), a set of message content encodings (supportedEncoding), and a set of ontologies (supportedOntology) they support. This set of meta-attributes can be extended by AML users if needed.

Instances of SocializedSemiEntityTypes are referred to as *socialized semi-entities*.

**Attributes**

| | |
|---|---|
| supportedAcl: ValueSpecification[*] | A set of supported agent communication languages. |
| supportedCl: ValueSpecification[*] | A set of supported content languages. |
| supportedEncoding: ValueSpecification[*] | A set of supported message content encodings. |
| supportedOntology: ValueSpecification[*] | A set of supported ontologies. |

**Associations**

| | |
|---|---|
| /socialAttribute: SocialProperty[*] | A set of all SocialProperties owned by the SocializedSemiEntityType. This association is ordered and derived. Subsets UML Class::ownedAttribute. |

**Constraints**  1. The socialAttribute meta-association refers to all ownedAttributes of the kind SocialProperty:

socialAttribute = self.ownedAttribute->
select(oclIsKindOf(SocialProperty))

**Notation**  There is no general notation for SocializedSemiEntityType. The specific subclasses of the SocializedSemiEntityType define their own notation.

The meta-attributes are shown as a property string of the owning SocializedSemiEntityType. The following keywords are used:

❑ acl,

❑ cl,

❑ encoding,

❑ ontology.

Their values represent arbitrary lists of ValueSpecifications, but the most commonly used types are enumerations or string literals.

**Examples** An example of a specification of the meta-attributes for an agent type called Surgeon is depicted in Fig. 10-22.

Fig. 10-22 Example of specification of meta-attributes for a Socialized-SemiEntityType

**Rationale** SocializedSemiEntityType is introduced to define the features common to all its subclasses.

## 10.5.3 SocialProperty

**Semantics** SocialProperty is a specialized ServicedProperty used to specify social relationships that can or must occur between instances of its type and:

☐ instances of its owning class (when the SocialProperty is an attribute of a Class), or

☐ instances of the associated class (when the SocialProperty is a member end of an Association).

SocialProperty can be only of a SocializedSemiEntityType type.

SocialProperties can be owned only by:

☐ SocializedSemiEntityTypes as attributes, or

☐ SocialAssociations as member ends.

When a SocialProperty is owned by a SocializedSemiEntityType, it represents a *social attribute*. In this case the SocialProperty can explicitly declare a social role of its type in regard to the owning class. The social role of the owning SocializedSemiEntityType in regard to the social property's type is implicitly derived according to the rules described in Tab. 10-1.

| Social role of attribute's type | Derived social role of attribute owner |
|---|---|
| *peer* | *peer* |
| *superordinate* | *subordinate* |
| *subordinate* | *superordinate* |

Tab. 10-1 Rules for determining a social role of the SocialProperty owner

Ownership of a SocialProperty by a SocializedSemiEntityType can be considered as an implicit declaration of a binary SocialAssociation between owning SocializedSemiEntityType and a type of the attribute. It is usually used to model social relationships of structured socialized classes (e.g. EnvironmentTypes) and their parts.

When a SocialProperty is owned by a SocialAssociation, it represents a non-navigable end of the association. In this case the SocialProperty declares a social relation of its type (connected SocializedSemiEntity-Type) in regard to the other association end types (SocializedSemiEntityTypes connected to the other association ends).

**Attributes**

| | |
|---|---|
| socialRole: SocialRoleKind[0..1] | The kind of a social relationship between So-cialProperty's type and the owning Social-izedSemiEntityType. |

**Associations**

| | |
|---|---|
| association: SocialAssociation[0..1] | The owning SocialAssociation of which this SocialProperty is a member, if any. Redefines UML Property::association. |
| type: SocializedSemiEntity-Type[0..1] | The type of a SocialProperty. Redefines UML TypedElement::type. |

**Constraints**

1. If SocialProperty is a member end of a SocialAssociation and its socialRole is set to *peer*, the socialRoles of all other member ends must be set to *peer* as well:

   (self.association->notEmpty() and self.socialRole=#peer) implies
       self.association.memberEnd->forAll(socialRole=#peer)

2. If SocialProperty is a member end of a SocialAssociation and its socialRole is set to *superordinate*, the socialRoles of all other member ends must be set to *subordinate*:

   (self.association->notEmpty() and self.socialRole=#superordinate)
       implies self.association.memberEnd->
       forAll(me|me <> self and me.socialRole=#subordinate)

3. If SocialProperty is a member end of a SocialAssociation and its socialRole is set to *subordinate*, the socialRole of some another member end must be set to *superordinate*:

   (self.association->notEmpty() and self.socialRole=#subordinate)
       implies self.association.memberEnd->
       exists(socialRole=#superordinate)

**Notation**  When shown as an association end, the SocialProperty is depicted as a UML association end with a stereotype specifying the social role kind. The keyword is defined by the SocialRoleKind enumeration. See Fig. 10-23.

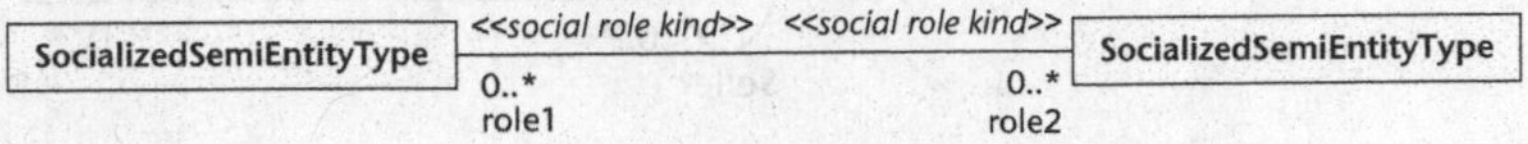

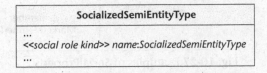

**Fig. 10-23** Notation of SocialProperty shown as an association end

When shown as an attribute, the SocialProperty is depicted as a UML attribute with an additional keyword specifying the social role kind. The keyword is defined by the SocialRoleKind enumeration. See Fig. 10-24.

| SocializedSemiEntityType |
|---|
| ... |
| <<social role kind>> name:SocializedSemiEntityType |
| ... |

**Fig. 10-24** Notation of SocialProperty shown as an attribute

**Presentation options**  An iconic notation for particular social role kinds can be used instead of textual labels. Alternative notation is depicted in Fig. 10-25.

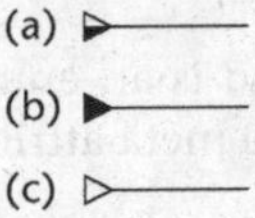

**Fig. 10-25** Alternative notation for SocialProperty shown as an association end: (a) peer, (b) superordinate, (c) subordinate.

The same icons can be used also for a SocialProperty specified as an attribute. See Fig. 10-26.

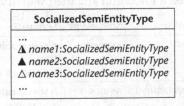

**Fig. 10-26** Alternative notation of SocialProperty shown as an attribute

**Examples**  Fig. 10-27 (a) shows an example of peer-to-peer social relationship between sellers and buyers. In case (b), an OrganizationUnitType Market comprises many market members who are subordinated to their home market. The case (c) is semantically similar to the case (b), but the Market is depicted as a StructuredClassifier and its market members are represented as a part.

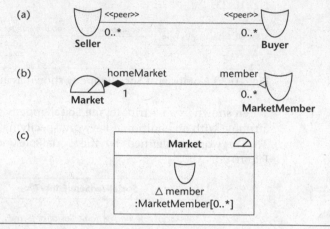

**Fig. 10-27** Examples of SocialProperty

**Rationale**  SocialProperty is introduced to model social relationships between entities in multi-agent systems.

### 10.5.4 SocialRoleKind

**Semantics**  SocialRoleKind is an enumeration which specifies allowed values for the socialRole meta-attribute of the SocialProperty.

AML supports modeling of superordinate-subordinate and peer-to-peer relationships, but this set can be extended as required (e.g. to model producer-consumer, competition, or cooperation relationships).

**Enumeration values**  Tab. 10-2 specifies SocialRoleKind's enumeration literals, stereotypes used for notation and their semantics.

| Value | Stereotype | Semantics |
|---|---|---|
| *peer* | <<peer>> | A social role kind used in the peer-to-peer relationships of the entities with the same social status and equal authority. |
| *superordinate* | <<super>> | A social role kind specifying higher authority and power for its owner than for other associated subordinate entities. Superordinate entity is able to constrain the behavior of its subordinates. |
| *subordinate* | <<sub>> | A social role kind specifying lower authority and power than associated superordinate entity. |

**Tab. 10-2** SocialRoleKind's enumeration literals

**Rationale** SocialRoleKind is introduced to define allowed values for the social-Role meta-attribute of the SocialProperty.

## 10.5.5 SocialAssociation

**Semantics** SocialAssociation is a specialized Association (from UML) used to model social relationships that can occur between SocializedSemiEntityTypes. It redefines the type of the memberEnd property of Association to SocialProperty.

An instance of the SocialAssociation is called *social link*.

**Associations**

| | |
|---|---|
| memberEnd:<br>SocialProperty[2..*] | At least two SocialProperties representing participation of socialized semi-entities in a social link. This is an ordered association. Redefines UML Association::memberEnd. |

**Notation** SocialAssociation is depicted as a UML Association with stereotype <<social>>. Ends of SocialAssociation can use a special notation that is described in section 10.5.3. Notation of binary SocialAssociation is shown in Fig. 10-28.

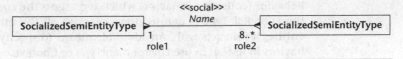

**Fig. 10-28** Notation of binary SocialAssociation

Notation of n-ary social association is shown in Fig. 10-29.

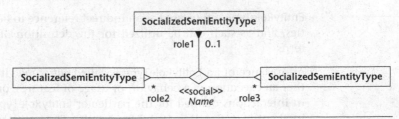

**Fig. 10-29** Notation of n-ary SocialAssociation

**Style** The Association's stereotype is usually omitted if the association ends are stereotyped by social role kinds.

**Examples**  Fig. 10-30 shows a peer-to-peer SocialAssociation named Deal of two entity role types Seller and Buyer.

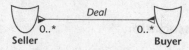

**Fig. 10-30** Example of SocialAssociation

Other examples of SocialAssociations can be found in Fig. 10-11, Fig. 10-19, Fig. 10-20, Fig. 10-27, Fig. 10-33, and Fig. 10-40.

**Rationale**  SocialAssociation is introduced to model social relationships between entities in multi-agent systems in the form of an Association.

## 10.5.6  EntityRoleType

**Semantics**  EntityRoleType is a specialized BehavioredSemiEntityType, Mental-SemiEntityType, and SocializedSemiEntityType, used to represent a coherent set of features, behaviors, participation in interactions, and services offered or required by BehavioralEntityTypes in a particular context (e.g. interaction or social).

Each EntityRoleType thus should be defined within a specific larger behavior (collective behavior) which represents the context in which the EntityRoleType is defined together with all the other behavioral entities it interacts with. An advisable means to specify collective behaviors in AML is to use EnvironmentType or Context.

Each EntityRoleType should be realized by a specific implementation possessed by a BehavioralEntityType which may play that EntityRoleType (for details see sections 10.5.7 and 10.5.8).

EntityRoleType can be used as an indirect reference to behavioral entities, and as such can be utilized for the definition of reusable patterns.

An instance of an EntityRoleType is called *entity role*. It represents either an execution of a behavior, or usage of features, or participation in interactions defined for the particular EntityRoleType by a behavioral entity (see section 10.1.2 for details). The entity role exists only while a behavioral entity plays it.

An entity role represented in a model as an InstanceSpecification classified by an EntityRoleType represents an instance of any BehavioralEntityType that may play that EntityRoleType, if the player (a behavioral entity which plays that entity role) is not specified explicitly.

When an EntityRoleType is used to specify the type of a TypedElement, values represented by that TypedElement are constrained to be in-

stances of those BehavioralEntityTypes that may play given EntityRole-
Type.

An EntityRoleType, composed of other EntityRoleTypes (i.e. owning aggregated attributes having types of EntityRoleType), represents a *position type*. Its instantiation results in particular *positions*. A position can
also be expressed implicitly by specifying several entity roles representing a specific position to be played by one behavioral entity hold-
ing this position.

**Notation** EntityRoleType is depicted as a UML Class with the stereotype
<<entity role>> and/or a special icon, see Fig. 10-31.

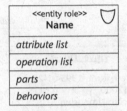

**Fig. 10-31** Notation of EntityRoleType

**Examples** Fig. 10-32 shows an example of detailed modeling of EntityRoleTypes.
The abstract EntityRoleType called Employee is used to model a type of
employees. It defines a set of attributes which characterize their playing, namely employed_from, salary, and responsibilities. A social association Work for represents the social relationship of employees (instances of the Employee EntityRoleType) who are subordinated to their
employer(s) (instances of the Employer EntityRoleType). EntityRole-
Type Driver is a specialized Employee used to model profesional car
drivers who drive and maintain cars. In addition to the structural features defined by Employee, it models also the connection of a driver
with the farmed out car modeled by the Drive association, and two capabilities driveCar and maintainCar.

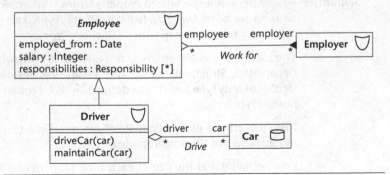

**Fig. 10-32** EntityRoleType example—employee and driver

Fig. 10-33 shows instantiation of EntityRoleTypes. In this example an agent Oliver plays an entity role master (depicted as an instantiated PlayAssociation). An agent John holds an implicitly specified position of a driver and a valet which can be possibly played simultaneously. Slots shown for the driver entity role specify its property values. An agent Mary plays an entity role cook. The figure shows also the links which represent instances of social associations defined on respective EntityRoleTypes. The corresponding class diagram is depicted in Fig. 10-37.

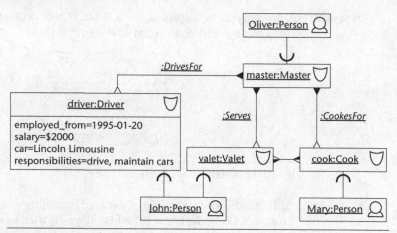

**Fig. 10-33** EntityRoleType example—instances

Other examples of EntityRoleTypes can be found in Fig. 10-19, Fig. 10-20, and Fig. 10-21.

**Rationale**  EntityRoleType is introduced to model roles in multi-agent systems.

## 10.5.7 RoleProperty

**Semantics**  RoleProperty is a specialized Property (from UML) used to specify that an instance of its owner, a BehavioralEntityType, can play one or several entity roles of the specified EntityRoleType.

The owner of a RoleProperty is responsible for implementation of all Capabilities, StructuralFeatures and metaproperties defined by SocializedSemiEntityType which are defined by RoleProperty's type (an EntityRoleType).

Instances of the played EntityRoleType represent (can be substituted by) instances of the RoleProperty owner.

One behavioral entity can at each time play (instantiate) several entity roles. These entity roles can be of the same as well as of different types. The multiplicity defined for a RoleProperty constrains the number of entity roles of a given type that the particular behavioral entity can play concurrently.

**Associations**

| association:<br>PlayAssociation[0..1] | The owning PlayAssociation of which this Role-Property is a member, if any.<br>Redefines UML Property::association. |
|---|---|
| type:<br>EntityRoleType[0..1] | The type of a RoleProperty.<br>Redefines UML TypedElement::type. |

**Constraints**   1.  The aggregation meta-attribute of the RoleProperty is composite:

self.aggregation = #composite

**Notation**   When shown as the end of a PlayAssociation, the RoleProperty is depicted as a UML association end.

When shown as an attribute, the RoleProperty is depicted as a UML attribute with the stereotype <<role>>, see Fig. 10-34.

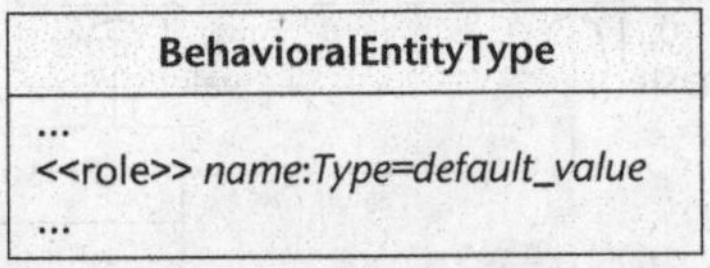

| **BehavioralEntityType** |
|---|
| ...<br><<role>> *name:Type=default_value*<br>... |

Fig. 10-34 Notation of RoleProperty shown as an attribute

**Presentation options**   The role properties of a BehavioralEntityType can be placed in a special class compartment named <<roles>>. The stereotype <<role>> of a particular RoleProperty is in this case omitted. See Fig. 10-35.

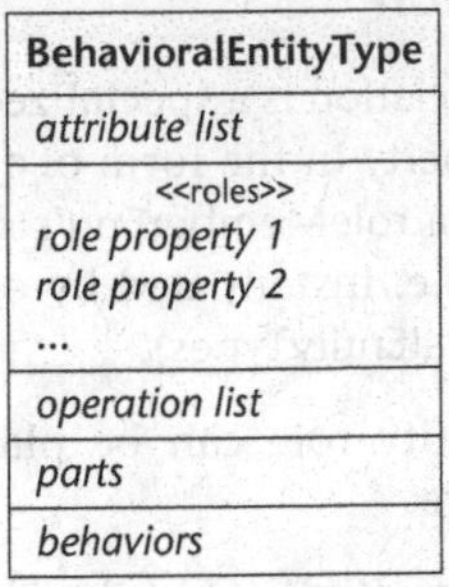

| **BehavioralEntityType** |
|---|
| *attribute list* |
| <<roles>><br>*role property 1*<br>*role property 2*<br>... |
| *operation list* |
| *parts* |
| *behaviors* |

Fig. 10-35 Alternative notation for RoleProperty placed in a special class compartment

**Examples**  Fig. 10-36 shows an example of specifying RoleProperties as attributes in a special class compartment. An agent Person can play four kinds of entity roles: master, valet, driver and cook.

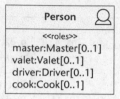

Fig. 10-36 Example of RoleProperties specified as attributes

Fig. 10-37 shows a semantically identical model, but the RoleProperties are specified as ends of PlayAssociations.

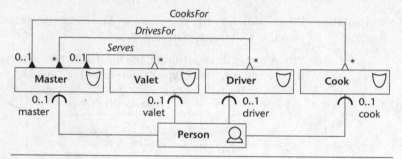

**Fig. 10-37** Example of RoleProperties specified as association ends

**Rationale**  RoleProperty is introduced to model the possibility of playing entity roles by behavioral entities.

## 10.5.8 PlayAssociation

**Semantics**  PlayAssociation is a specialized Association (from UML) used to specify RoleProperty in the form of an association end. It specifies that entity roles of a roleMemberEnd's type (which is an EntityRoleType) can be played, i.e. instantiated by entities of the other end type (which are BehavioralEntityTypes).

Each entity role can be played by at most one behavioral entity. Therefore:

❏ The multiplicity of the PlayAssociation at the BehavioralEntityType side is always 0..1, and thus is not shown in diagrams.

❏ If there are more than one PlayAssociations attached to an EntityRoleType then an implicit constraint applies, stating that no more than one PlayAssociation link can exist at any given moment. These constraints are implicit and thus not shown in diagrams.

Multiplicity on the entity role side of the PlayAssociation constrains the number of entity roles the particular BehavioralEntityType can instantiate concurrently.

An instance of the PlayAssociation is called *play link*.

Other notation parts defined for UML Association (qualifier, property string, navigability, etc.) can be specified for the PlayAssociation as well. Their semantics are specified in UML 2.0 Superstructure [104].

**Associations**

| memberEnd:<br>Property[2] | Two associated Properties. This is an ordered association.<br>Redefines UML Association::memberEnd. |
|---|---|
| roleMemberEnd:<br>RoleProperty[1] | Associated RoleProperty.<br>Subsets PlayAssociation::memberEnd. |

**Notation** PlayAssociation is depicted as a UML Association with the <<play>> stereotype, see Fig. 10-38. The multiplicity at the BehavioralEntityType side is unspecified.

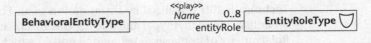

**Fig. 10-38** Notation of PlayAssociation

**Presentation options** Instead of a stereotyped Association, the PlayAssociation can be depicted as an association line with a small thick semicircle as an arrow head at the end of EntityRoleType. See Fig. 10-39.

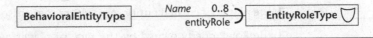

**Fig. 10-39** Alternative notation of PlayAssociation

**Style** Stereotype labels or icons of association ends are usually omitted because their end types determine them implicitly. An association end connected to an EntityRoleType represents a RoleProperty and therefore the <<role>> stereotype may be omitted.

Even if the aggregation meta-attribute of the RoleProperty is always composite, a solid filled diamond is usually not shown in the PlayAssociation.

**Examples** Fig. 10-40 shows an example where each instance of an AgentType Person and an OrganizationUnitType Bank can play several entity roles of type Buyer. Each of these entity roles is used to specify a deal with a specific seller.

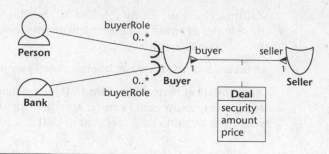

**Fig. 10-40** Example of PlayAssociation relationship

**Rationale** PlayAssociation is introduced to model the possibility of playing entity roles by behavioral entities.

## 10.5.9 CreateRoleAction

**Semantics** CreateRoleAction is a specialized CreateObjectAction (from UML) and AddStructuralFeatureValueAction (from UML), used to model the action of creating and starting to play an entity role by a behavioral entity.

Technically this is realized by instantiation of an EntityRoleType into an entity role of that type, and adding this instance as a value to the RoleProperty of its player (a behavioral entity) which starts to play it.

The CreateRoleAction specifies:

❑ what EntityRoleType is being instantiated (roleType meta-association),

❑ the entity role being created (role meta-association),

❑ the player of created entity role (player meta-association), and

❑ the RoleProperty owned by the type of player, where the created entity role is being placed (roleProperty meta-association).

If the RoleProperty referred to by the roleProperty meta-association is ordered, the insertAt meta-association (inherited from the AddStructuralFeatureValueAction) specifies a position at which to insert the entity role.

Because the value meta-association (inherited from UML WriteStructuralFeatureAction) represents the same entity role as is already represented by the role meta-association, the properties of the InputPin referred to by the value meta-association are ignored in CreateRoleAction, and can be omitted in its specification.

**Associations**

| | |
|---|---|
| roleType: EntityRoleType[1] | Instantiated EntityRoleType. Redefines UML CreateObjectAction::classifier. |
| role: OutputPin[1] | The OutputPin on which the created entity role is put. Redefines UML CreateObjectAction::result. |
| player: InputPin[1] | The InputPin specifying the player of the created entity role. Redefines UML StructuralFeatureAction::object. |
| roleProperty: RoleProperty[1] | The RoleProperty where the created entity role is being placed. Redefines UML StructuralFeatureAction::structuralFeature. |

**Constraints**  1. If the type of the InputPin referred to by the player meta-association is specified, it must be a BehavioralEntityType:

self.player.type->notEmpty() implies
    self.player.type.oclIsKindOf(BehavioralEntityType)

2. If the type of the OutputPin referred to by the role meta-association is specified, it must conform to the EntityRoleType referred to by the roleType meta-association:

self.role.type->notEmpty() implies
    self.role.type.conformsTo(self.roleType)

3. If the type of the RoleProperty referred to by the roleProperty meta-association is specified, the EntityRoleType referred to by the roleType meta-association must conform to it:

self.roleProperty.type->notEmpty() implies
    self.roleType.conformsTo(self.roleProperty.type)

**Notation**  CreateRoleAction is shown as a UML Action with the stereotype <<create role>> and/or a special icon, see Fig. 10-41.

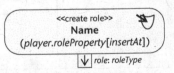

**Fig. 10-41** Notation of CreateRoleAction

Optionally, the name of the player, delimited by a period from the name of the RoleProperty referred to by the roleProperty meta-association, may be specified in parentheses below the action's name. If the RoleProperty is ordered, the value of the insertAt meta-association can be placed after the RoleProperty's name in brackets.

If the player itself executes the CreateRoleAction, it can be identified by the keyword 'self' in place of player name.

A created entity role is specified as an OutputPin. All notational variations for the UML OutputPin are allowed. The EntityRoleType referred to by the roleType meta-association is specified as the type of the OutputPin.

A mandatory InputPin referred to by the value meta-association has unspecified properties and is not drawn in diagrams.

**Examples**   Fig. 10-42 shows an example of the activity describing the scenario of creating and matching a sell order at the stock exchange.

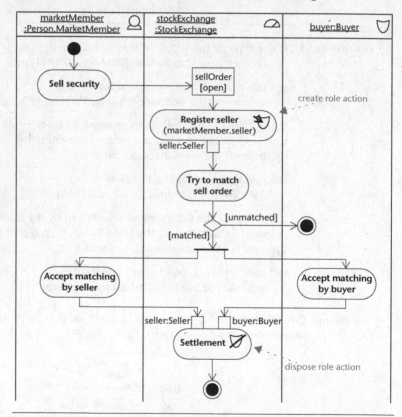

**Fig. 10-42** Example of CreateRoleAction and DisposeRoleAction

The activity comprises three activity partitions: an agent marketMember representing a Person who is playing an entity role of type MarketMember, organization unit stockExchange, and an entity role buyer.

The marketMember, wanting to sell some securities, creates a sellOrder and submits it to the stockExchange. The stockExchange registers this order and creates a new seller entity role (we can say: "a new seller position is opened at the stock exchange"). The marketMember becomes a seller by this registration. Then the stockExchange tries to match the sellOrder. If the matching was unsuccessful, the scenario terminates. If the matching was successful, the marketMember (now also seller) and the buyer concurrently confirm the match. When complete, the stockExchange performs a settlement and both the seller and buyer entity roles are disposed.

**Rationale** CreateRoleAction is introduced to model an action of creating and playing entity roles by behavioral entities.

## 10.5.10 DisposeRoleAction

**Semantics** DisposeRoleAction is a specialized DestroyObjectAction (from UML) used to model the action of stopping to play an entity role by a behavioral entity.

Technically it is realized by destruction of the corresponding entity role(s). As a consequence, all behavioral entities that were playing the destroyed entity roles stop to play them.

**Associations**

| role: InputPin[1..*] | The InputPins representing the entity roles to be disposed. Redefines UML DestroyObjectAction::target. |
| --- | --- |

**Constraints** 1. If the types of the InputPins referred to by the role meta-association are specified, they must be EntityRoleTypes:

self.role->forAll(ro | ro.type->notEmpty() implies
  ro.type.oclIsKindOf(EntityRoleType))

**Notation** DisposeRoleAction is drawn as a UML Action with the stereotype <<dispose role>> and/or a special icon, see Fig. 10-43. Disposed entity roles are depicted as InputPins.

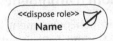

**Fig. 10-43** Notation of DisposeRoleAction

**Examples** See Fig. 10-42.

**Rationale** DisposeRoleAction is introduced to model the action of disposing of entity roles by behavioral entities.

## 10.6  MAS Deployment

**Overview** The *MAS Deployment* package defines the metaclasses used to model deployment of a multi-agent system to a physical environment.

**Abstract** The diagrams of the MAS Deployment package are shown in figures
**syntax** Fig. 10-44 and Fig. 10-45.

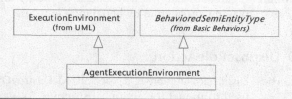

**Fig. 10-44** MAS Deployment—agent execution environment

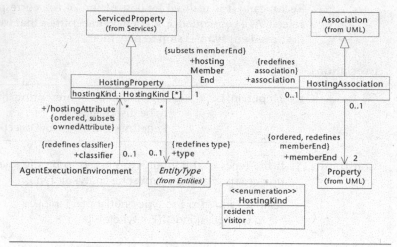

**Fig. 10-45** MAS Deployment—hosting

## 10.6.1  AgentExecutionEnvironment

**Semantics** AgentExecutionEnvironment is a specialized ExecutionEnvironment (from UML) and BehavioredSemiEntityType, used to model types of execution environments of multi-agent systems. AgentExecutionEnvironment thus provides the physical infrastructure in which MAS entities can run. One entity can run at most in one AgentExecutionEnvironment instance at one time.

If useful, it may be further subclassed into more specific agent execution environments, for example, agent platform, or agent container.

AgentExecutionEnvironment can provide (use) a set of services that deployed entities use (provide) at run time. AgentExecutionEnvironment, being a BehavioredSemiEntityType, can explicitly specify such services by means of ServiceProvisions and ServiceUsages respectively.

Owned HostingProperties specify kinds of entities hosted by (running at) the AgentExecutionEnvironment. Internal structure of the AgentExecutionEnvironment can also contain other features and behaviors that characterize it.

**Associations**

| | |
|---|---|
| /hostingAttribute: HostingProperty[*] | A set of all HostingProperties owned by the AgentExecutionEnvironment. This association is ordered and derived. Subsets UML Class::ownedAttribute. |

**Constraints**  1. The internal structure of an AgentExecutionEnvironment can also consist of other attributes than parts of the type Node. The constraint [1] defined for UML Node, and inherited by the AgentExecutionEnvironment, is therefore discarded (see [104] for details).

2. The hostingAttribute meta-association refers to all ownedAttributes of the kind HostingProperty:

hostingAttribute = self.ownedAttribute->
    select(oclIsKindOf(HostingProperty))

**Notation**  AgentExecutionEnvironment is depicted as a UML ExecutionEnvironment with the stereotype <<agent execution environment>> and/or a special icon, see Fig. 10-46.

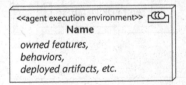

**Fig. 10-46** Notation of AgentExecutionEnvironment

**Examples**  Fig. 10-47 shows the example of a MAS deployment model. A Node called StockExchangeServer runs an AgentExecutionEnvironment of type TradingServer and this in turn enables the hosting of agents of type Broker (modeled by a HostingProperty), resources of type Account and one environment of type OrderPool. A Node ClientPC runs an AgentExecutionEnvironment of type TradingClient in which agents of type Broker can be hosted. All hosting entities are modeled as hosting-Attributes.

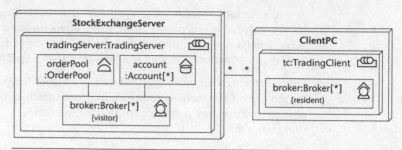

**Fig. 10-47** MAS deployment example—class diagram

Fig. 10-48 shows an instance-level example of the AgentExecutionEnvironment called AgentPlatform, distributed over several Nodes. Each Node contains its own specific AgentContainer, where the local agents operate. The mainNode, in addition to the main agent container mainAc, has also deployed the central database centralDB used by the agent container.

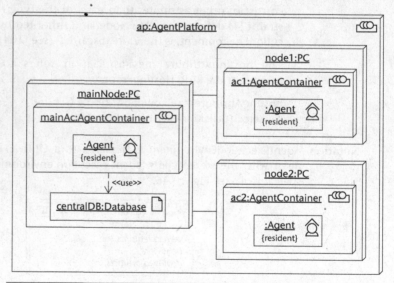

**Fig. 10-48** MAS deployment example—instance diagram

For another example see also Fig. 11-117.

**Rationale** AgentExecutionEnvironment is introduced to model execution environments of multi-agent systems, i.e. the environments in which the entities exist and operate.

## 10.6.2 HostingProperty

**Semantics**  HostingProperty is a specialized ServicedProperty used to specify what EntityTypes can be hosted by what AgentExecutionEnvironments.

Type of a HostingProperty can be only an EntityType.

HostingProperties can be owned only by:

☐ AgentExecutionEnvironments as attributes, or

☐ HostingAssociations as member ends.

The owned meta-attribute hostingKind specifies the relation of the referred EntityType to the owning AgentExecutionEnvironment (for details see section 10.6.3).

**Attributes**

| | |
|---|---|
| hostingKind: HostingKind[*] | A set of hosting kinds that the owning AgentExecutionEnvironment provides to the HostingProperty's type. |

**Associations**

| | |
|---|---|
| association: HostingAssociation [0..1] | The owning HostingAssociation of which this HostingProperty is a member, if any. It represents a hosting place. Redefines UML Property::association. |
| type: EntityType[0..1] | The type of a HostingProperty. It represents an entity that resides at the hosting AgentExecutionEnvironment. Redefines UML TypedElement::type. |
| /move: Move[*] | A set of the Move dependencies that refer to the HostingProperty as source of moving. This is a derived association. |
| /moveFrom: Move[*] | A set of the Move dependencies that refer to the HostingProperty as destination of moving. This is a derived association. |
| /clone: Clone[*] | A set of the Clone dependencies that refer to the HostingProperty as source of cloning. This is a derived association. |
| /cloneFrom: Clone[*] | A set of the Clone dependencies that refer to the HostingProperty as destination of cloning. This is a derived association. |

**Constraints**  1. The move meta-association refers to all clientDependencies of the
kind Move:

move = self.clientDependency->select(oclIsKindOf(Move))

2. The moveFrom meta-association refers to all supplierDependencies
of the kind Move:

moveFrom = self.supplierDependency->select(oclIsKindOf(Move))

3. The clone meta-association refers to all clientDependencies of the
kind Clone:

clone = self.clientDependency->select(oclIsKindOf(Clone))

4. The cloneFrom meta-association refers to all supplierDependencies
of the kind Clone:

cloneFrom = self.supplierDependency->select(oclIsKindOf(Clone))

**Notation**  When shown as the end of a HostingAssociation, the HostingProperty
is depicted as a UML association end (see section 10.6.4 for details).

When shown as an attribute, the HostingProperty is depicted as a UML
attribute with the stereotype <<hosting>>, see Fig. 10-49.

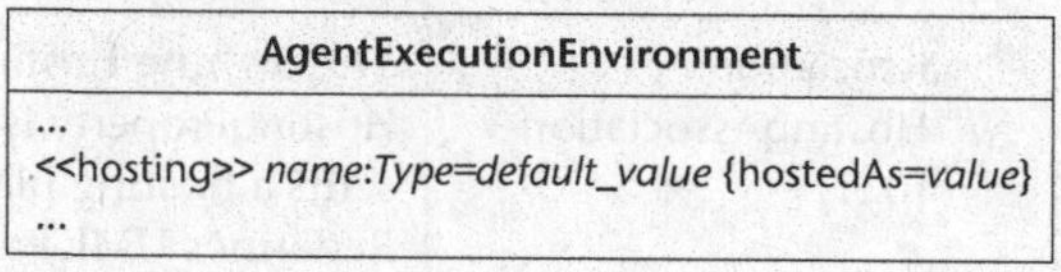

| **AgentExecutionEnvironment** |
|---|
| ... |
| <<hosting>> *name:Type=default_value* {hostedAs=*value*} |
| ... |

**Fig. 10-49** Notation of HostingProperty shown as an attribute

The hostingKind meta-attribute is specified as a tagged value with the
keyword 'hostedAs' and a value containing a list of HostingKind literals separated by ampersands ('&').

Alternatively, the HostingProperty can be depicted as a ConnectableElement with the stereotype <<hosting>>, see Fig. 10-50.

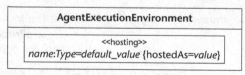

**Fig. 10-50** Notation of HostingProperty shown as a ConnectableElement

**Presentation**  All HostingProperties of an AgentExecutionEnvironment can be placed
**options**  in a special compartment named <<hosting>>. The stereotype
<<hosting>> of a particular HostingProperty is in this case omitted. See
Fig. 10-51.

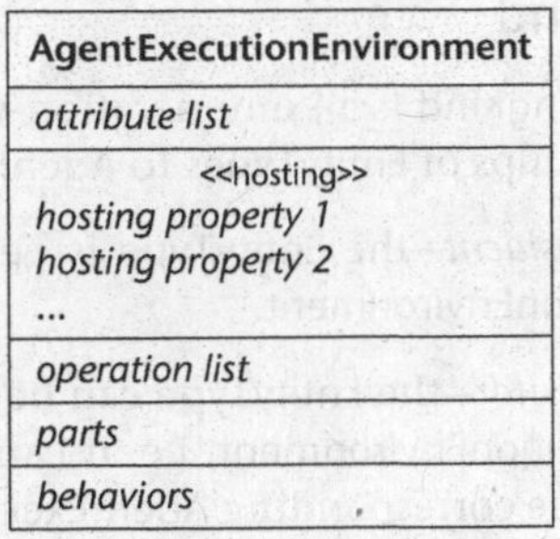

| AgentExecutionEnvironment |
| --- |
| *attribute list* |
| *<<hosting>>* <br> *hosting property 1* <br> *hosting property 2* <br> *...* |
| *operation list* |
| *parts* |
| *behaviors* |

**Fig. 10-51** Alternative notation for HostingProperty placed in a special class compartment

To recognize the fundamental type of HostingProperty's type visually and to specify just one stereotype, AML offers a notation shortcut to combine both stereotypes when the HostingProperty is depicted as a ConnectableElement. The basic shape of the modified stereotype icon represents an original EntityType's stereotype icon placed under a "shelter", which means hosting. Variants of stereotype icons for all concrete EntityTypes are depicted in Fig. 10-52.

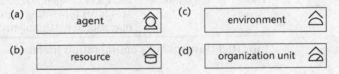

**Fig. 10-52** Alternative notation for HostingProperty depicting a stereotype of its type's fundamental type: (a) hosting of an agent, (b) hosting of a resource, (c) hosting of an environment, (d) hosting of an organization unit.

If the only displayed tagged value is the hostingKind, its keyword may be omitted and only its value is specified. Alternatively, the property string may be placed under the name/type string.

**Examples**  See Fig. 10-47, Fig. 10-48, and Fig. 11-117.

**Rationale**  HostingProperty is introduced to model the hosting of EntityTypes by AgentExecutionEnvironments.

### 10.6.3  HostingKind

**Semantics**  HostingKind is an enumeration which specifies possible hosting relationships of EntityTypes to AgentExecutionEnvironments. These are:

- ❒ *resident*—the EntityType is perpetually hosted by the AgentExecutionEnvironment.

- ❒ *visitor*—the EntityType can be temporarily hosted by the AgentExecutionEnvironment, i.e. it can be temporarily moved or cloned to
  the corresponding AgentExecutionEnvironment.

If needed, the set of available hosting kinds can be extended.

**Enumeration**  Tab. 10-3 specifies HostingKind's enumeration literals, keywords used
**values**  for notation and their semantics.

| Value | Keyword | Semantics |
|---|---|---|
| *resident* | resident | Instances of AgentExecutionEnvironment represent home for resident entities, i.e. execution environments where the entities are deployed and operate perpetually. |
| *visitor* | visitor | Instances of AgentExecutionEnvironment represent hosts for visiting entities, i.e. temporary operational environments. |

**Tab. 10-3** HostingKind's enumeration literals

**Rationale**  HostingKind is introduced to define possible values of the hostingKind
meta-attribute of the HostingProperty metaclass.

### 10.6.4  HostingAssociation

**Semantics**  HostingAssociation is a specialized Association (from UML) used to
specify HostingProperty in the form of an association end. It specifies
that entities classified according to a hostingMemberEnd's type
(which is an EntityType) can be hosted by instances of an AgentExecutionEnvironment representing the other end type.

HostingAssociation is a binary association.

An instance of the HostingAssociation is called *hosting link*.

Other notation parts defined for UML Association (qualifier, property
string, navigability, etc.) can be specified for the HostingAssociation as
well. Their semantics are specified in UML 2.0 Superstructure [104].

**Associations**

| | |
|---|---|
| memberEnd: Property[2] | Two associated Properties. This is an ordered association.<br>Redefines UML Association::memberEnd. |
| hostingMemberEnd: HostingProperty[1] | Associated HostingProperty.<br>Subsets HostingAssociation::memberEnd. |

**Notation** HostingAssociation is depicted as a UML Association with the stereotype <<hosting>>, see Fig. 10-53.

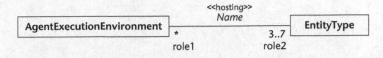

**Fig. 10-53** Notation of HostingAssociation

**Presentation options** Instead of a stereotyped Association, the HostingAssociation can be depicted as an association line with a small thick "V" shape at the end of EntityRoleType, pointing in the direction of the AgentExecutionEnvironment. See Fig. 10-54.

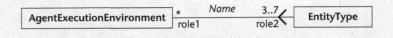

**Fig. 10-54** Alternative notation of HostingAssociation

**Examples** Fig. 10-55 shows an example of hosting Broker, Account and an Order-Pool EntityTypes by the TradingServer AgentExecutionEnvironment. Broker is hosted as a visitor.

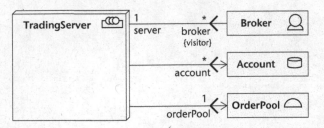

**Fig. 10-55** Example of HostingAssociation

**Rationale** HostingAssociation is introduced to model the hosting of EntityTypes by AgentExecutionEnvironments in the form of an Association.

# Chapter 11

# Behaviors

**Overview** The *Behaviors* package defines the metaclasses used to model behavioral aspects of multi-agent systems.

**Package structure** Fig. 11-1 depicts the package diagram of the Behaviors package.

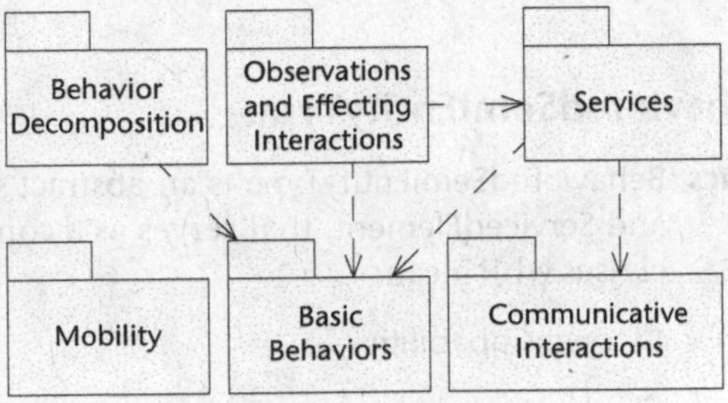

Fig. 11-1 Behaviors—package structure

## 11.1 Basic Behaviors

**Overview** The *Basic Behaviors* package defines the core, frequently referred metaclasses used to model behavior in AML.

**Abstract syntax**  The diagram of the Basic Behaviors package is shown in Fig. 11-2.

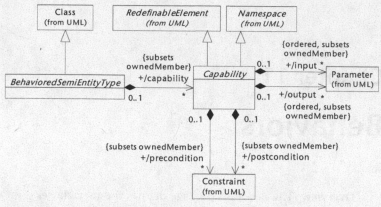

**Fig. 11-2** Basic Behaviors—behaviored semi-entity type and capability

## 11.1.1 BehavioredSemiEntityType

**Semantics**  BehavioredSemiEntityType is an abstract specialized Class (from UML) and ServicedElement, that serves as a common superclass to all meta-classes which can:

- ☐ own Capabilities,

- ☐ observe and/or effect their environment by means of Perceptors and Effectors, and

- ☐ provide and/or use services by means of ServicedPorts.

Furthermore, behavior of BehavioredSemiEntityTypes (and related features) can be explicitly (and potentially recursively) decomposed into BehavioralFragments.

In addition to the services provided and used directly by the BehavioredSemiEntityType (see the serviceUsage and the serviceProvision meta-associations inherited from the ServicedElement), it is also responsible for implementation of the services specified by all ServiceProvisions and ServiceUsages owned by the ServicedProperties and ServicedPorts having the BehavioredSemiEntityType as their type.

Instances of BehavioredSemiEntityTypes are referred to as *behaviored semi-entities*.

**Associations**

| | |
|---|---|
| /capability: Capability[*] | A set of all Capabilities owned by a BehavioredSemiEntityType. This is a derived association. |
| /behaviorFragment: BehaviorFragment[*] | A set of all BehaviorFragments that decompose a BehavioredSemiEntityType. This is a derived association. |
| /ownedServicedPort: ServicedPort[*] | A set of all ServicedPorts owned by a BehavioredSemiEntityType. This is a derived association. |
| /ownedPerceptor: Perceptor[*] | All owned Perceptors. This is a derived association.<br>Subsets BehavioredSemiEntityType:: ownedServicedPort. |
| /ownedEffector: Effector[*] | All owned Effectors. This is a derived association.<br>Subsets BehavioredSemiEntityType:: ownedServicedPort. |

**Constraints**

1. The capability meta-association is union of owned BehavioralFeatures and Behaviors:

   capability = self.ownedBehavior->union(self.feature->
       select(oclIsKindOf(BehavioralFeature)))

2. The behaviorFragment meta-association comprises types of all owned aggregate or composite attributes having the type of a BehaviorFragment:

   behaviorFragment = self.ownedAttribute->
       select(oa|(oa.aggregation=#shared
       or oa.aggregation=#composite)
       and oa.type->notEmpty()
       and oa.type.oclIsKindOf(BehaviorFragment)).type

3. The ownedServicedPort meta-association refers to all owned ports of the kind ServicedPort:

   ownedServicedPort = self.ownedPort->
       select(oclIsKindOf(ServicedPort))

4. The ownedPerceptor meta-association refers to all owned service ports of the kind Perceptor:

   ownedPerceptor = self.ownedServicedPort->
       select(oclIsKindOf(Perceptor))

5. The ownedEffector meta-association refers to all owned service ports of the kind Effector:

ownedEffector = self.ownedServicedPort->
    select(oclIsKindOf(Effector))

**Notation**  There is no general notation for BehavioredSemiEntityType. The specific subclasses of BehavioredSemiEntityType define their own notation.

**Rationale**  BehavioredSemiEntityType is introduced as a common superclass to all metaclasses which can have capabilities, can observe and/or effect their environment, and can provide and/or use services.

## 11.1.2 Capability

**Semantics**  Capability is an abstract specialized RedefinableElement (from UML) and Namespace (from UML), used to model an abstraction of a behavior in terms of its inputs, outputs, pre-conditions, and post-conditions. Such a common abstraction allows use of the common features of all the concrete subclasses of the Capability metaclass uniformly, and thus reason about and operate on them in a uniform way.

To maintain consistency with UML, which considers pre-conditions as aggregates (see Operation and Behavior in *UML 2.0 Superstructure* [104]), all pre-conditions specified for one Capability are understood to be logically AND-ed to form a single logical expression representing an overall pre-condition for that Capability. This is analogously the case for post-conditions.

Capability, being a RedefinableElement, allows the redefinition of specifications (see UML Constraint::specification) of its pre- and post-conditions, e.g. when inherited from a more abstract Capability. Specification of redefined conditions are logically combined with the specification of redefining conditions (of the same kind), following the rules:

❑ overall pre-conditions are logically OR-ed, and

❑ overall post-conditions are logically AND-ed.

Input and output parameters must be the same for redefining Capability as defined in the context of redefined Capability.

The set of meta-attributes defined by the Capability can be further extended in order to accommodate specific requirements of users and/or implementation environments.

Capabilities can be owned by BehavioredSemiEntityTypes.

Capability is part of the non-conservative extension of UML, while it is a common superclass to two UML metaclasses: BehavioralFeature and Behavior.

**Associations**

| | |
|---|---|
| /input: Parameter[*] | An ordered list of input parameters of the Capability. This is a derived association. Subsets UML Namespace::ownedMember. |
| /output: Parameter[*] | An ordered list of output parameters of the Capability. This is a derived association. Subsets UML Namespace::ownedMember. |
| /precondition: Constraint[*] | An optional set of Constraints on the state of the system in which the Capability can be invoked. This is a derived association. Subsets UML Namespace::ownedMember. |
| /postcondition: Constraint[*] | An optional set of Constraints specifying the expected state of the system after the Capability is completed. This is a derived association. Subsets UML Namespace::ownedMember. |

**Constraints**  1. The input meta-association refers to all parameters having the direction set either to *in* or *inout*:

```
input = if self.oclIsKindOf(BehavioralFeature) then
        self.oclAsType(BehavioralFeature).parameter->
        select(direction=#in or direction=#inout)
    else
        self.oclAsType(Behavior).parameter->
        select(direction=#in or direction=#inout)
    endif
```

2. The output meta-association refers to all parameters having the direction set either to *out* or *inout*:

```
output = if self.oclIsKindOf(BehavioralFeature) then
        self.oclAsType(BehavioralFeature).parameter->
        select(direction=#out or direction=#inout)
    else
        self.oclAsType(Behavior).parameter->
        select(direction=#in or direction=#inout)
    endif
```

3. The precondition meta-association is identical either to the pre-condition meta-association from Operation or the precondition meta-association from Behavior:

precondition = if self.oclIsKindOf(Behavior) then
    self.oclAsType(Behavior).precondition
else
    if self.oclIsKindOf(Operation) then
        self.oclAsType(Operation).precondition
    else
        Set{} -- self.oclIsKindOf(Reception)
    endif
endif

4. The postcondition meta-association is identical either to the post-condition meta-association from Operation or the postcondition meta-association from Behavior:

postcondition = if self.oclIsKindOf(Behavior) then
    self.oclAsType(Behavior).postcondition
else
    if self.oclIsKindOf(Operation) then
        self.oclAsType(Operation).postcondition
    else
        Set{} -- self.oclIsKindOf(Reception)
    endif
endif

**Notation**  There is no general notation for Capability. The specific subclasses of Capability define their own notation.

Usually, the capability conditions are specified as a hidden informa-tion, not shown in the diagram. However, if a user needs to express them explicitly in the diagram, the conditions can be shown as a note symbol structured into sections specifying pre-conditions and post-conditions, see Fig. 11-3. Any of the sections can be omitted.

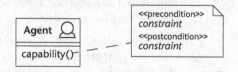

**Fig. 11-3** Notation of the Capability meta-attribute specification

**Presentation** Each single capability condition can be depicted as a separate note
**options** symbol connected to the Capability itself, see Fig. 11-4.

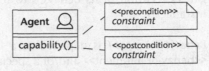

**Fig. 11-4** Alternative notation of the Capability meta-attribute specification

**Rationale** Capability is introduced to define common meta-attributes for all
"behavior-specifying" modeling elements in order to refer them uniformly, e.g. while reasoning.

## 11.2 Behavior Decomposition

**Overview** The *Behavior Decomposition* package defines the BehaviorFragment
which allows the decomposition of complex behaviors of Behaviored-
SemiEntityTypes and the means to build reusable libraries of behaviors and related features.

**Abstract** The diagram of the Behavior Decomposition package is shown in
**syntax** Fig. 11-5.

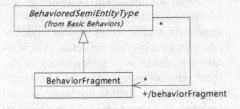

**Fig. 11-5** Behavior Decomposition—behavior fragment

### 11.2.1 BehaviorFragment

**Semantics** BehaviorFragment is a specialized BehavioredSemiEntityType used to
model coherent and reusable fragments of behavior and related structural and behavioral features, and to decompose complex behaviors
into simpler and (possibly) concurrently executable fragments.

BehaviorFragments can be shared by several BehavioredSemiEntity-
Types and a behavior of a BehavioredSemiEntityType can, possibly recursively, be decomposed into several BehaviorFragments.

The decomposition of a behavior of a BehavioredSemiEntityType to its
sub-behaviors is modeled by owned aggregate attributes (having the

aggregation meta-attribute set either to *shared* or *composite*) of the BehaviorFragment type. At run time, the behaviored semi-entity delegates execution of its behavior to the containing BehaviorFragment instances.

**Notation** BehaviorFragment is depicted as a UML Class with the stereotype <<behavior fragment>> and/or a special icon, see Fig. 11-6.

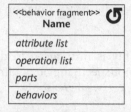

| <<behavior fragment>>   ↻ |
| :--- |
| **Name** |
| *attribute list* |
| *operation list* |
| *parts* |
| *behaviors* |

**Fig. 11-6** Notation of BehaviorFragment

**Style** Decomposition of a BehavioredSemiEntityType into sub-behaviors is usually depicted as an aggregation or composition relating the BehavioredSemiEntityType to the BehaviorFragments, or as a structuring of the BehavioredSemiEntityType into parts (or attributes not owned by composition) of the BehaviorFragment type (see UML StructuredClassifier).

**Examples** Fig. 11-7 shows an example of a decomposition of an AgentType into BehaviorFragments. The behavior of the SoccerRobot AgentType is decomposed into four BehaviorFragments: Localization, Mobility, BallManipulation and SoccerPlayerThinking. Localization manages the robot's position in a pitch, enables it to observe surrounding objects, and to measure distances between them. It requires Observing and Measurement services provided by a pitch. Mobility allows movement within a physical space. BallManipulation is used to manipulate the ball. SoccerPlayerThinking comprises different strategies and ad-hoc behaviors of a soccer player. Strategy allows the execution of a certain strategy which influences global long-term behavior of a player. AdHocReaction allows short-term behaviors triggered by a particular situation, e.g. certain pre-learned tricks.

Another example of BehaviorFragment is in Fig. 10-5.

**Rationale** BehaviorFragment is introduced to: (a) decompose complex behaviors of BehavioredSemiEntities, and (b) build reusable libraries of behaviors and related features.

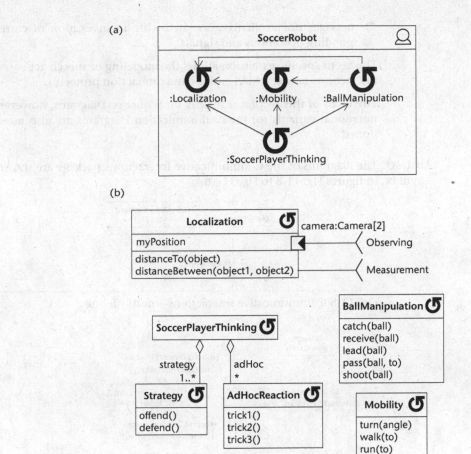

**Fig. 11-7** Example of BehaviorFragment: (a) decomposition of a behavior of an AgentType into BehaviorFragments, (b) definition of used BehaviorFragments.

## 11.3 Communicative Interactions

**Overview** The *Communicative Interactions* package contains metaclasses that provide generic as well as agent specific extensions to UML Interactions.

The generic extension allows the modeling of:

❐ interactions between groups of objects,

❐ dynamic change of an object's attributes induced by interactions, and

❏ messages not explicitly associated with an invocation of corresponding operations and signals.

The agent specific extension allows the modeling of speech act based interactions between MAS entities and interaction protocols.

The focus of this section is mainly on Sequence Diagrams, however, notational variants for the Communication Diagrams are also mentioned.

**Abstract syntax** The diagrams of the Communicative Interactions package are shown in figures Fig. 11-8 to Fig. 11-18.

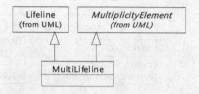

**Fig. 11-8** Communicative Interactions—multi-lifeline

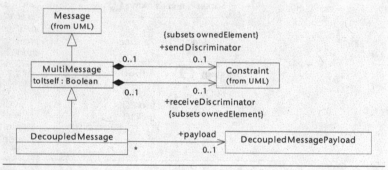

**Fig. 11-9** Communicative Interactions—multi-message and decoupled message

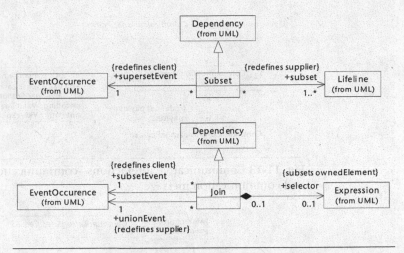

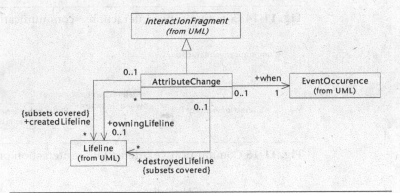

**Fig. 11-10** Communicative Interactions—subset and join relationships

**Fig. 11-11** Communicative Interactions—attribute change

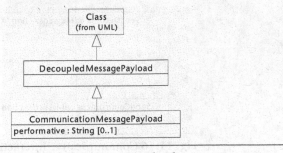

**Fig. 11-12** Communicative Interactions—payloads

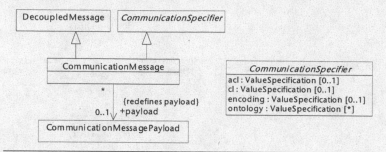

**Fig. 11-13** Communicative Interactions—communication specifier and communication message

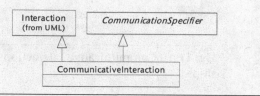

**Fig. 11-14** Communicative Interactions—communicative interaction

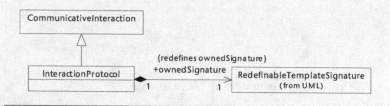

**Fig. 11-15** Communicative Interactions—interaction protocol

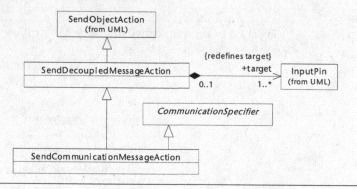

**Fig. 11-16** Communicative Interactions—send message actions

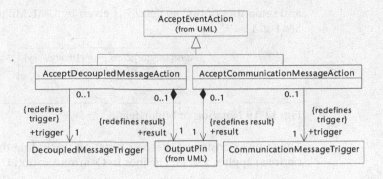

**Fig. 11-17** Communicative Interactions—accept message actions

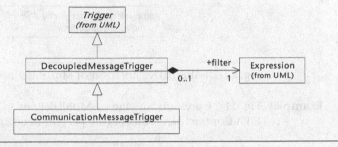

**Fig. 11-18** Communicative Interactions—message triggers

## 11.3.1 MultiLifeline

**Semantics** MultiLifeline is a specialized Lifeline (from UML) and MultiplicityElement (from UML) used to represent a multivalued ConnectableElement (i.e. ConnectableElement with multiplicity > 1) participating in an Interaction (from UML). The multiplicity meta-attribute of the MultiLifeline determines the number of instances it represents. If the multiplicity is equal to 1, MultiLifeline is semantically identical with Lifeline (from UML).

The selector of a MultiLifeline may (in contrary to Lifeline) specify more than one participant represented by the MultiLifeline.

**Notation** MultiLifeline is depicted by a Lifeline symbol having specified the multiplicity mark. Information identifying the MultiLifeline has following format:

> *lifelineident* ::= [*connectable_element_name* ['[' *selector* ']']]
> [':'*class_name* '['*multiplicity*']'] [*decomposition*] |
> 'self' '['*multiplicity*']'

Syntax and semantics of *connectable_element_name*, *selector*, *class_name*, *decomposition*, and 'self' is defined in UML Lifeline. Syntax and semantics of the *multiplicity* is given by UML MultiplicityElement. See Fig. 11-19.

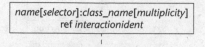

*name[selector]:class_name[multiplicity]*
ref *interactionident*

**Fig. 11-19** Notation of MultiLifeline

The same extension of Lifeline's notation (including the presentation options) applies also for Lifelines in Communication Diagrams.

**Presentation options** The multiplicity for a MultiLifeline may also be shown as a multiplicity mark in the top right corner of the "head" box, see Fig. 11-20.

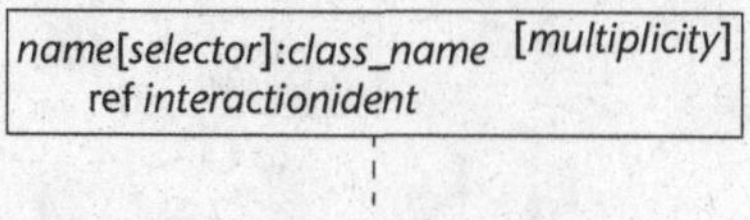

*name[selector]:class_name* [*multiplicity*]
ref *interactionident*

**Fig. 11-20** Alternative notation of MultiLifeline

**Examples** Fig. 11-21 presents a usage of MultiLifelines in a specification of the FIPA Contract Net Protocol (see [47] for details).

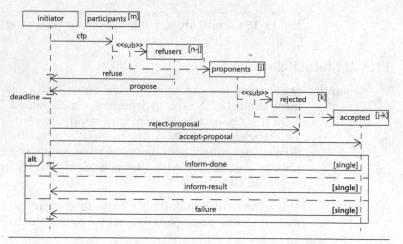

**Fig. 11-21** FIPA Contract Net Protocol

The initiator issues call for proposal (cfp) messages to m participants. The participants generate n responses (n<=m). Within the participants two subgroups can be identified: n-j refusers who refuse the cfp and j proponents who propose to perform the task, by sending the propose message (j<=n). Once the deadline passes, the initiator evaluates the received j proposals and selects agents to perform the task. The k (k<=j) rejected agents will be sent a reject-proposal message and the remaining j-k accepted proponents will receive an accept-proposal message. Once each single accepted proponent has completed the task, it sends a completion message to the initiator in the form of an inform-done or an inform-result act. If the task completion fails, a failure message is sent back to the initiator.

**Rationale** MultiLifeline is introduced to represent a multivalued ConnectableElement participating in an Interaction.

## 11.3.2 MultiMessage

**Semantics** MultiMessage is a specialized Message (from UML) which is used to model a particular communication between MultiLifelines of an Interaction.

If the sender of a MultiMessage is a MultiLifeline, the MultiMessage represents a set of messages of a specified kind sent from all instances (potentially constrained by the sendDiscriminator) represented by that MultiLifeline.

If the receiver of a MultiMessage is a MultiLifeline, the MultiMessage represents a set of messages of a specified kind multicasted to all instances (potentially constrained by the receiveDiscriminator) represented by that MultiLifeline.

If a message end of a MultiMessage references a simple Lifeline (from UML), it represents a single sender or receiver.

When a sender and/or receiver of a MultiMessage are represented by MultiLifelines, the owned constraints sendDiscriminator and receiveDiscriminator can be used to specify what particular representatives of the group of ConnectableElements represented by the particular MultiLifeline are involved in the communication modeled by that MultiMessage.

Within an alternative CombinedFragment (from UML), it is useful to differentiate between:

☐ *all* of the ConnectableElements represented by the MultiLifeline, and

☐ *each* of the ConnectableElements represented by the MultiLifeline.

The keyword 'single' used as the corresponding discriminator indicating the latter of the above cases.

The receiver of a MultiMessage can be a group of instances containing also the senders themselves. In this case the MultiMessage can specify (by the toItself meta-attribute) whether the message is sent also to the senders themselves or not.

**Attributes**

| | |
|---|---|
| toItself: Boolean[1] | If *true*, the MultiMessage is sent also to its sender when the sender belongs to the group of receivers. If *false*, the sender is excluded from the group of receivers. |

**Associations**

| | |
|---|---|
| sendDiscriminator: Constraint[0..1] | The Constraint which specifies the subset of MultiMessage senders when it is sent from a MultiLifeline. Senders are those instances represented by the MultiLifeline for which the sendDiscriminator is evaluated to *true*. Subsets UML Element::ownedElement. |
| receiveDiscriminator: Constraint[0..1] | The Constraint which specifies the MultiMessage receivers when it is sent to a MultiLifeline. Receivers are those instances represented by the MultiLifeline for which the receiveDiscriminator is evaluated to *true*. Subsets UML Element::ownedElement. |

**Constraints**  1. At least one end of the MultiMessage must be a MultiLifeline:

self.sendEvent.covered.oclIsKindOf(MultiLifeline) or
    self.receiveEvent.covered.oclIsKindOf(MultiLifeline)

2. The sendDiscriminator meta-association can be specified only if the sender is represented by a MultiLifeline:

self.sendDiscriminator->notEmpty() implies
    self.sendEvent.covered.oclIsKindOf(MultiLifeline)

3. The receiveDiscriminator meta-association can be specified only if the receiver is represented by a MultiLifeline:

self.receiveDiscriminator->notEmpty() implies
    self.receiveEvent.covered.oclIsKindOf(MultiLifeline)

**Notation**  MultiMessage is depicted as a UML Message having the discriminator labels placed within brackets near the message ends and the keyword toItself, shown as a property string, placed near the name, if it is *true*. The <<multi>> stereotype label , or a small icon placed near the arrowhead, can be shown as well. See Fig. 11-22.

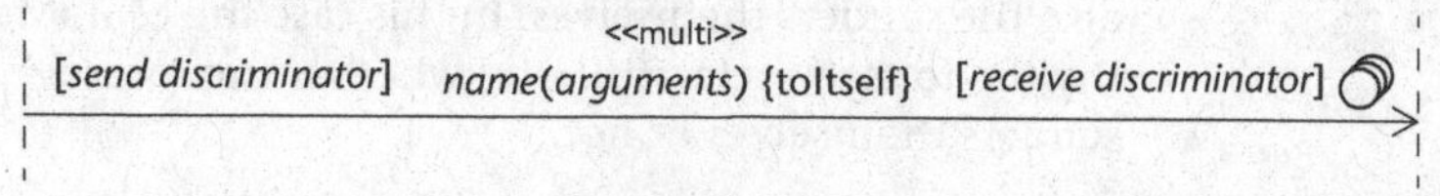

**Fig. 11-22** Notation of MultiMessage

The previous picture shows just an extension of an asynchronous message, but all other types of messages defined by UML (e.g. synchronous, reply, signal, and object creation messages) can be used for MultiMessage. Their notation is identical with standard UML notation, but it is extended by the multi message-specific parts as in the case of the asynchronous message.

MultiMessages in Communication Diagrams use the following format:

> *multimessageident* ::= [*sequence_expression*]
> ['[' *send_discriminator* ']'] *messageident*
> ['[' *receive_discriminator* ']'] ['/']

The syntax and semantics of *sequence_expression* and *messageident* are defined in UML [104] Communication Diagrams and Message sections respectively. The *send_discriminator* and *receive_discriminator* variables represent constraint expressions of the discriminators described above. A slash character ('/') is specified if the toItself meta-attribute is *false*.

**Presentation options** Alternatively, if the toItself meta-attribute is *false*, a small slanted bar is placed near the arrow head instead of the slash character specified in the name. See Fig. 11-23.

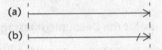

**Fig. 11-23** Alternative notation of MultiMessage: (a) toItself = true, (b) toItself = false.

**Style** The stereotype is usually omitted.

**Examples** Examples of MultiMessages can be found in Fig. 11-21.

**Rationale** MultiMessage is introduced to model messages with multiple senders and/or recipients.

### 11.3.3 DecoupledMessage

**Semantics** DecoupledMessage is a specialized MultiMessage which is used to model a specific kind of communication within an Interaction (from UML), particularly the asynchronous sending and receiving of a DecoupledMessagePayload instance without explicit specification of the behavior invoked on the side of the receiver. The decision of which behavior should be invoked when the DecoupledMessage is received is up to the receiver (for details see sections 11.3.17 and 11.3.15).

The objects transmitted in the form of DecoupledMessages are De-coupledMessagePayload instances.

Because all the decoupled messages are asynchronous, the message-Sort meta-attribute (inherited from the UML Message) is ignored.

**Associations**

| | |
|---|---|
| payload: Decoupled-MessagePayload[0..1] | The type of the object transmitted. |

**Constraints** 1. The constraints [2], [3], and [4] imposed on the UML Message are released, i.e. the DecoupledMessage's signature does not need to refer to either an Operation or a Signal.

**Notation** DecoupledMessage is shown as an asynchronous MultiMessage, but the stereotype label is <<decoupled>>, or a different small icon is placed near the arrowhead. See Fig. 11-24.

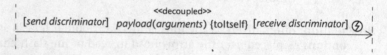

**Fig. 11-24** Notation of DecoupledMessage

Syntax for the DecoupledMessage name is the following:

*dm-messageident* ::= *payload*['(' *arguments* ')']

If the meta-attribute payload is specified, the DecoupledMessage's signature must refer to the DecoupledMessagePayload, in other words:

❑ the payload must correspond to the referred DecoupledMessage-Payload's name, and

❑ the *arguments* use the same notation as defined for UML Message, and must correspond to the attributes of the DecoupledMessage-Payload (i.e. the name of an argument must be the same as the name of one of the attributes of the referenced DecoupledMes-sagePayload, and the type of the argument must be of the same kind as the type of the attribute with the corresponding name).

If the meta-attribute payload is not specified, the *payload* can be any string and the *arguments* can be any values.

**Presentation options** As for MultiMessage.

**Style** The stereotype is usually omitted.

Argument names may by omitted if mapping of argument values to the payload attributes is unambiguous.

**Examples** An example can be obtained by the replacement of all MultiMessages in Fig. 11-21 by DecoupledMessages.

For another example see Fig. 11-26.

**Rationale** DecoupledMessage is introduced to model autonomy in message processing.

## 11.3.4 DecoupledMessagePayload

**Semantics** DecoupledMessagePayload is a specialized Class (from UML) used to model the type of objects transmitted in the form of DecoupledMessages.

**Notation** DecoupledMessagePayload is depicted as a UML Class with the stereotype <<dm payload>> and/or a special icon, see Fig. 11-25.

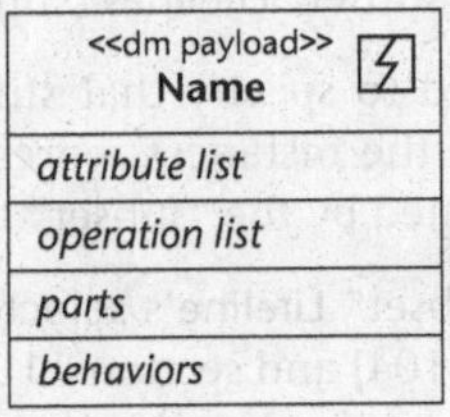

| <<dm payload>> **Name** ⚡ |
| :--- |
| *attribute list* |
| *operation list* |
| *parts* |
| *behaviors* |

Fig. 11-25 Notation of DecoupledMessagePayload

**Style** The DecoupledMessagePayload usually specifies only attributes, and possibly also corresponding access operations.

**Examples** Fig. 11-26 (a) shows an example of DecoupledMessagePayload named SendOrder. Its instances represent the payloads of the DecoupledMessages used to send an order from broker to the stock exchange.

Example of such a DecoupledMessage is depicted in Fig. 11-26 (b).

**Rationale** DecoupledMessagePayload is introduced to model objects transmitted in the form of DecoupledMessages.

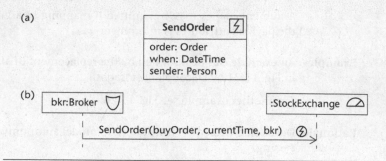

**Fig. 11-26** Example of DecoupledMessagePayload

## 11.3.5 Subset

**Semantics**  Subset is a specialized Dependency (from UML) used to specify that instances represented by one Lifeline are a subset of instances represented by another Lifeline. The Subset relationship is between:

❑ an EventOccurrence owned by the "superset" Lifeline (client), and

❑ the "subset" Lifelines (suppliers).

It is used to specify that since the occurrence of the supersetEvent, some of the instances represented by the "superset" Lifeline are also represented by the "subset" Lifeline.

The "subset" Lifeline's selector (for the details about the selector see Lifeline [104] and section 11.3.1) specifies the instances of the "superset" Lifeline that are also represented by the "subset" Lifeline.

All instances represented by the "subset" Lifeline are still represented also by the "superset" Lifeline.

One Lifeline can represent a "subset" of several "superset" Lifelines, i.e. more than one Subset relationships can lead to one "subset" Lifeline.

Termination of the "subset" Lifeline (the Stop is placed at the end of Lifeline) destroys all instances it represents.

**Associations**

| supersetEvent:<br>EventOccurrence[1] | An EventOccurrence owned by the "superset" Lifeline. It specifies the time point when the subset of represented instances is identified.<br>Redefines UML Dependency::client. |
|---|---|
| subset: Lifeline[1..*] | The "subset" Lifeline.<br>Redefines UML Dependency::supplier. |

**Constraints**   1. All types of the "subset" Lifelines must conform to the type of the "superset" Lifeline:

self.subset->forAll((represents.type->notEmpty() and
    self.supersetEvent.covered.represents.type->notEmpty())
implies self.subset.represents.type.conformsTo(
    self.supersetEvent.covered.represents.type))

**Notation**   The Subset relationship is depicted as a UML Dependency with the stereotype <<sub>>. The dependency arrowhead is always connected to the "subset" Lifeline "head". See Fig. 11-27 and Fig. 11-28.

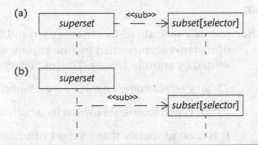

**Fig. 11-27** Notation of Subset: (a) the subset is identified from the beginning of the superset's existence, (b) the subset is identified during the life time of the superset.

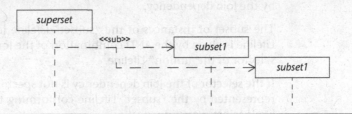

**Fig. 11-28** Notation of Subset—multiple subsets created at once

When shown in a Communication Diagram, the Subset relationship can also specify a sequence-expression in order to identify a relative time since which the subset Lifeline has been identified. If the Subset relationship does not specify a sequence-expression, the subset Lifeline exists from the time when the superset Lifeline exists in the interaction. See Fig. 11-29.

**Style**   The name is usually omitted.

**Examples**   Examples of Subset relationship can be found in Fig. 11-21, and Fig. 11-32.

**Rationale**   Subset is introduced to specify that instances represented by one Lifeline are a subset of instances represented by another Lifeline.

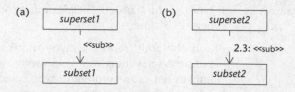

**Fig. 11-29** Notation of Subset in Communication Diagram: (a) subset1 starts to be identified from when superset1 occurs, (b) subset2 is identified when an "event" 2.3 occurs during Interaction.

## 11.3.6 Join

**Semantics** Join is a specialized Dependency (from UML) used to specify joining of instances represented by one Lifeline with a set of instances represented by another Lifeline. The Join relationship is between:

☐ an EventOccurrence owned by a "subset" Lifeline (client), and

☐ an EventOccurrence owned by a "union" Lifeline (supplier).

It is used to specify that a subset of instances, which have been until the subsetEvent represented by the "subset" Lifeline, is, after the unionEvent represented only by the "union" Lifeline. Thus after the unionEvent occurrence, the "union" Lifeline represents the union of the instances it has previously represented and the instances specified by the Join dependency.

The subset of instances of the "subset" Lifeline joining the "union" Lifeline is given by the AND combination of the Join's selector and the selector of the "union" Lifeline.

If the selector of the Join dependency is not specified, all the instances represented by the "subset" Lifeline conforming to the "union" Lifeline's selector are joined.

Between subsetEvent and unionEvent occurrences, the set of instances joining the "union" Lifeline is not represented by any of the two Lifelines.

One EventOccurrence can be a client or a supplier of several Joins.

**Associations**

| | |
|---|---|
| selector: Expression [0..1] | Specifies the subset of instances represented by the "subset" Lifeline, which are being joined. Subsets UML Element::ownedElement. |

| subsetEvent: EventOccurrence[1] | An EventOccurrence owned by the subset Lifeline. It specifies the time point when the subset of instances resented by the "subset" Lifeline is detached from others. Redefines UML Dependency::client. |
|---|---|
| unionEvent: EventOccurrence[1] | An EventOccurrence owned by the "union" Lifeline. It specifies the time point when the subset instances are joined with the union set of instances. Redefines UML Dependency::supplier. |

**Constraints** 1. The Lifeline owning the EventOccurrence referred to by the union-Event meta-association must be a MultiLifeline:

self.unionEvent.covered.oclIsKindOf(MultiLifeline)

2. The type of the subsetEvent's Lifeline must conform to the type of the unionEvent's MultiLifeline:

(self.subsetEvent.covered.represents.type->notEmpty() and
    self.unionEvent.covered.represents.type->notEmpty()) implies
    self.subsetEvent.covered.represents.type.conformsTo(
    self.unionEvent.covered.represents.type)

**Notation** The Join relationship is depicted as UML Dependency with the stereotype <<join>>. The dependency arrowhead is always connected to the union Lifeline. Optionally a selector expression can be specified in brackets. See Fig. 11-30.

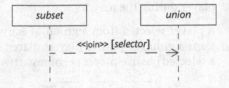

**Fig. 11-30** Notation of Join

When shown in a Communication Diagram, the Join relationship can optionally specify a sequence-expression in order to identify a relative time when it occurs. See Fig. 11-31.

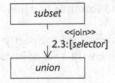

**Fig. 11-31** Notation of Join in Communication Diagrams

**Style**  The name is usually omitted.

**Examples**  Fig. 11-32 shows an interaction representing a communication of parties concerned with the processing of a job application, which exploits the Join relationship.

The Applicant sends a message applyForJob to a Company. The Company replies with an invitation message that specifies all the details about the interview. The interview is described by a separate interaction between the Applicant and a StaffManager. If the applicant is accepted after the Interview, she/he becomes an employee (joins a group of employees) and the entity role apl is disposed (but the instance which was playing that entity role still exist).

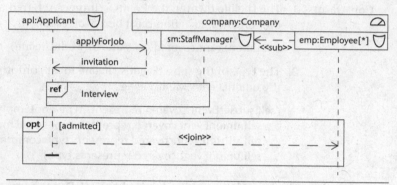

Fig. 11-32 Example of Join

Fig. 11-33 shows a part of an interaction representing a situation when an actively playing soccer player is substituted by another player during the match.

A player selected from a group of actively (currently) playing players joins a group of passive players placed outside the soccer pitch. Then a selected passive player becomes active.

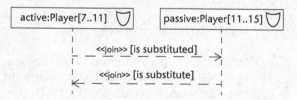

Fig. 11-33 Example of a Join with selector

**Rationale**  Join is introduced to specify the joining of instances represented by one Lifeline with a set of instances represented by another Lifeline.

## 11.3.7 AttributeChange

**Semantics** AttributeChange is a specialized InteractionFragment (from UML) used to model the change of attribute values (state) of the ConnectableElements (from UML) represented by Lifelines (from UML) within Interactions (from UML).

AttributeChange enables to add, change or remove attribute values in time, as well as to express added attribute values by Lifelines (from UML). Attributes are represented by inner ConnectableElements.

AttributeChange can also be used to model dynamic changing of entity roles played by behavioral entities represented by Lifelines. Furthermore, it allows the modeling of entity interaction with respect to the played entity roles, i.e. each "sub-lifeline" representing a played entity role (or entity roles in the case of MultiLifeline) is used to model the interaction of its player with respect to this/these entity role(s).

If an AttributeChange is used to destroy played entity roles, it represents disposal of the entity roles while their former players still exist as instances in the system. To also destroy the player of an entity role, the Stop element (from UML) must be used instead. Usage of the Stop element thus leads to the disposal of the player as well as all the entity roles it has been playing.

**Associations**

| | |
|---|---|
| createdLifeline: Lifeline[*] | A set of Lifelines representing the added or changed attribute values. Subsets UML InteractionFragment::covered. |
| destroyedLifeline: Lifeline[*] | A set of lifelines representing the removed attribute values. Subsets UML InteractionFragment::covered. |
| owningLifeline: Lifeline[0..1] | The Lifeline representing an owner of the created attribute values. |
| when: EventOccurrence[1] | The EventOccurrence specifying a time point when the AttributeChange occurs. |

**Constraints** 1. If createdLifeline is specified, the owningLifeline must be specified as well:

self.createdLifeline->notEmpty() implies
self.owningLifeline->notEmpty()

2. Each createdLifeline must represent an attribute of the Classifier used as the type of the ConnectableElement represented by the owningLifeline meta-association:

(self.createdLifeline->notEmpty() and
    self.owningLifeline.represents.type->notEmpty()) implies
    self.owningLifeline.represents.type.attribute->
    includesAll(self.createdLifeline.represents)

**Notation** AttributeChange is depicted as a bold horizontal line. The created Lifelines are shown as Lifelines with the top sides of their "heads" attached to the AttributeChange line. The owner of new Lifelines is identified by drawing a small solid circle at the intersection of its Lifeline and AttributeChange's line. If necessary, the AttributeChange's line is enlarged to touch the owner's Lifeline. Vertical lines of Lifelines representing the destroyed attribute values terminate at the AttributeChange's line. Lifelines that's vertical lines cross the AttributeChange's line and continue below are unaffected by the AttributeChange. See Fig. 11-34.

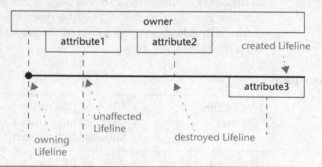

**Fig. 11-34** Notation of AttributeChange

In Communication Diagrams, the AttributeChange is shown as a small solid circle placed into a Lifeline representing the owner of newly created or destroyed Lifelines. A sequence number can be placed near the circle, to identify the relative time at which the AttributeChange occurs. Destroyed Lifelines are identified by arrows with bold crossing bars as arrow heads and lead from the AttributeChange circle. Created Lifelines are identified by arrows with open arrow heads leading from the AttributeChange circle. Fig. 11-35 shows a Communication Diagram semantically identical to the Sequence Diagram shown in Fig. 11-34.

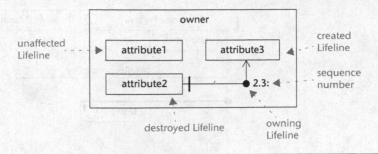

**Fig. 11-35** Notation of AttributeChange in Communication Diagrams

**Style** The name is usually omitted.

**Examples** The change of an entity role played by one entity is shown in Fig. 11-36. An agent worker is a programmer. After receiving a message advancement from the ProjectBoard it changes its entity role to the projectManager. At this point he is no longer a programmer. The argument values of the advancement message specify details of advancement (including the type of a new entity role) but for simplicity they are hidden in the diagram.

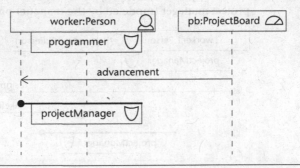

**Fig. 11-36** Example of AttributeChange—entity role change

An addition of a new entity role to the entity is shown in Fig. 11-37. An agent worker is an analyst. At a certain time the projectManager decides to also allocate this worker to testing. He informs the worker about this decision by sending a takeResponsibility message. The worker then also becomes a tester, but still remains an analyst. The argument values of the takeResponsibility message specify details of the new entity role being played but for simplicity they are hidden in the diagram.

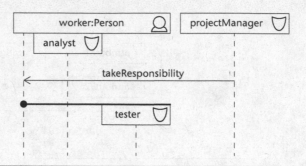

**Fig. 11-37** Example of AttributeChange—entity role addition

Fig. 11-38 shows an example of swapping the players of (virtually) one entity role played within an organization unit. The diagram realizes the scenario of replacing an existing project manager by another person. The agent worker1 is a project manager (modeled by its role property projectManager). After receiving a message resignResponsibility from the project board (pb) it stops playing the role of a project manager. At the same time another person, named worker2, takes the responsibility, as the result of previously received message takeResponsibility sent by the project board, and starts to play the role of the project manager (modeled by the manager property of worker2).

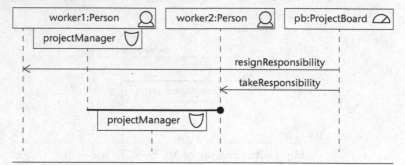

**Fig. 11-38** Example of AttributeChange—change of entity role players

Fig. 11-39 shows the difference between destroying the entity role's Lifeline by the AttributeChange and stopping the Lifeline by the Stop element. The diagram shows two employees, John and Robert. After John betrayed the confidential company information he is fired and is no longer an employee. But he still exists. The AttributeChange was used in this case. The owning Lifeline does not need to be specified because no Lifeline was created.

On the other hand, after a fatal injury Robert dies, i.e. Robert as a person no longer exists. The Stop was used in this case.

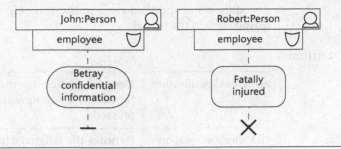

**Fig. 11-39** Example of destruction and stopping of an entity role's Lifeline

**Rationale** AttributeChange is introduced to model a change of the attribute values (state) of ConnectableElements in the context of Interactions.

## 11.3.8 CommunicationSpecifier

**Semantics** CommunicationSpecifier is an abstract metaclass which defines meta-properties of its concrete subclasses, i.e. CommunicationMessage, CommunicativeInteraction, and ServiceSpecification, which are used to model different aspects of communicative interactions.

CommunicationMessages can occur in CommunicativeInteractions, and parameterized CommunicativeInteractions can be parts of Service-Specifications. All of them can specify values of the meta-attributes inherited from the CommunicationSpecifier. Potential conflicts in specifications of the CommunicationSpecifier's meta-property values are resolved by the overriding principle that defines which concrete subclasses of the CommunicationSpecifier have higher priority in specification of those meta-attributes. Thus, if specified on different priority levels, the values at higher priority levels override those specified at lower priority levels.

The priorities, from the highest to the lowest are defined as follows:

1. CommunicationMessage,

2. CommunicativeInteraction,

3. ServiceSpecification.

For example, if an encoding value is specified for a particular CommunicationMessage it overrides the encoding specified for the owning CommunicativeInteraction. If the encoding is not specified for the CommunicationMessage, its value is specified by the owning CommunicativeInteraction. If not specified for the owning CommunicativeInteraction and the CommunicativeInteraction is a part of a ServiceSpecification, the value is taken from that ServiceSpecification. If the encoding is not specified even in the ServiceSpecification, it remains unspecified in the model.

**Attributes**

| acl: ValueSpecification [0..1] | Denotes the agent communication language in which CommunicationMessages are expressed. |
|---|---|
| cl: ValueSpecification [0..1] | Denotes the language in which the CommunicationMessage's content is expressed, also called the content language. |
| encoding: ValueSpecification [0..1] | Denotes the specific encoding of the CommunicationMessage's content. |
| ontology: ValueSpecification[*] | Denotes the ontologies used to give a meaning to the symbols in the CommunicationMessage's content expression. |

**Notation** There is no general notation for CommunicationSpecifier. Its specific subclasses define their own notation.

The CommunicationSpecifier's meta-attributes are specified as tagged values. The following keywords are used:

❏ acl,

❏ cl,

❏ encoding, and

❏ ontology.

Their values represent arbitrary ValueSpecifications, but the most commonly used types are: enumerations, string literals, or lists of literals (used for the ontology specification).

**Style** Usually, the CommunicationSpecifier's meta-attributes are specified as a hidden information, not shown in diagrams.

**Rationale** CommunicationSpecifier is introduced to define meta-properties which are used to model different aspects of communicative interactions. It is used in definitions of its subclasses.

## 11.3.9 CommunicationMessage

**Semantics** CommunicationMessage is a specialized DecoupledMessage and CommunicationSpecifier, which is used to model communicative acts of *speech act based communication* in the context of Interactions.

The objects transmitted in the form of CommunicationMessages are CommunicationMessagePayload instances.

**Associations**

| | |
|---|---|
| payload: Communication- MessagePayload[0..1] | The type of the object transmitted. Redefines DecoupledMessage::payload. |

**Notation** CommunicationMessage is shown as a DecoupledMessage, but the stereotype label is <<communication>>, or a different small icon is placed near the arrowhead. See Fig. 11-40.

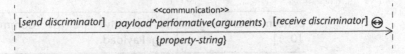

**Fig. 11-40** Notation of CommunicationMessage

Syntax for the CommunicationMessage name is the following:

*cm-messageident* ::= [ *payload* '^'] *performative*['(' *arguments* ')']

If the meta-attribute payload is specified, the CommunicationMessage's signature must refer to the CommunicationMessagePayload, in other words:

❐ the *payload* (optional) must correspond to the referred CommunicationMessagePayload's name,

❐ the *performative* must correspond to the performative of the CommunicationMessagePayload, and

❐ the *arguments* use the same notation as defined for UML Message, and must correspond (for details see section 11.3.3) to the attributes of the CommunicationMessagePayload.

If the meta-attribute payload is not specified, the *performative* can be any string and the *arguments* can be any values. In this case the *payload* part is omitted from the signature.

**Presentation options** As for MultiMessage.

**Style** When used in a CommunicativeInteraction containing only CommunicationMessages, their stereotypes are usually omitted.

Argument names may by omitted if mapping of argument values to the payload attributes is unambiguous.

Usually, the specification of tagged values is a hidden information, not shown in diagrams.

**Examples**  See Fig. 11-42 and Fig. 11-48.

**Rationale**  CommunicationMessage is introduced to model speech act based communication in the context of Interactions.

## 11.3.10 CommunicationMessagePayload

**Semantics**  CommunicationMessagePayload is a specialized Class (from UML) used to model the type of objects transmitted in the form of CommunicationMessages.

**Attributes**

| | |
|---|---|
| performative: String [0..1] | Performative of the CommunicationMessagePayload. |

**Notation**  CommunicationMessagePayload is depicted as a UML Class with the stereotype <<cm payload>> and/or a special icon, see Fig. 11-41.

If specified, the value of the meta-attribute performative is depicted as a property string (tagged value) with name 'performative', placed in the name compartment.

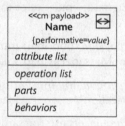

**Fig. 11-41** Notation of CommunicationMessagePayload

**Presentation options**  If the only displayed tagged value is the performative, its keyword may be omitted and only its value is specified.

**Style**  The CommunicationMessagePayload usually specifies only performative, attributes, and possibly also corresponding access operations.

**Examples**  Fig. 11-42 (a) shows an example of a CommunicationMessagePayload named PerformTask. Its instances represent the payloads of the CommunicationMessages used to send the request to perform a task.

Examples of such CommunicationMessages are depicted in Fig. 11-42 (b). Presented notational alternatives are semantically equivalent (for details see section 11.3.9).

(a)

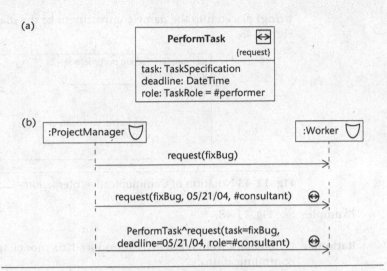

(b)

Fig. 11-42 Example of CommunicationMessagePayload

**Rationale** CommunicationMessagePayload is introduced to model objects transmitted in the form of CommunicationMessages.

## 11.3.11 CommunicativeInteraction

**Semantics** CommunicativeInteraction is a specialized Interaction (from UML) and CommunicationSpecifier, used to model speech act based communications, i.e. Interactions containing CommunicationMessages.

CommunicativeInteraction, being a concrete subclass of the abstract CommunicationSpecifier, can specify some additional meta-attributes of interactions, which are not allowed to be specified within UML Interactions, particularly:

☐ acl, i.e. the agent communication language used within the CommunicativeInteraction,

☐ cl, i.e. the content language used within the CommunicativeInteraction,

☐ encoding, i.e. the content encoding used within the CommunicativeInteraction, and

☐ ontology, i.e. the ontologies used within the CommunicativeInteraction.

For the above meta-attributes, the overriding principle defined in section 11.3.8 holds.

**Notation** CommunicativeInteraction is depicted as UML Interaction with the optionally specified meta-attribute tagged values (shown as a property string) placed into the name compartment of the diagram frame. See Fig. 11-43.

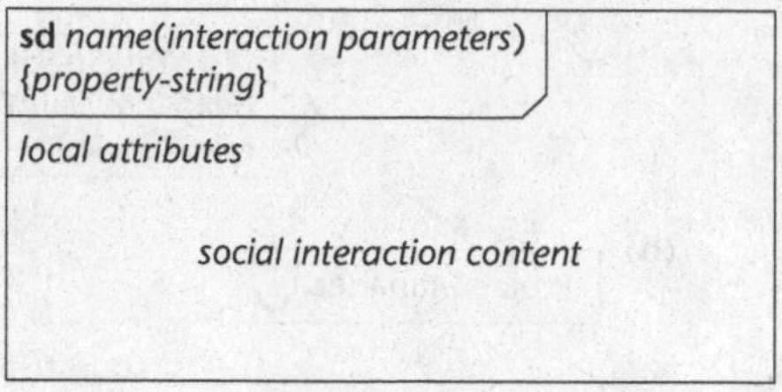

**Fig. 11-43** Notation of CommunicativeInteraction

**Examples** See Fig. 11-48.

**Rationale** CommunicativeInteraction is introduced to model speech act based communications.

## 11.3.12 InteractionProtocol

**Semantics** InteractionProtocol is a parameterized CommunicativeInteraction template used to model reusable templates of CommunicativeInteractions.

Possible TemplateParameters of an InteractionProtocol are:

❏ values of CommunicationSpecifier's meta-attributes,

❏ local variable names, types, and default values,

❏ Lifeline names, types, and selectors,

❏ Message names and argument values,

❏ MultiLifeline multiplicities,

❏ MultiMessage discriminators,

❏ CommunicationMessage meta-attributes,

❏ ExecutionOccurrence's behavior specification,

❏ guard expressions of InteractionOperands,

❏ specification of included Constraints, and

❏ included Expressions and their particular operands.

*Partial binding* of an InteractionProtocol (i.e. the TemplateBinding which does not substitute all the template parameters by actual parameters) results in a different InteractionProtocol.

A complete binding of an InteractionProtocol represents a CommunicativeInteraction.

**Associations**

| | |
|---|---|
| ownedSignature: RedefinableTemplate- Signature[1] | A template signature specifying the formal template parameters. Redefines UML Classifier::ownedSignature. |

**Notation**   InteractionProtocol is depicted as a parameterized Communica-tiveInteraction, with the keyword 'ip' used for the diagram frame kind. Specification of template parameters is placed into a dashed rectangle in the upper right corner of the diagram frame. See Fig. 11-44.

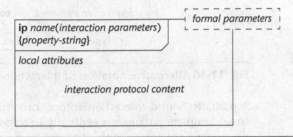

**Fig. 11-44** Notation of InteractionProtocol

Binding of an InteractionProtocol is shown either as a TemplateBind-ing relationship, or named bound CommunicativeInteraction, or as an anonymous bound CommunicativeInteraction, see Fig. 11-45.

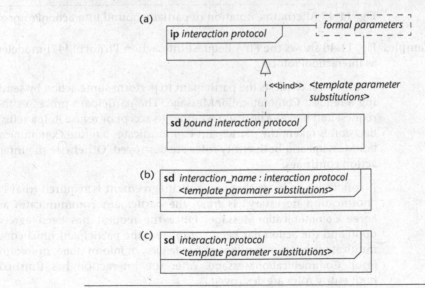

**Fig. 11-45** Notation of InteractionProtocol binding: (a) as a Template-Binding relationship, (b) as a named bound CommunicativeInterac-tion, (c) as an anonymous bound CommunicativeInteraction.

All notational variants are defined in UML 2.0 Superstructure [104].

**Presentation** Binding of a formal template parameter representing a type used
**options** within the InteractionProtocol (e.g. a type of comprised Lifeline) can
be alternatively shown as a dashed line from the bound Interaction-
Protocol to the Type substituting the formal parameter. The line is la-
belled with a name of the substituted template parameter. See Fig. 11-
46.

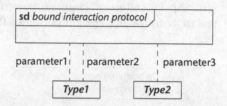

**Fig. 11-46** Alternative notation of InteractionProtocol binding

A partially bound InteractionProtocol can show remaining unbound
(free) template parameters explicitly in a dashed rectangle placed in
the upper right corner of the diagram frame, see Fig. 11-47.

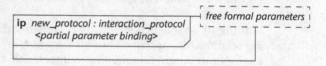

**Fig. 11-47** Alternative notation of partially bound InteractionProtocol

**Examples** Fig. 11-48 shows the FIPA Request Interaction Protocol [47] modeled
as InteractionProtocol.

The initiator requests the participant to perform some action by sending a request CommunicationMessage. The participant processes the
request and makes a decision whether to accept or refuse it. If a refuse
decision is taken, the participant communicates a refuse CommunicationMessage and both entity roles are destroyed. Otherwise the interaction continues.

If conditions indicate that an explicit agreement is required (that is,
"notification necessary" is *true*), the participant communicates an
agree CommunicationMessage. Once the request has been agreed
upon and the action has been completed, the participant must communicate the action result as either failure, or inform-done, or inform-
result CommunicationMessage. After the interaction has finished,
both entity roles are destroyed.

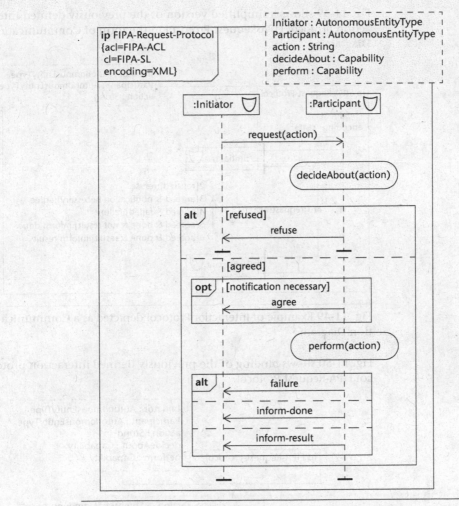

**Fig. 11-48** Example of InteractionProtocol depicted as a Sequence Diagram

Fig. 11-49 shows a simplified version of the previously defined interaction protocol FIPA-Request-Protocol in the form of Communication
Diagram.

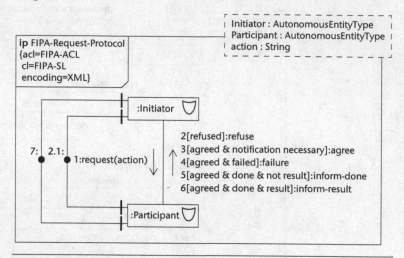

**Fig. 11-49** Example of InteractionProtocol depicted as a Communication Diagram

Fig. 11-50 shows binding of the previously defined interaction protocol FIPA-Request-Protocol.

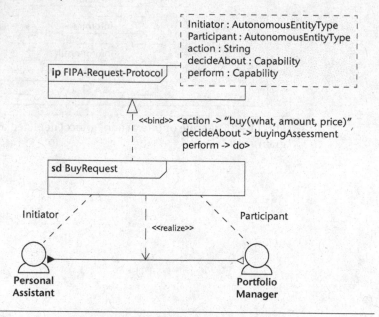

**Fig. 11-50** Example of InteractionProtocol binding

The result of the binding is a new CommunicativeInteraction called BuyRequest, used to model an interaction of a personal assistant agent with a portfolio manager agent when the personal assistant requests the portfolio manager to buy some securities.

The initiator template parameter is substituted by the PersonalAssistant AgentType, participant by the PortfolioManager AgentType, action by a string specifying the buying action, decideAbout by the buyingAssessment operation, and the parameter perform by the do operation. The diagram also shows that the SocialAssociation between the PersonalAssistant and the PortfolioManager is realized by the BuyRequest CommunicativeInteraction which specifies this relationship at the detailed level of abstraction.

**Rationale**  InteractionProtocol is introduced to model reusable templates of CommunicativeInteractions.

## 11.3.13  SendDecoupledMessageAction

**Semantics**  SendDecoupledMessageAction is a specialized SendObjectAction (from UML) used to model the action of sending of DecoupledMessagePayload instances, referred to by the request meta-association, in the form of a DecoupledMessage to its recipient(s), referred to by the target meta-association.

**Associations**

| | |
|---|---|
| target: InputPin[1..*] | The target objects to which the DecoupledMessage is sent.<br>Redefines UML SendObjectAction::target. |

**Notation**  SendDecoupledMessageAction is depicted as a rectangle with convex rounded right side, see Fig. 11-51.

Syntax of the SendDecoupledMessageAction name is the same as defined for the dm-messageident by DecoupledMessage:

   *dm-messageident* ::= *payload*['(' *arguments* ')']

The *payload* represents the type of the sent DecoupledMessagePayload instance, and the *arguments* can be used to indicate the values of the attributes of the sent payload instance. If the type of the InputPin referred to by the request meta-association is specified, the *payload* must correspond to the name, and *arguments* must correspond to its attributes of the type.

Recipients of the sent DecoupledMessage are indicated by a comma separated list of recipient names placed below the message name in parentheses.

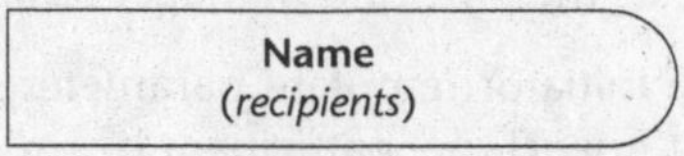

**Fig. 11-51** Notation of SendDecoupledMessageAction

**Presentation options** If the action's name does not conform to the syntax of the dm-messageident, the dm-messageident may optionally be placed after the list of recipients separated by the double colon. See Fig. 11-52.

**Fig. 11-52** Alternative notation of SendDecoupledMessageAction— indication of recipients and sent decoupled message

SendDecoupledMessageAction can be alternatively depicted as a UML Action with stereotype <<send decoupled message>> and/or a special decoration icon, see Fig. 11-53.

**Fig. 11-53** Alternative notation of SendDecoupledMessageAction— action with stereotype and/or decoration icon

**Examples** See Fig. 11-57. All SendCommunicationMessageActions from the diagram should be replaced by SendDecoupledMessageActions.

**Rationale** SendDecoupledMessageAction is introduced to model the sending of DecoupledMessages in Activities.

## 11.3.14 SendCommunicationMessageAction

**Semantics** SendCommunicationMessageAction is a specialized SendDecoupledMessageAction, which allows to specify the values of the CommunicationSpecifier's meta-attributes.

**Notation** SendCommunicationMessageAction is depicted as a rectangle with convex rounded right side and doubled left side, see Fig. 11-54.

Syntax of the SendCommunicationMessageAction name is the same as defined for the cm-messageident by CommunicationMessage:

*cm-messageident* ::= [ *payload* '^'] *performative*['(' *arguments* ')']

The *payload* represents the name, the *performative* denotes the performative, and the *arguments* the values of the attributes of the type of the sent CommunicationMessagePayload instance. If the type of the InputPin referred to by the request meta-association is specified, the *payload* must correspond to its name, the *performative* to its performative meta-attribute, and *arguments* must correspond to its attributes.

Recipients of the sent CommunicationMessage are indicated by the comma separated list of recipient names, placed below the message name in parentheses.

> **Name**
> *(recipients)*
> *{property-string}*

**Fig. 11-54** Notation of SendCommunicationMessageAction

If specified, the values of the CommunicationSpecifier's meta-attributes are depicted as a property string (tagged values).

**Presentation options** If the action's name does not conform to the syntax of the cm-messageident, the cm-messageident may optionally be placed after the list of recipients separated by the double colon. See Fig. 11-55.

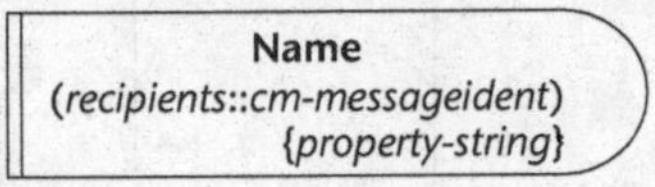

> **Name**
> *(recipients::cm-messageident)*
> *{property-string}*

**Fig. 11-55** Alternative notation of SendCommunicationMessageAction—indication of recipients and sent communication message

SendCommunicationMessageAction can be alternatively depicted as a UML Action with stereotype <<send communication message>> and/or a special decoration icon, see Fig. 11-56.

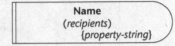

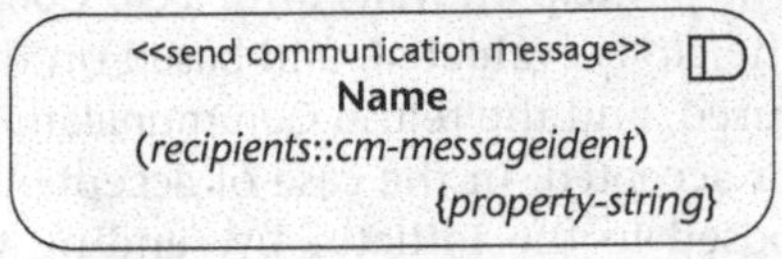

> <<send communication message>>
> **Name**
> *(recipients::cm-messageident)*
> *{property-string}*

**Fig. 11-56** Alternative notation of SendCommunicationMessageAction—action with stereotype and/or decoration icon

**Examples** An activity diagram of participant's behavior within the FIPA Contract Net Protocol (see [47] for details) is depicted in Fig. 11-57.

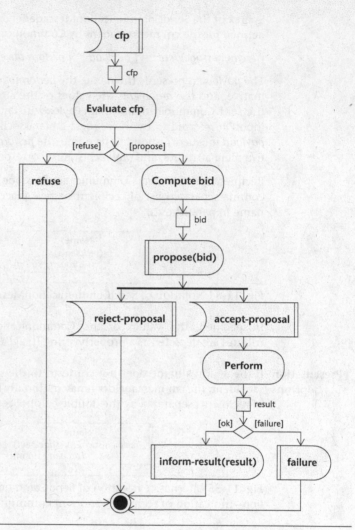

**Fig. 11-57** Example of SendCommunicationMessageAction and AcceptCommunicationMessageAction

The participant waits until a cfp CommunicationMessage arrives. If so, the cfp is evaluated, and based on this evaluation the cfp is either refused, and the refuse CommunicationMessage is sent to the initiator, or accepted. In the case of acceptance, the bid is computed and proposed to the initiator by sending the propose CommunicationMessage. Then the initiator sends either the reject-proposal, which terminates the algorithm, or the accept-proposal. In the second case the participant performs the action and informs the initiator of the result of the action execution, by sending the inform-result Communication-Message.

The diagram does not show recipients of CommunicationMessages because the only recipient is the initiator of the FIPA Contract Net Protocol.

For more examples see also Fig. 11-120 and Fig. 11-122.

**Rationale** SendCommunicationMessageAction is introduced to model the sending of CommunicationMessages in Activities.

## 11.3.15 AcceptDecoupledMessageAction

**Semantics** AcceptDecoupledMessageAction is a specialized AcceptEventAction (from UML) which waits for the reception of a DecoupledMessage that meets conditions specified by the associated trigger (for details see section 11.3.17). The received DecoupledMessagePayload instance is placed to the result OutputPin.

If an AcceptDecoupledMessageAction has no incoming edges, the action starts when the containing Activity (from UML) or StructuredActivityNode (from UML) starts. An AcceptDecoupledMessageAction with no incoming edges is always enabled to accept events regardless of how many are accepted. It does not terminate after accepting an event and outputting the value, but continues to wait for subsequent events.

**Associations**

| | |
|---|---|
| trigger: DecoupledMessage-Trigger[1] | The DecoupledMessageTrigger accepted by the action. Redefines UML AcceptEventAction::trigger. |
| result: OutputPin[1] | The OutputPin holding the event object that has been received as a DecoupledMessage. Redefines UML AcceptEventAction::result. |

**Constraints** 1. If the type of the OutputPin referred to by the result meta-association is specified, it must be a DecoupledMessagePayload:

self.result.type->notEmpty() implies
self.result.type.oclIsKindOf(DecoupledMessagePayload)

**Notation** AcceptDecoupledMessageAction is depicted as a rectangle with concave rounded left side, see Fig. 11-58.

**Fig. 11-58** Notation of AcceptDecoupledMessageAction

The name of the AcceptDecoupledMessageAction is the associated trigger.

The event object received as a DecoupledMessage may be specified as an OutputPin.

**Presentation options**  AcceptDecoupledMessageAction can be alternatively depicted as a UML Action with stereotype <<accept decoupled message>> and/or a special decoration icon, see Fig. 11-59.

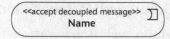

**Fig. 11-59** Alternative notation of AcceptDecoupledMessageAction

**Examples**  An example can be obtained by the replacement of all AcceptDecoupledMessageActions in Fig. 11-57 by AcceptCommunicationMessageActions.

**Rationale**  AcceptDecoupledMessageAction is introduced to model the reception of DecoupledMessages in Activities.

## 11.3.16 AcceptCommunicationMessageAction

**Semantics**  AcceptCommunicationMessageAction is a specialized AcceptEventAction (from UML) which waits for the reception of a CommunicationMessage that meets conditions specified by associated trigger (for details see section 11.3.18). The received CommunicationMessagePayload instance is placed to the result OutputPin.

If an AcceptCommunicationMessageAction has no incoming edges, then the action starts when the containing Activity (from UML) or StructuredActivityNode (from UML) starts. An AcceptCommunicationMessageAction with no incoming edges is always enabled to accept events regardless of how many are accepted. It does not terminate after accepting an event and outputting a value, but continues to wait for subsequent events.

**Associations**

| trigger: Communication-MessageTrigger[1] | The CommunicationMessageTrigger accepted by the action. Redefines UML AcceptEventAction::trigger. |
|---|---|
| result: OutputPin[1] | The OutputPin holding the event object that has been received as a CommunicationMessage. Redefines UML AcceptEventAction::result. |

**Constraints** 1. If the type of the OutputPin referred to by the result meta-association is specified, it must be a CommunicationMessagePayload:

    self.result.type->notEmpty() implies
        self.result.type.oclIsKindOf(CommunicationMessagePayload)

**Notation** AcceptCommunicationMessageAction is depicted as a rectangle with
concave rounded left side and doubled right side, see Fig. 11-60.

The name of the AcceptCommunicationMessageAction is the associated trigger.

The event object received as a CommunicationMessage may be specified as an OutputPin.

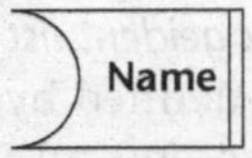

**Fig. 11-60** Notation of AcceptCommunicationMessageAction

**Presentation** AcceptCommunicationMessageAction can be alternatively depicted as
**options** a UML Action with stereotype <<accept communication message>>
and/or a special decoration icon, see Fig. 11-61.

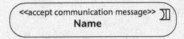

**Fig. 11-61** Alternative notation of AcceptCommunicationMessageAction

**Examples** See Fig. 11-57, Fig. 11-120, and Fig. 11-122.

**Rationale** AcceptCommunicationMessageAction is introduced to model the reception of CommunicationMessages in Activities.

## 11.3.17 DecoupledMessageTrigger

**Semantics** DecoupledMessageTrigger is a specialized Trigger (from UML) that
represents the event of reception of a DecoupledMessage, that satisfies the condition specified by the boolean-valued Expression (from
UML) referred to by the filter meta-association.

The Expression can constrain the signature name and argument values of the received DecoupledMessage, or alternatively, the type and
attribute values of the received DecoupledMessagePayload instance.

**Associations**

| filter: Expression[1] | A boolean-valued Expression filtering received DecoupledMessages. |
|---|---|

**Notation**    DecoupledMessageTrigger is denoted as a boolean-valued Expression which represents the value of the filter meta-attribute.

**Style**    In the case of simple filtering, the following syntax of the Decoupled-MessageTrigger can be used:

>   *triggerident ::= dm-messageident-list*
>   *dm-messageident-list ::= dm-messageident [',' dm-messageident-list ]*

The *dm-messageident-list* represents a comma-separated list of *dm-messageidents* as defined by the DecoupledMessage. The DecoupledMessageTrigger accepts all DecoupledMessages that match the specified payload and argument values.

**Examples**    The DecoupledMessageTrigger specified as:

>   CancelOrder, SendOrder(when=today)

accepts all DecoupledMessages CancelOrder, or SendOrder from today.

**Rationale**    DecoupledMessageTrigger is introduced to model events representing reception of DecoupledMessages.

## 11.3.18 CommunicationMessageTrigger

**Semantics**    CommunicationMessageTrigger is a specialized DecoupledMessage-Trigger that represents the event of reception of a Communication-Message, that satisfies the condition specified by the boolean-valued Expression (from UML) referred to by the filter meta-association.

The Expression can constrain the signature name and argument values of the received CommunicationMessage, or alternatively, the type, value of performative meta-attribute, and attribute values of the received CommunicationMessagePayload instance.

**Notation**    The same as for DecoupledMessageTrigger.

**Style**    In the case of simple filtering, the following syntax of the CommunicationMessageTrigger can be used:

>   *triggerident ::= cm-messageident-list*
>   *cm-messageident-list ::= cm-messageident [',' cm-messageident-list ]*

The *cm-messageident-list* represents a comma-separated list Communi-cationMessage names as defined by the CommunicationMessage. The CommunicationMessageTrigger accepts all CommunicationMessages that match the specified payload, performative and argument values.

**Examples** The CommunicationMessageTrigger specified as:

> accept-proposal

accepts all CommunicationMessages with performative accept-pro-posal.

**Rationale** CommunicationMessageTrigger is introduced to model events repre-senting reception of CommunicationMessages.

## 11.4 Services

**Overview** The *Services* package defines metaclasses used to model services, par-ticularly their specification, provision and usage.

**Abstract** The diagrams of the Services package are shown in figures Fig. 11-62
**syntax** to Fig. 11-66.

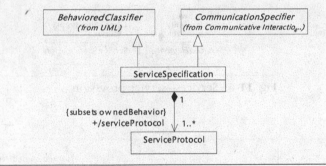

**Fig. 11-62** Services—service specification

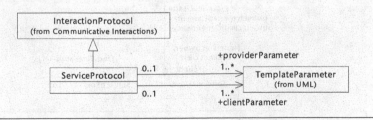

**Fig. 11-63** Services—service protocol

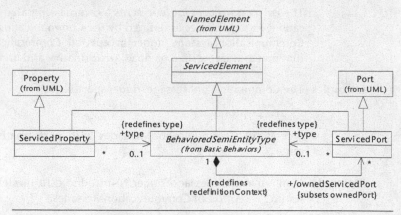

**Fig. 11-64** Services—serviced elements

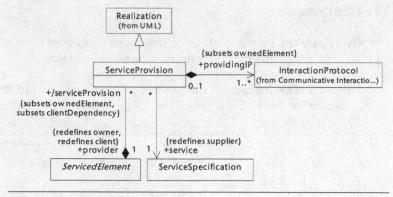

**Fig. 11-65** Services—service provision

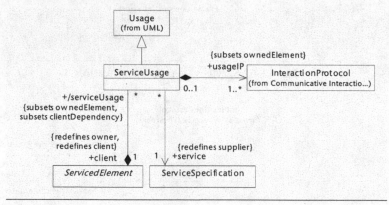

**Fig. 11-66** Services—service usage

## 11.4.1 ServiceSpecification

Semantics ServiceSpecification is a specialized BehavioredClassifier (from UML) and CommunicationSpecifier, used to specify services.

A *service* is a coherent block of functionality provided by a behaviored semi-entity, called *service provider*, that can be accessed by other behaviored semi-entities (which can be either external or internal parts of the service provider), called *service clients*. The ServiceSpecification is used to specify properties of such services, particularly:

❏ the functionality of the services and

❏ the way the specified service can be accessed.

The specification of the functionality and the accessibility of a service is modeled by owned ServiceProtocols, i.e. InteractionProtocols extended with an ability to specify two mandatory, disjoint and non-empty sets of (not bound) parameters of their TemplateSignatures, particularly:

❏ provider template parameters, and

❏ client template parameters.

The *provider template parameters* (providerParameter meta-association) of all contained ServiceProtocols specify the set of template parameters that must be bound by the service providers, and the *client template parameters* (clientParameter meta-association) of all contained ServiceProtocols specify the set of template parameters that must be bound by the service clients. Binding of all these complementary template parameters results in the specification of the CommunicativeInteractions between the service providers and the service clients.

For the meta-attributes defined by CommunicationSpecifier the overriding priority principle defined in section 11.3.8 applies.

**Note 1:** The ServiceSpecification can, in addition to the ServiceProtocols, also own other Behaviors (from UML) describing additional behavioral aspects of the service. For instance, *Interaction Overview Diagrams* (see UML for details) used to describe the overall algorithm (also called the process) of invoking particular ServiceProtocols.

**Note 2:** The ServiceSpecification can also contain StructuralFeatures to model additional structural characteristics of the service, e.g. attributes can be used to model the service parameters.

Associations

| | |
|---|---|
| serviceProtocol: ServiceProtocol[1..*] | Owned ServiceProtocols. Subsets UML BehavioredClassifier:: ownedBehavior. |

**Notation** ServiceSpecification is depicted as a UML Classifier symbol (i.e. a solid-outline rectangle containing the Classifier's name, and optionally also compartments separated by horizontal lines containing features or other members of the Classifier). A ServiceSpecification is marked with the stereotype <<service specification>> and/or a special decoration icon placed in the name compartment. The name compartment can also contain specification of tagged values, e.g. setting of meta-attributes inherited from the CommunicativeInteractionSpecifier meta-class.

The ServiceSpecification shows a compartment which comprises owned ServiceProtocols, but other standard UML or user-defined compartments can be used as well.

Notation of the ServiceSpecification is depicted in Fig. 11-67.

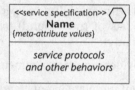

**Fig. 11-67** Notation of the ServiceSpecification

**Style** When defined, the ServiceSpecification usually uses the rectangular notation with the compartment showing owned ServiceProtocols.

When used to specify provision or usage of the service, the ServiceSpecification is usually depicted just as an icon.

**Examples** Fig. 11-68 presents the specification of the FIPA-compliant Directory-Facilitator [47] service with its functions: Register, Deregister, Modify, and Search. All functions use the Fipa-Request-Protocol, see [47] and Fig. 11-48 for details. Binding of the template parameters decide-About and perform is omitted from this example, for the purpose of simplicity. The DirectoryFacilitator also specifies the acl, cl, and ontology meta-attributes used commonly in all comprised ServiceProtocols.

**Rationale** ServiceSpecification is introduced to model the specification of services, particularly (a) the functionality of the service, and (b) the way the service can be accessed.

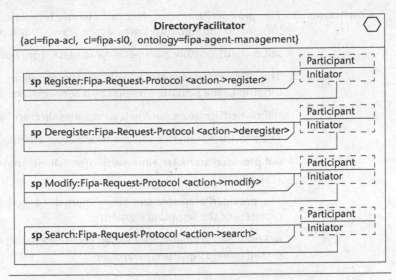

**Fig. 11-68** Example of ServiceSpecification

## 11.4.2 ServiceProtocol

**Semantics** ServiceProtocol is a specialized InteractionProtocol, used only within the context of its owning ServiceSpecification, extended with an ability to specify two mandatory, disjoint and non-empty sets of (not bound) parameters of its TemplateSignature (from UML), particularly:

☐ providerParameter, i.e. a set of parameters which must be bound by providers of the service, and

☐ clientParameter, i.e. a set of parameters which must be bound by clients of the service.

Usually at least one of the provider/client parameters is used as a Lifeline's type which represents a provider/client or its inner ConnectableElements (see UML StructuredClassifier).

The ServiceProtocol can be defined either as a unique InteractionProtocol (a parameterized CommunicativeInteraction) or as a partially bound, already defined InteractionProtocol.

**Associations**

| | |
|---|---|
| providerParameter:<br>TemplateParameter<br>[1..*] | The set of TemplateParameters which must be bound by a provider of the service. |
| clientParameter:<br>TemplateParameter<br>[1..*] | The set of TemplateParameters which must be bound by a client of the service. |

**Constraints**  1.  The providerParameter refer only to the template parameters belonging to the signature owned by a ServiceProtocol:

self.ownedSignature.parameter->includesAll(providerParameter)

2.  The clientParameter refers only to the template parameters belonging to the signature owned by a ServiceProtocol:

self.ownedSignature.parameter->includesAll(clientParameter)

3.  The providerParameter and clientParameter are disjoint:

self.providerParameter->intersection(self.clientParameter)->
    isEmpty()

4.  The providerParameter and clientParameter together cover all parameters of the template signature:

self.providerParameter->union(self.clientParameter) =
    self.ownedSignature.paramater

**Notation**  ServiceProtocol is shown as an InteractionProtocol, having a list of formal template parameters divided into two parts: provider parameters and client parameters. The provider parameters are preceded with the keyword <<provider>> and the client parameters with the keyword <<client>>. The keyword 'sp' used for the diagram frame kind. Notation of ServiceProtocol is depicted in Fig. 11-69.

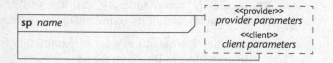

**Fig. 11-69** Notation of ServiceProtocol

**Presentation**  Alternatively, the provider parameters can be separated from the cli-
**options**  ent parameters by a solid horizontal line, see Fig. 11-70.

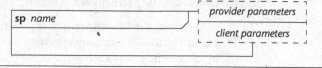

**Fig. 11-70** Alternative notation of ServiceProtocol

Alternatively a ServiceProtocol can be shown textually with the following format:

*service_protocol ::= name '/' provider_parameters '/' client_parameters*

The *name* is the name of the ServiceProtocol, the *provider_parameters* is a comma-separated list of the provider parameters, and the *client_parameters* is a comma-separated list of the client parameters.

**Examples** Fig. 11-71 shows the FIPA Propose Interaction Protocol [47] modeled as ServiceProtocol.

The initiator sends a propose CommunicationMessage to the participant indicating that it will perform some action if the participant agrees. The participant responds by either rejecting or accepting the proposal, communicating this with the reject-proposal or accept-proposal CommunicationMessage, accordingly.

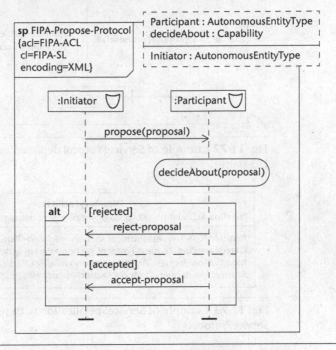

**Fig. 11-71** Example of ServiceProtocol depicted as a Sequence Diagram

Fig. 11-72 shows a simplified version of the previously defined service protocol FIPA-Propose-Protocol in the form of Communication Diagram.

Fig. 11-68 shows an example of the FIPA DirectoryFacilitator service containing several ServiceProtocols obtained by binding of the Fipa-Request-Proposal InteractionProtocol's template parameters to the actual, provider and client parameters. Semantically identical specification of the DirectoryFacilitator service using the textual notation of the contained ServiceProtocols is depicted in Fig. 11-73.

**Rationale** ServiceProtocol is introduced to specify the parameters of an InteractionProtocol that must be bound by service providers and clients. ServiceProtocols are necessary to define ServiceSpecifications.

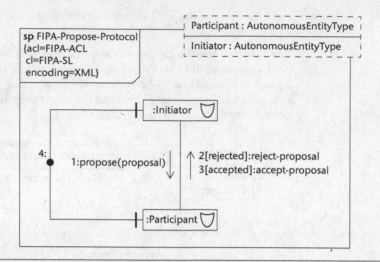

**Fig. 11-72** Example of ServiceProtocol depicted as a Communication Diagram

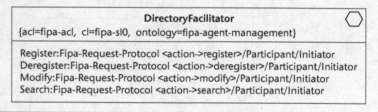

**Fig. 11-73** Example of ServiceSpecification with textual notation of ServiceProtocols

## 11.4.3 ServicedElement

**Semantics**  ServicedElement is an abstract specialized NamedElement (from UML) used to serve as a common superclass to all the metaclasses that can provide or use services (i.e. BehavioralSemiEntitiyType, ServicedPort, and ServicedProperty).

Technically, the service provision and usage is modeled by ownership of ServiceProvisions and ServiceUsages.

**Associations**

| | |
|---|---|
| /serviceProvision: ServiceProvision[*] | The ServiceProvision relationships owned by a ServicedElement. This is a derived association.<br>Subsets UML Element::ownedElement and NamedElement::clientDependency. |

| /serviceUsage: ServiceUsage[*] | The ServiceUsage relationships owned by a ServicedElement. This is a derived association.<br>Subsets UML Element::ownedElement and NamedElement::clientDependency. |

Constraints  1. The serviceProvision meta-association refers to all client dependencies of the kind ServiceProvision:

serviceProvision = self.clientDependency->
  select(oclIsKindOf(ServiceProvision))

2. The serviceUsage meta-association refers to all client dependencies of the kind ServiceUsage:

serviceUsage = self.clientDependency->
  select(oclIsKindOf(ServiceUsage))

Notation  There is no general notation for ServicedElement. The specific subclasses of ServicedElement define their own notation.

Rationale  ServicedElement is introduced to define a common superclass for all metaclasses that may provide or require services.

## 11.4.4 ServicedProperty

Semantics  ServicedProperty is a specialized Property (from UML) and ServicedElement, used to model attributes that can provide or use services. It determines what services are provided and used by the behaviored semi entities when occur as attribute values of some objects.

The type of a ServicedProperty is responsible for processing or mediating incoming and outgoing communication. The ServiceProvisions and ServiceUsages owned by the the ServicedProperty are handled by its type. For details see section 11.1.1.

Associations

| type: BehavioredSemiEntity-Type[0..1] | The type of a ServicedProperty. Redefines UML TypedElement::type. |

Notation  ServicedProperty is depicted as a UML Property with the stereotype <<serviced>>.

Additionally, it can be connected to the ServiceProvision and the ServiceUsage relationships, to specify the provided and the required services respectively. See Fig. 11-74.

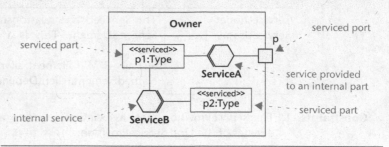

**Fig. 11-74** Notation of ServicedProperty

**Style** The stereotype label is usually omitted and the ServicedProperty is identified only by the owned ServiceProvision and the ServiceUsage relationships.

**Examples** A model of a simple mobile robot is is shown in Fig. 11-75. The diagram demonstrates the use of all kinds of ServicedElements, but does not specify details about ServiceSpecification bindings (for details see sections 11.4.6 and 11.4.7).

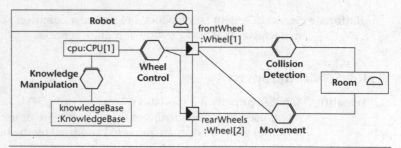

**Fig. 11-75** Example of ServicedElements—simple model of a mobile robot

The AgentType called Robot, which models the type of a mobile robot capable of movement in a room, owns two Effectors (special Serviced-Ports): frontWheel and rearWheels. They both provide the service Movement enabling to change position of the robot in the room, and the service WheelControl to the internal ServicedProperty called cpu, representing the central robot controller. The frontWheel, in order to detect collisions of the robot, requires from the Room Environment-Type a service CollisionDetection.

The Robot also contains two ServicedProperties: the already described cpu, and knowledgeBase. The knowledgeBase is used to store and manipulate a representation of the robot's environment and state. It offers a KnowledgeManipulation service that is internally used by the cpu.

The Wheel EffectorType is responsible for realization of the Movement and the WheelControl services, and for accessing the CollisionDetection service. Type CPU is responsible for usage of the WheelControl and the KnowledgeManipulation services. The KnowledgeBase type handles the KnowledgeManipulation service.

For another example see also Fig. 11-77.

**Rationale** ServicedProperty is introduced to model attributes that can provide or use services.

## 11.4.5 ServicedPort

**Semantics** ServicedPort is a specialized Port (from UML) and ServicedElement that specifies a distinct interaction point between the owning BehavioredSemiEntityType and other ServicedElements in the model. The nature of the interactions that may occur over a ServicedPort can, in addition to required and provided interfaces, be specified also in terms of required and provided services, particularly by associated provided and/or required ServiceSpecifications.

The required ServiceSpecifications of a ServicedPort determine services that the owning BehavioredSemiEntityType expects from other ServicedElements and which it may access through this interaction point. The provided ServiceSpecifications determine the services that the owning BehavioredSemiEntityType offers to other ServicedElements at this interaction point.

The type of a ServicedPort is responsible for processing or mediating incoming and outgoing communication. The ServiceProvisions and ServiceUsages owned by the the ServicedPort are handled by its type. For details see section 11.1.1.

**Associations**

| | |
|---|---|
| type:<br>BehavioredSemiEntity-<br>Type[0..1] | The type of a ServicedPort.<br>Redefines UML TypedElement::type. |

**Notation** ServicedPort is depicted as a UML Port with the stereotype <<serviced>>.

Additionally, it can be connected to the ServiceProvision and the ServiceUsage relationships, to specify the provided and the required services respectively. See Fig. 11-76.

**Style** The stereotype label is usually omitted and the ServicedPort is identified only by the owned ServiceProvision and the ServiceUsage relationships.

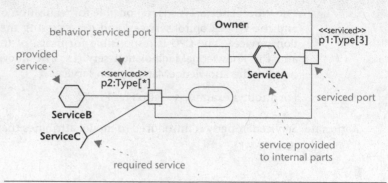

**Fig. 11-76** Notation of ServicedPort

**Examples**  Fig. 11-77 shows an example of the deployment diagram of a FIPA compliant agent platform (for details see FIPA Abstract Architecture Specification at [47]).

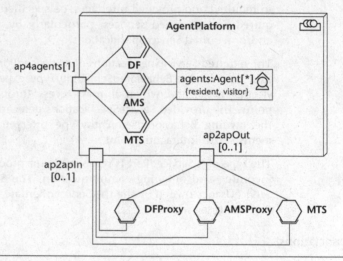

**Fig. 11-77** Example of ServicedPort

The platform is modeled as an AgentExecutionEnvironment named AgentPlatform which hosts agents. The AgentPlatform provides three services to the contained agents: DF (Directory Facilitator), AMS (Agent Management System), and MTS (Message Transport System). All these services are provided through the ServicedPort called ap4agents.

The AgentPlatform also provides services (DFProxy, AMSProxy, and MTS) to the other agent platforms over the ap2apOut (agent platform-to-agent platform output) ServicedPort, and requires the same services from other agent platforms via the ap2apIn ServicedPort. The proxy services represent restricted versions of corresponding plat-form-internal services.

For another example see also Fig. 11-75.

**Rationale** ServicedPort is introduced to model the distinct interaction points be-tween the owning BehavioredSemiEntityTypes and other ServicedEle-ments which can be used to provide and/or use services.

## 11.4.6 ServiceProvision

**Semantics** ServiceProvision is a specialized Realization dependency (from UML) between a ServiceSpecification and a ServicedElement, used to specify that the ServicedElement provides the service specified by the related ServiceSpecification.

The details of the service provision are specified by means of owned InteractionProtocols, which are partially bound counterparts to all Ser-viceProtocols comprised within the related ServiceSpecification.

Owned InteractionProtocols (specified by the providingIP meta-associ-ation) must bind all (and only those) template parameters of the cor-responding ServiceProtocol, which are declared to be bound by a ser-vice provider.

The constraints put on bindings performed by service providers and clients of a service (see section 11.4.7) guarantee complementarity of those bindings. Therefore the InteractionProtocols of a ServiceProvi-sion and a ServiceUsage, which correspond to the same ServiceSpecifi-cation, can be merged to create concrete CommunicativeInteractions according to which the service is accessed.

**Associations**

| | |
|---|---|
| provider: ServicedElement[1] | The ServicedElement that provides the ser-vice specified by the ServiceProvision. Redefines UML Element::owner and Dependency::client. |
| service: ServiceSpecification[1] | The ServiceSpecification that specifies the service provided by the provider. Redefines UML Dependency::supplier. |
| providingIP: InteractionProtocol [1..*] | A set of InteractionProtocols each of which represents a partial binding of the related service's serviceProtocol, where all declared provider parameters are bound by the pro-vider. Subsets UML Element::ownedElement. |

**Constraints**  1. The providingIP binds all (and only) the provider parameters from all the service's ServiceProtocols:

self.providingIP.templateBinding.parameterSubstitution.formal = self.service.serviceProtocol.providerParameter

**Notation**  ServiceProvision is depicted as a UML Dependency relationship with the stereotype <<provides>>. The ServicedElement providing the service represents a client and the ServiceSpecification is a supplier. The provider template parameter substitutions are placed in a Comment symbol attached to the relationship's arrow. See Fig. 11-78.

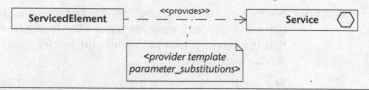

**Fig. 11-78** Notation of ServiceProvision

The provider template parameter substitutions use the following syntax:

'<' template-parameter-substitutions '>'

The template-parameter-substitutions is a comma separated list of template-parameter-substitution defined in UML. The template-parameter-name can be prefixed with a name of owning ServiceProtocol followed by the scope operator (::) to avoid ambiguity in naming of template parameters with the same names but from different ServiceProtocols.

**Presentation options**  ServiceProvision can be alternatively depicted as a solid line connecting the ServicedElement which provides the service with the ServiceSpecification, see Fig. 11-79.

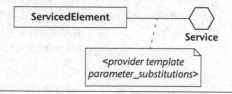

**Fig. 11-79** Alternative notation of ServiceProvision

To simplify the diagram, the Comment containing the provider template parameter substitutions can be hidden.

**Examples**  See Fig. 11-75 and Fig. 11-77.

**Rationale**  ServiceProvision is introduced to specify that the ServicedElement provides the service specified by the related ServiceSpecification.

## 11.4.7 ServiceUsage

**Semantics** ServiceUsage is a specialized Usage dependency (from UML) between a ServiceSpecification and a ServicedElement, used to specify that the ServicedElement uses or requires (can request) the service specified by the related ServiceSpecification.

The details of the service usage are specified by means of owned InteractionProtocols, which are partially bound counterparts to all ServiceProtocols comprised within the related ServiceSpecification.

Owned InteractionProtocols (specified by the usageIP meta-association) must bind all (and only those) template parameters of the corresponding ServiceProtocol, which are declared to be bound by a client of the service.

The constraints put on bindings performed by service providers (see section 11.4.6) and clients of a service guarantee complementarity of those bindings. Therefore the InteractionProtocols of a ServiceProvision and a ServiceUsage, which correspond to the same ServiceSpecification, can be merged to create concrete CommunicativeInteractions according to which the service is accessed.

**Associations**

| | |
|---|---|
| client:<br>ServicedElement[1] | The ServicedElement that uses the service specified by the ServiceUsage.<br>Redefines UML Element::owner and Dependency::client. |
| service:<br>ServiceSpecification[1] | The ServiceSpecification that specifies the service used by the client.<br>Redefines UML Dependency::supplier. |
| usageIP:<br>InteractionProtocol<br>[1..*] | A set of InteractionProtocols each of which represents a partial binding of related service's serviceProtocol, where all declared client parameters are bound by the client.<br>Subsets UML Element::ownedElement. |

**Constraints** 1. The usageIP binds all and only the client parameters from all service's ServiceProtocols:

self.usageIP.templateBinding.parameterSubstitution.formal = self.service.serviceProtocol.clientParameter

**Notation** ServiceUsage is depicted as a UML Dependency relationship with the stereotype <<uses>>. The ServicedElement using the service represents a client and the ServiceSpecification is a supplier. The client template parameter substitutions are placed in a Comment symbol attached to the relationship's arrow. See Fig. 11-80.

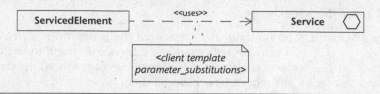

**Fig. 11-80** Notation of ServiceUsage

The client template parameter substitutions use the same notation as the provider template parameter substitutions described in section 11.4.6.

**Presentation** The ServiceUsage relationship can also be shown by representing the **options** used ServiceSpecification by an angular icon, called *service socket*, labeled with the name of the ServiceSpecification, attached by a solid line to the ServicedElement that uses this ServiceSpecification. See Fig. 11-81.

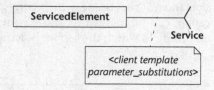

**Fig. 11-81** Alternative notation of ServiceUsage

Where two ServicedElements provide and require the same ServiceSpecification, respectively, the iconic notations may be combined as shown in Fig. 11-82. This notation hints at that the ServiceSpecification in question serves to mediate interactions between the two ServicedElements.

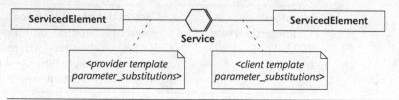

**Fig. 11-82** Combination of ServiceProvision with ServiceUsage

To simplify the diagram, the Comment containing the client template parameter substitutions can be hidden.

**Examples** See Fig. 11-75 and Fig. 11-77.

**Rationale** ServiceUsage is introduced to specify that the ServicedElement uses the service specified by the related ServiceSpecification.

## 11.5 Observations and Effecting Interactions

Overview  The *Observations and Effecting Interactions* package defines metaclasses used to model structural and behavioral aspects of observations (i.e. the ability of entities to observe features of other entities) and effecting interactions (i.e. the ability of entities to manipulate or modify the state of other entities).

Abstract  The diagrams of the Observations and Effecting Interactions package
syntax  are shown in figures Fig. 11-83 to Fig. 11-90.

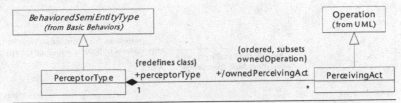

Fig. 11-83 Observations and Effecting Interactions—perceiving act and perceptor type

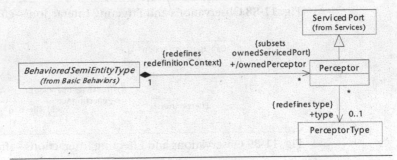

Fig. 11-84 Observations and Effecting Interactions—perceptor

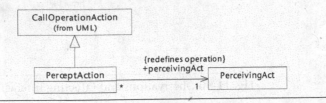

Fig. 11-85 Observations and Effecting Interactions—percept action

Fig. 11-86 Observations and Effecting Interactions—perceives

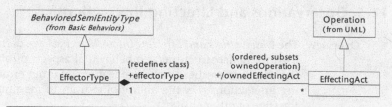

**Fig. 11-87** Observations and Effecting Interactions—effecting act and effector type

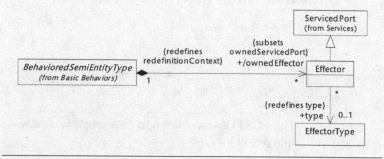

**Fig. 11-88** Observations and Effecting Interactions—effector

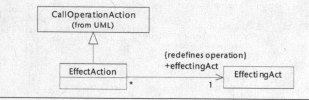

**Fig. 11-89** Observations and Effecting Interactions—effect action

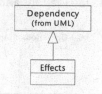

**Fig. 11-90** Observations and Effecting Interactions—effects

## 11.5.1 PerceivingAct

**Semantics**   PerceivingAct is a specialized Operation (from UML) which is owned by a PerceptorType and thus can be used to specify what perceptions the owning PerceptorType, or a Perceptor of that PerceptorType, can perform.

Associations

| | |
|---|---|
| perceptorType: PerceptorType[1] | The PerceptorType that owns this Perceiving-Act. Redefines UML Operation::class. |

Notation    PerceivingAct is shown using the same notation as for UML Operation with the stereotype <<pa>>, see Fig. 11-91.

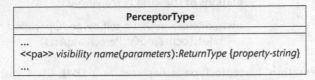

| PerceptorType |
|---|
| ... <br> <<pa>> *visibility name(parameters):ReturnType {property-string}* <br> ... |

Fig. 11-91 Notation of PerceivingAct

Presentation options    PerceivingAct can be placed in a special class compartment of the owning PerceptorType named <<perceiving acts>>. The stereotype <<pa>> of a particular PerceivingAct is in this case omitted. See Fig. 11-92.

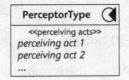

Fig. 11-92 Alternative notation of PerceivingAct—placed in a special class compartment

Examples    See Fig. 11-95.

Rationale    PerceivingAct is introduced to specify which perceptions the owning PerceptorType, or a Perceptor of that PerceptorType, can perform.

## 11.5.2 PerceptorType

Semantics    PerceptorType is a specialized BehavioredSemiEntityType used to model the type of Perceptors, in terms of owned:

❑ Receptions (from UML) and

❑ PerceivingActs.

**Associations**

| | |
|---|---|
| /ownedPerceivingAct: PerceivingAct[*] | A set of all PerceivingActs owned by the PerceptorType. The association is ordered and derived. Subsets UML Class::ownedOperation. |

**Constraints**  1. The ownedPerceivingAct meta-association refers to all ownedOperations of the kind PerceivingAct:

ownedPerceivingAct = self.ownedOperation->
select(oclIsKindOf(PerceivingAct))

**Notation**  PerceptorType is depicted as a UML Class with the stereotype label <<perceptor type>> and/or a special icon, see Fig. 11-93.

**Fig. 11-93** Notation of PerceptorType

**Presentation options**  Alternatively, the PerceptorType can, for owned PerceivingActs and Receptions, specify special compartments marked with the stereotypes <<perceiving acts>> and <<signals>> respectively. Stereotypes of particular PerceivingActs and Receptions are omitted in this case. See Fig. 11-94.

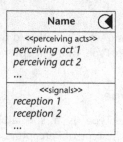

**Fig. 11-94** Alternative notation of PerceptorType

**Examples**  Fig. 11-95 shows a specification of the Eye, which is a PerceptorType used to provide information about status of the environment where the Robot, described in Fig. 11-98, is placed. The Eye provides two PerceivingActs (isOnFloor and isOnCube) returning an information about positions of cubes, and can process the signal newCubeAppeared, which is raised when a new cube appears in the environment.

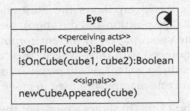

**Fig. 11-95** Example of PerceptorType

**Rationale** PerceptorType is introduced to model types of Perceptors.

## 11.5.3 Perceptor

**Semantics** Perceptor is a specialized ServicedPort used to model capability of its owner (a BehavioredSemiEntityType) to observe, i.e. perceive a state of and/or to receive a signal from observed objects. What observations a Perceptor is capable of is specified by its type, i.e. PerceptorType.

**Associations**

| type: PerceptorType[0..1] | The type of a Perceptor. Redefines UML TypedElement::type. |
| --- | --- |

**Notation** Perceptor is depicted as a ServicedPort with the stereotype <<perceptor>>. See Fig. 11-96.

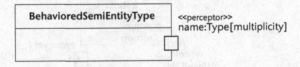

**Fig. 11-96** Notation of Perceptor

**Presentation options** Perceptor can also be depicted as a ServicedPort with a small filled triangle pointing from the outside to the middle of owner's shape. The stereotype label is usually omitted in this case. See Fig. 11-97.

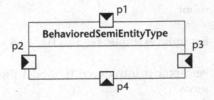

**Fig. 11-97** Alternative notation of Perceptor

**Examples** Fig. 11-98 (a) shows the illustration of a robot able to move (to change position and direction), see its environment and manipulate the cubes placed in the environment. The robot for this purpose is equipped with three wheels, two "eyes" (cameras with a picture recognition system able to perceive and reason about the environment), and one manipulator used to move and lift the cubes.

Fig. 11-98 (b) shows a model of the robot. It is modeled as an Agent-Type with attributes position and direction, and respective Perceptors (eyes) and Effectors (wheels and manipulator). The diagram also depicts Perceives and Effects relationships between the robot and cubes (meaning that the robot is able to see and to manipulate the cubes), and the robot itself (because it is able to change its own position and direction by means of wheels).

See also models of perceptor and effector types Eye in Fig. 11-95 and Manipulator in Fig. 11-107.

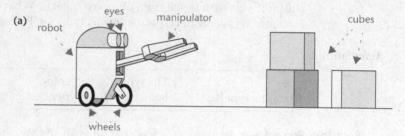

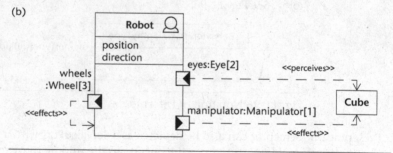

**Fig. 11-98** Example of non-communicative interaction modeling— mobile robot: (a) illustration of the robot, (b) AML model of the robot.

For more examples see also Fig. 10-5 and Fig. 11-7.

**Rationale** Perceptor is introduced to model the capability of its owner to observe.

## 11.5.4 PerceptAction

**Semantics**  PerceptAction is a specialized CallOperationAction (from UML) which can call PerceivingActs. As such, PerceptAction can transmit an operation call request to a PerceivingAct, what causes the invocation of the associated behavior.

PerceptAction being a CallOperationAction allows to call PerceivingActs both synchronously and asynchronously.

**Associations**

| perceivingAct: PerceivingAct[1] | The PerceivingAct to be invoked by the action execution. Redefines UML CallOperationAction:: operation. |
|---|---|

**Notation**  PerceptAction is drawn as a UML CallOperationAction with the stereotype <<percept>> and/or a special icon, see Fig. 11-99. Action's name represents a PerceivingAct's call, i.e. its name and possibly also parameter values.

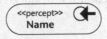

**Fig. 11-99** Notation of PerceptAction

**Presentation options**  If the action's name is different from the PerceivingAct's call, the call may appear in parentheses below the action's name. To indicate the Perceptor owning the called PerceivingAct, its name postfixed by a period may precede the PerceivingAct's call. See Fig. 11-100.

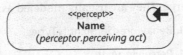

**Fig. 11-100** Alternative notation of PerceptAction—indication of PerceivingAct's call

PerceptAction can use all presentation options from UML CallOperationAction.

**Examples**  Fig. 11-101 shows an example of the Plan describing how the robot, as in Fig. 11-98, can achieve the placement of the red cube on the blue one. The application logic is described solely by the PerceptActions (isOnFloor) and the EffectActions (putOn and putOnFloor).

For details on how the called PerceivingAct and EffectingActs are defined see Fig. 11-95 and Fig. 11-107 respectively.

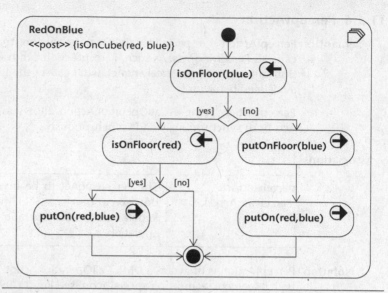

**Fig. 11-101** Example of Plan, PerceptAction and EffectAction

**Rationale**   PerceptAction is introduced to model observations in Activities.

## 11.5.5 Perceives

**Semantics**   Perceives is a specialized Dependency (from UML) used to model which elements can observe others.

Suppliers of the Perceives dependency are the observed elements, particularly NamedElements (from UML).

Clients of the Perceives dependency represent the objects that observe. They are usually modeled as:

☐ BehavioredSemiEntityTypes,

☐ PerceivingActs,

☐ PerceptorTypes, or

☐ Perceptors.

**Notation**   Perceives is depicted as a UML Dependency relationship with the stereotype <<perceives>>. See Fig. 11-102.

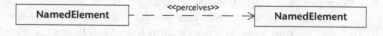

**Fig. 11-102** Notation of Perceives

Presentation
options

Alternatively, the Perceives dependency can be depicted as a dashed
line with a filled triangle as an arrowhead. One side of the triangle is
oriented toward the icon of the observed element. The stereotype label is usually omitted in this case. See Fig. 11-103.

**Fig. 11-103** Alternative notation of Perceives

Examples　See Fig. 11-98.

Rationale　Perceives is introduced to model which elements can observe others.

## 11.5.6　EffectingAct

Semantics

EffectingAct is a specialized Operation (from UML) which is owned by
an EffectorType and thus can be used to specify what effecting acts the
owning EffectorType, or an Effector of that EffectorType, can perform.

Associations

| effectorType:<br>EffectorType[1] | The EffectorType that owns this EffectingAct.<br>Redefines UML Operation::class. |
|---|---|

Notation

EffectingAct is shown using the same notation as for UML Operation
with the stereotype <<ea>> , see Fig. 11-104.

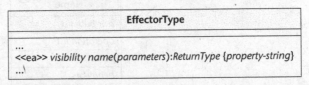

**Fig. 11-104** Notation of EffectingAct

Presentation
options

EffectingAct can be placed in a special class compartment of the owning EffectorType named <<effecting acts>>. The stereotype <<ea>> of a
particular EffectingAct is in this case omitted. See Fig. 11-105.

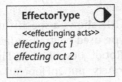

**Fig. 11-105** Alternative notation of EffectingAct—placed in a special
class compartment

**Examples** See Fig. 11-107.

**Rationale** EffectingAct is introduced to specify which effecting acts the owning EffectorType, or an Effector of that EffectorType, can perform.

## 11.5.7 EffectorType

**Semantics** EffectorType is a specialized BehavioredSemiEntityType used to model type of Effectors, in terms of owned EffectingActs.

**Associations**

| /ownedEffectingAct: EffectingAct[*] | A set of all EffectingActs owned by the EffectorType. The association is ordered and derived.<br>Subsets UML Class::ownedOperation. |
| --- | --- |

**Constraints** 1. The ownedEffectingAct meta-association refers to all ownedOperations of the kind EffectingAct:

ownedEffectingAct = self.ownedOperation-> select(oclIsKindOf(EffectingAct))

**Notation** EffectorType is depicted as a UML Class with the stereotype label <<effector type>> and/or a special icon, see Fig. 11-106.

**Fig. 11-106** Notation of EffectorType

**Presentation options** Alternatively, the EffectorType can for owned EffectingActs specify a special compartment marked with the <<effecting acts>> keyword. See Fig. 11-105.

**Examples** Fig. 11-107 shows a specification of the Manipulator, which is an EffectorType used to manipulate the cubes placed in the environment of the Robot, described in Fig. 11-98. The Manipulator provides two EffectingActs: putOnFloor enabling the placement of a cube on the floor, and putOn enabling the placement of one cube on another.

**Rationale** EffectorType is introduced to model types of Effectors.

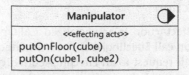

Fig. 11-107 Example of EffectorType

## 11.5.8 Effector

**Semantics** Effector is a specialized ServicedPort used to model the capability of its owner (a BehavioredSemiEntityType) to bring about an effect on others, i.e. to directly manipulate with (or modify a state of) some other objects. What effects an Effector is capable of is specified by its type, i.e. EffectorType.

**Associations**

| type: EffectorType[0..1] | The type of an Effector. Redefines UML TypedElement::type. |
|---|---|

**Notation** Effector is depicted as a ServicedPort with the stereotype <<effector>>. See Fig. 11-108.

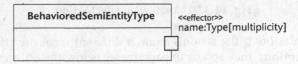

Fig. 11-108 Notation of Effector

**Presentation options** Effector can also be depicted as a ServicedPort with a small filled triangle pointing from middle of the owner's shape to the outside. The stereotype label is usually omitted in this case. See Fig. 11-109.

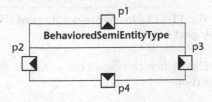

Fig. 11-109 Alternative notation of Effector

**Examples** See Fig. 10-5, Fig. 11-75, and Fig. 11-98.

**Rationale** Effector is introduced to model the capability of its owner to bring about an effect on other objects.

## 11.5.9 EffectAction

**Semantics**  EffectAction is a specialized CallOperationAction (from UML) which can call EffectingActs. Thus, an EffectAction can transmit an operation call request to an EffectingAct, which causes the invocation of the associated behavior.

EffectAction being a CallOperationAction allows calling EffectingActs both synchronously and asynchronously.

**Associations**

| | |
|---|---|
| effectingAct: EffectingAct[1] | The EffectingAct to be invoked by the action execution. Redefines UML CallOperationAction:: operation. |

**Notation**  EffectAction is drawn as a UML CallOperationAction with the stereotype <<effect>> and/or a special icon, see Fig. 11-110. The action's name represents an EffectingAct's call, i.e. its name and possibly also parameter values.

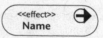

**Fig. 11-110** Notation of EffectAction

**Presentation options**  If the action's name is different from the EffectingAct's call, the call may appear in parentheses below the action's name. To indicate the Effector owning the called EffectingAct, its name postfixed by a period may precede the EffectingAct's call. See Fig. 11-111.

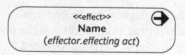

**Fig. 11-111** Alternative notation of EffectAction—indication of EffectingAct's call

EffectAction can use all presentation options from UML CallOperationAction.

**Examples**  See Fig. 11-101.

**Rationale**  EffectAction is introduced to model effections in Activities.

### 11.5.10 Effects

**Semantics** Effects is a specialized Dependency (from UML) used to model which elements can effect others.

Suppliers of the Effects dependency are the effected elements, particularly NamedElements (from UML).

Clients of the Effects dependency represent the objects which effect. They are usually modeled as:

☐ BehavioredSemiEntityTypes,

☐ EffectingActs,

☐ EffectorTypes, or

☐ Effectors.

**Notation** Effects is depicted as a UML Dependency relationship with the stereotype <<effects>>. See Fig. 11-112.

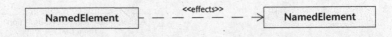

**Fig. 11-112** Notation of Effects

**Presentation options** Alternatively, the Effects dependency can be depicted as a dashed line with a filled triangle as an arrowhead. One point of the triangle touches an icon of the the observed element. The stereotype label is usually omitted in this case. See Fig. 11-113.

**Fig. 11-113** Alternative notation of Effects

**Examples** See Fig. 11-98.

**Rationale** Effects is introduced to model which elements can effect others.

## 11.6 Mobility

**Overview** The *Mobility* package defines metaclasses used to model structural and behavioral aspects of entity mobility[29].

---

[29] Agents are special entities and therefore agent mobility is also covered by the AML mobility mechanisms.

**Abstract**   The diagrams of the Mobility package are shown in figures Fig. 11-
**syntax**   114 and Fig. 11-115.

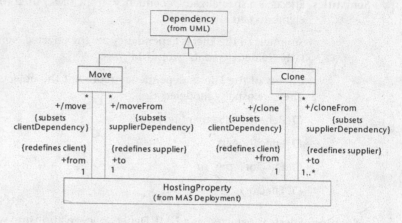

**Fig. 11-114** Mobility—mobility relationships

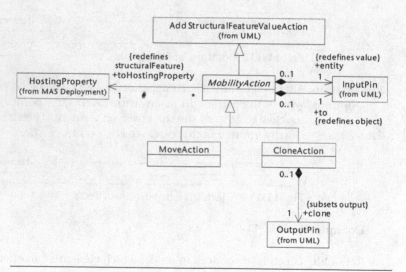

**Fig. 11-115** Mobility—mobility-related actions

## 11.6.1 Move

**Semantics**   Move is a specialized Dependency (from UML) between two Hosting-
Properties used to specify that the entities represented by the source
HostingProperty (specified by the from meta-association) can be
moved/transferred to the instances of the AgentExecutionEnvironment
owning the destination HostingProperty (specified by the to meta-association).

For example, a Move dependency between a HostingProperty A of type T (owned by AgentExecutionEnvironment AEE1) and a HostingProperty B of the same type T (owned by another AgentExecutionEnvironment AEE2) means that entities of type T can be moved from AEE1 to AEE2.

AML does not specify the type and other details of moving, which may be technology dependent. If needed, they can be specified as specific tagged values, comments, constraints, linked/attached information, etc.

**Associations**

| from: HostingProperty[1] | The HostingProperty representing the source of moving. Redefines UML Dependency::client. |
|---|---|
| to: HostingProperty[1] | The HostingProperty representing the destination of moving. Redefines UML Dependency::supplier. |

**Constraints**  1. If both specified, the type of the HostingProperty referred to by the to meta-association must conform to the type of the HostingProperty referred to by the from meta-association:

(self.from.type->notEmpty() and self.to.type->notEmpty()) implies
self.to.type.conformsTo(self.from.type)

**Notation**  Move is depicted as a UML Dependency relationship with the stereotype <<move>>. The from HostingProperty is specified as a dependency client and the to HostingProperty is a dependency supplier. See Fig. 11-116.

**Fig. 11-116** Notation of Move

**Examples**  Fig. 11-117 extends the example from Fig. 10-47 by modeling load balancing and agent mobility. Agents of type Broker residing in the TradingClient can be cloned to the TradingServer instances running at the MainStockExchangeServers. Each TradingServer can control the load of its machine, and if necessary, it can move some brokers (agents of type Broker) to any of the BackupStockExchangeServers. The LoadBalanceManager agents are concerned with monitoring of machine load and moving brokers to other machines. The brokers can move back to the MainStockExchangeServers.

**Rationale**  Move is introduced to model the movement of entities between instances of AgentExecutionEnvironments.

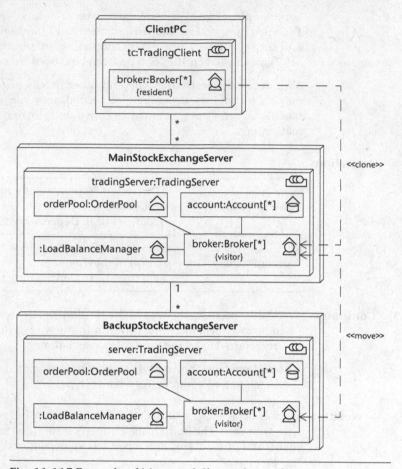

**Fig. 11-117** Example of Move and Clone relationships

## 11.6.2 Clone

**Semantics** Clone is a specialized Dependency (from UML) between HostingProperties used to specify that entities represented by the source HostingProperty (specified by the from meta-association) can be cloned to the instances of the AgentExecutionEnvironment owning the destination HostingProperties (specified by the to meta-association).

For example, a Clone dependency between a HostingProperty A of type T (owned by AgentExecutionEnvironment AEE1) and a HostingProperty B of the same type T (owned by another AgentExecutionEnvironment AEE2) means that entities of type T can be cloned from AEE1 to AEE2.

AML does not specify the type and other details of cloning, which may be technology dependent. If needed, they can be specified as

specific tagged values, comments, constraints, linked/attached information, etc.

**Associations**

| | |
|---|---|
| from:<br>HostingProperty[1] | The HostingProperty representing the source of cloning.<br>Redefines UML Dependency::client. |
| to:<br>HostingProperty[1..*] | The HostingProperties representing the desti-nation of cloning.<br>Redefines UML Dependency::supplier. |

**Constraints** 1. If specified, the types of the HostingProperties referred to by the to
meta-association must conform to the type of the HostingProperty
referred to by the from meta-association:

(self.from.type->notEmpty() and self.to.type->notEmpty()) implies
self.to.type->forAll(conformsTo(self.from.type))

**Notation** Clone is depicted as a UML Dependency relationship with the stereotype <<clone>>. The from HostingProperty is specified as a dependency
client and the to HostingProperty is a dependency supplier. See
Fig. 11-118.

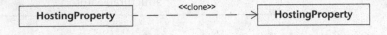

**Fig. 11-118** Notation of Clone

**Examples** See Fig. 11-117.

**Rationale** Clone is introduced to model the cloning of entities among instances
of AgentExecutionEnvironments.

## 11.6.3 MobilityAction

**Semantics** MobilityAction is an abstract specialized AddStructuralFeatureValueAction (from UML) used to model mobility actions of entities, i.e. actions that cause movement or cloning of an entity from one AgentExecutionEnvironment to another one. MobilityAction specifies:

❑ which entity is being moved or cloned (entity meta-association),

❑ the destination AgentExecutionEnvironment instance where the
entity is being moved or cloned (to meta-association), and

❑ the HostingProperty owned by the destination AgentExecutionEnvironment, where the moved or cloned entity is being placed (to-
HostingProperty meta-association).

If the destination HostingProperty is ordered, the insertAt meta-association (inherited from AddStructuralFeatureValueAction) specifies the position at which to insert the entity.

MobilityAction has two concrete subclasses:

❑ MoveAction and

❑ CloneAction.

**Associations**

| entity: InputPin[1] | The InputPin specifying the entity being moved or cloned. Redefines UML WriteStructuralFeatureValueAction::value. |
|---|---|
| to: InputPin[1] | The InputPin specifying the destination AgentExecutionEnvironment instance where the entity is being moved or cloned. Redefines UML StructuralFeatureAction:: object. |
| toHostingProperty: HostingProperty[1] | The HostingProperty where the moved or cloned entity is being placed. Redefines UML StructuralFeatureAction:: structuralFeature. |

**Constraints**  1. If the type of the InputPin referred to by the entity meta-association is specified, it must be an EntityType:

self.entity.type->notEmpty() implies
    self.entity.type.oclIsKindOf(EntityType)

2. If the type of the InputPin referred to by the to meta-association is specified, it must be an AgentExecutionEnvironment:

self.to.type->notEmpty() implies
    self.to.type.oclIsKindOf(AgentExecutionEnvironment)

3. If the type of the InputPin referred to by the to meta-association is specified, the HostingProperty referred to by the toHostingProperty meta-association must be an owned attribute of that type:

self.to.type->notEmpty() implies
    self.to.type.ownedAttribute->includes(self.toHostingProperty)

**Notation**  There is no general notation for MobilityAction. The specific subclasses of MobilityAction define their own notation.

**Rationale**  MobilityAction is introduced to define the common features of all its subclasses.

## 11.6.4 MoveAction

**Semantics**  MoveAction is a specialized MobilityAction used to model an action that results in a removal of the entity (specified by the entity meta-association, inherited from MobilityAction) from its current hosting location, and its insertion as a value to the destination HostingProperty (specified by the toHostingProperty meta-association, inherited from MobilityAction) of the owning AgentExecutionEnvironment instance (specified as the to meta-association, inherited from MobilityAction).

**Notation**  MoveAction is drawn as a UML Action with the stereotype <<move>> and/or a special icon, see Fig. 11-119.

**Fig. 11-119** Notation of MoveAction

Optionally, the name of the moved entity, followed by a greater-than character ('>') and a specification of the destination may appear in parentheses below the action's name. The movement destination is specified as the name of the destination AgentExecutionEnvironment instance (given by the to meta-association), delimited by a period from the name of the destination HostingProperty (given by the to-HostingProperty meta-association). If the destination HostingProperty is ordered, the value of the insertAt meta-association can be placed after the destination HostingProperty's name in brackets.

If the entity being moved is an instance which executes the MoveAction, it can be identified by the keyword 'self' in place of the entity name.

**Examples**  The diagram in Fig. 11-120 shows the Plan of the AgentType Broker (defined in Fig. 11-117) describing how to behave if the LoadBalanceManager (defined also in Fig. 11-117) sends a move command.

After accepting the move command, the Broker evaluates the move. If not possible, the Broker sends a reject CommunicationMessage to the LoadBalanceManager. If the movement is possible, the Broker sends an accept CommunicationMessage to the LoadBalanceManager and moves to the destination AgentExecutionEnvironment instance, specified by the moveCommand, where it is placed in the HostingProperty named broker.

**Rationale**  MoveAction is introduced to model the movement of entities in Activities.

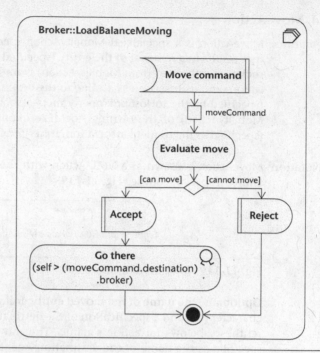

**Fig. 11-120** Example of Plan and MoveAction

## 11.6.5 CloneAction

**Semantics**  CloneAction is a specialized MobilityAction used to model an action that results in a insertion of a clone of the entity (specified by the entity meta-association, inherited from MobilityAction) as a value to the destination HostingProperty (specified by the toHostingProperty meta-association, inherited from MobilityAction) of the owning AgentExecutionEnvironment instance (specified as the to meta-association, inherited from MobilityAction). The original entity remains running at its current hosting location.

The entity clone is represented by the action's OutputPin (specified by the clone meta-association).

**Associations**

| | |
|---|---|
| clone: OutputPin[1] | The OutputPin representing the entity clone. Subsets UML Action::output. |

**Constraints**  1.  If the type of the OutputPin referred to by the clone meta-association is specified, it must be an EntityType:

self.clone.type->notEmpty() implies
    self.clone.type.oclIsKindOf(EntityType)

2. The type of the OutputPin referred to by the clone meta-association must conform to the type of the InputPin referred to by the entity meta-association, if the both specified:

(self.clone.type->notEmpty() and self.entity.type->notEmpty())
   implies self.clone.type.conformsTo(self.entity.type)

**Notation**  CloneAction is drawn as a UML Action with the stereotype <<clone>> and/or a special icon see Fig. 11-121.

**Fig. 11-121** Notation of CloneAction

Optionally, the name of the cloned entity, followed by a greater-than character ('>') and a specification of the destination may appear in parentheses below the action's name. The movement destination is specified as the name of the destination AgentExecutionEnvironment instance (given by the to meta-association), delimited by a period from the name of the destination HostingProperty (given by the to-HostingProperty meta-association). If the destination HostingProperty is ordered, the value of the insertAt meta-association can be placed after the destination HostingProperty's name in brackets. The clone entity is specified as an OutputPin.

If the entity being cloned is an instance which executes the CloneAction, it can be identified by the keyword 'self' in place of the entity name.

**Examples**  The activity diagram in Fig. 11-122 shows the behavior of the broker agent (its type is defined in Fig. 11-117), running at the client, after reception of a new order from a user. The broker checks the order, and if incorrect, a report is produced. In the case of a correct order, the broker selects the most appropriate trading server and clones itself to the selected server. In addition to the broker's code and status information, the clone (called brokerClone), also carries the order information.

When the brokerClone starts to run at the server, it tries to register. If unsuccessful, it announces to the broker the registration refusal which in turn reports this fact to the user. If registration was successful, the brokerClone places the order onto the orderPool (see Fig. 11-117) and negotiates the order with other brokers. If finished, the negotiation result is sent back to the broker which reports the result to the user. After sending the result, the brokerClone terminates its execution at the server.

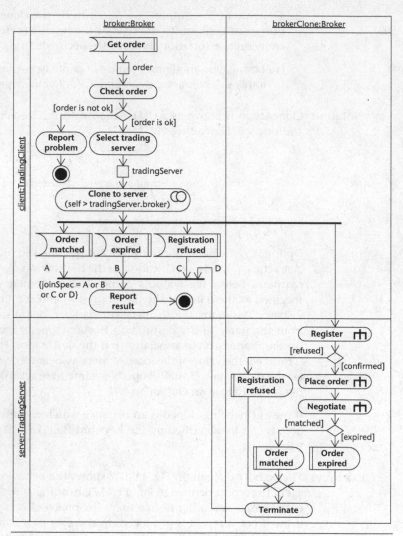

**Fig. 11-122** Example of CloneAction

The diagram is partitioned by two-dimensional ActivityPartitions. The first dimension contains ActivityPartitions representing entities responsible for performing actions. The second dimension contains ActivityPartitions representing the AgentExecutionEnvironment instances where the entities perform relevant actions. If the diagram was specified at the class level, the ActivityPartitions would represent EntityTypes and AgentExecutionEnvironments (and possibly also their HostingProperties) respectively. This is a usual way of partitioning mobility-related Activities, that enables the specification of which entities perform what actions at what hosting places, and also allows modeling the synchronization of activities performed by different entities.

Orientation of partitioning can be arbitrary, i.e. ActivityPartitions representing entities can be either horizontal or vertical, and the ActivityPartitions representing the hosting places should be orthogonal.

**Rationale** CloneAction is introduced to model the cloning of entities in Activities.

# Chapter 12

# Mental

**Overview** The *Mental* package defines the metaclasses which can be used to:

□ support analysis of complex problems/systems, particularly by:

- modeling intentionality in use case models,
- goal-based requirements modeling,
- problem decomposition, etc.

□ model mental attitudes of autonomous entities, which represent their informational, motivational and deliberative states.

**Package structure** The package diagram of the Mental package is depicted in Fig. 12-1.

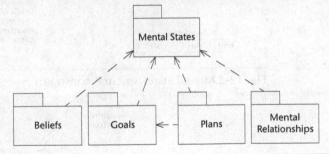

Fig. 12-1 Mental—package structure

## 12.1 Mental States

**Overview** The *Mental States* package comprises common fundamental meta-classes used to define concrete metaclasses contained within the rest of the Mental sub-packages, i.e. Beliefs, Goals, Plans and Mental Relationships.

**Abstract** The diagrams of the Mental State package are shown in figures
**syntax**  Fig. 12-2 to Fig. 12-5.

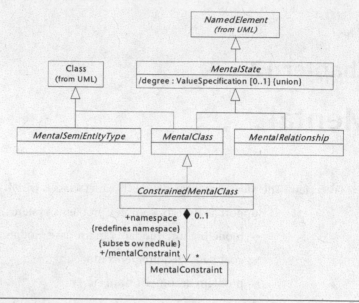

**Fig. 12-2** Mental States—mental states and mental semi-entity type

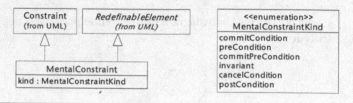

**Fig. 12-3** Mental States—mental constraint

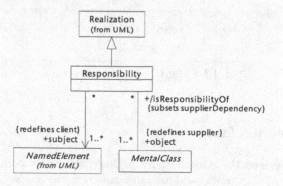

**Fig. 12-4** Mental States—responsibility

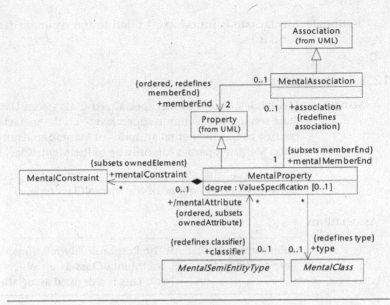

**Fig. 12-5** Mental States—mental property and mental association

## 12.1.1 MentalState

**Semantics** MentalState is an abstract specialized NamedElement (from UML) serving as a common superclass to all metaclasses which can be used for:

❑ modeling mental attitudes of MentalSemiEntityTypes, which represent their informational, motivational and deliberative states, and

❑ support for the human mental process of requirements specification and analysis of complex problems/systems, particularly by:

- expressing intentionality in use case models,

- goal-based requirements modeling,

- problem decomposition, etc.

**Attributes**

| /degree: ValueSpecification [0..1] | The degree of a MentalState. Its specific semantics varies depending on the context of MentalState's subclasses that subset it. This is a derived union. |
| --- | --- |

**Notation** There is no general notation for MentalState. The specific subclasses of MentalState define their own notation.

**Rationale** MentalState is introduced to define the common features of all its subclasses.

## 12.1.2 MentalClass

**Semantics** MentalClass is an abstract specialized Class (from UML) and Mental-State serving as a common superclass to all the metaclasses which can be used to specify mental attitudes of MentalSemiEntityTypes. Technically, MentalProperties can only be of the MentalClass type.

Furthermore, the object meta-association of the Responsibility relationship can also only be of the MentalClass type.

**Associations**

| /isResponsibilityOf: Responsibility[*] | The Responsibility relationships that refer to the MentalClass as an object of responsibility. This is a derived association. |
|---|---|

**Constraints** 1. The isResponsibilityOf meta-association refers to all supplierDependencies of the kind Responsibility:

isResponsibilityOf = self.supplierDependency->
    select(oclIsKindOf(Responsibility))

**Notation** There is no general notation for MentalClass. The specific subclasses of MentalClass define their own notation.

**Rationale** MentalClass is introduced to specify the mental attitudes of Mental-SemiEntityTypes and objects of Responsibility relationship.

## 12.1.3 ConstrainedMentalClass

**Semantics** ConstrainedMentalClass is an abstract specialized MentalClass which allows its concrete subclasses to specify MentalConstraints.

**Note:** To avoid misinterpretation of a set of multiple MentalConstraints of the same kind defined within one ConstrainedMentalClass, AML allows the specification of only one MentalConstraint of a given kind within one ConstrainedMentalClass.

**Associations**

| /mentalConstraint: MentalConstraint[*] | A set of the MentalConstraints owned by the ConstrainedMentalClass. This is a derived association. Subsets UML Namespace::ownedRule. |
|---|---|

**Constraints** 1. Each mentalConstraint must have a different kind:

self.mentalConstraint->forAll(mc1, mc2 | mc1.kind<>mc2.kind)

2. The mentalConstraint meta-association refers to all ownedRules of the kind MentalConstraint:

mentalConstraint = self.ownedRule->
select(oclIsKindOf(MentalConstraint))

**Notation** There is no general notation for ConstrainedMentalClass. The specific subclasses of ConstrainedMentalClass define their own notation.

**Rationale** ConstrainedMentalClass is introduced to allow the specification of MentalConstraints for all its subclasses.

## 12.1.4 MentalConstraint

**Semantics** MentalConstraint is a specialized Constraint (from UML) and RedefinableElement (from UML), used to specify properties of ConstrainedMentalClasses which can be used within mental (reasoning) processes of owning MentalSemiEntityTypes, i.e. pre- and post-conditions, commit conditions, cancel conditions and invariants. MentalConstraint, in addition to Constraint, allows specification of the kind of the constraint (for details see section 12.1.5).

MentalConstraints can be owned only by ConstrainedMentalClasses.

MentalConstraint, being a RedefinableElement, allows the redefinition of the values of constraint specifications (given by the specification meta-association inherited from UML Constraint), e.g. in the case of inherited owned ConstrainedMentalClasses, or redefinition specified by MentalProperties. Specification of a redefined MentalConstraint is logically combined with the specification of the redefining MentalConstraint (of the same kind), following the rules specified in Tab. 12-1.

| MentalConstraintKind | Combination kind |
|---|---|
| *commitCondition* | OR-ed |
| *preCondition* | OR-ed |
| *invariant* | Overridden |
| *cancelCondition* | OR-ed |
| *postCondition* | AND-ed |

**Tab. 12-1** Redefinition rules of MentalConstraints

**Attributes**

| kind:MentalConstraint-Kind[1] | A kind of the MentalConstraint. |
| --- | --- |

**Constraints**  1. The *commitPreCondition* literal cannot be used as the value of the kind meta-attribute.

self.kind <> #commitPreCondition

**Notation**  In general, the MentalConstraint is depicted as a text string in braces ('{' '}') with the same format as defined in UML.

MentalConstraint can occur only within the context of an (a) owning ConstrainedMentalClass, or (b) owning MentalProperty. These meta-classes define specific notation for MentalConstraint and its placement.

**Examples**  Pre-condition of the DecidableGoal named InterceptBall (shown in Fig. 12-21) is specified as:

pre = {not self.team.hasBall(ball) and self.isFree()}

The pre-condition checks whether the robot is free and and its team already has the ball. The keyword 'self' is used to refer to an instance of the SoccerRobot AgentType ( see Fig. 11-7 for details).

For other examples see Fig. 11-101, Fig. 12-21, Fig. 12-29, and Fig. 12-31.

**Rationale**  MentalConstraint is introduced to specify the properties of ConstrainedMentalClasses which can be used within mental (reasoning) processes of owning MentalSemiEntityTypes.

## 12.1.5 MentalConstraintKind

**Semantics**  MentalConstraintKind is an enumeration which specifies kinds of MentalConstraints, as well as kinds of constraints specified for contributor and beneficiary in the Contribution relationship.

If needed, the set of MentalConstraintKind enumeration literals can be extended.

**Enumeration values** Tab. 12-2 specifies MentalConstraintKind's enumeration literals, keywords used for notation, and their semantics.

| Value | Keyword | Semantics |
|---|---|---|
| *commitCondition* | commit | An assertion identifying the situation under which an autonomous entity commits to the particular ConstrainedMentalClass (if also the precondition holds). |
| *preCondition* | pre | The condition that must hold before the ConstrainedMentalClass can become effective (i.e. a goal can be committed to or a plan can be executed). |
| *commitPreCondition* | commpre | AND-ed combination of commitCondition and preCondition. Used only within Contribution. |
| *invariant* | inv | The condition that holds during the period the ConstrainedMentalClass remains effective. |
| *cancelCondition* | cancel | An assertion identifying the situation under which an autonomous entity cancels attempting to accomplish the ConstrainedMentalClass. |
| *postCondition* | post | The condition that holds after the ConstrainedMentalClass has been accomplished (i.e. a goal has been achieved or a plan has been executed). |

**Tab. 12-2** MentalConstraintKind's enumeration literals

**Rationale** MentalConstraintKind is introduced to specify the kinds of MentalConstraints and ends of a Contribution relationship.

## 12.1.6 MentalRelationship

**Semantics** MentalRelationship is an abstract specialized MentalState, a superclass to all metaclasses defining the relationships between MentalStates.

There is one concrete subclass of the MentalRelationship—Contribution.

**Notation** There is no general notation for MentalRelationship. The specific subclasses of MentalRelationship define their own notation.

**Rationale** MentalRelationship is introduced as a superclass to all metaclasses defining the relationships between MentalStates.

### 12.1.7 MentalSemiEntityType

**Semantics** MentalSemiEntityType is a specialized abstract Class (from UML), a superclass to all metaclasses which can own MentalProperties, i.e. AutonomousEntityType and EntityRoleType.

The ownership of a MentalProperty of a particular MentalClass type means that instances of the owning MentalSemiEntityType have control over instances of that MentalClass, i.e. they have (at least to some extent) a power or authority to manipulate those MentalClass instances (their decisions about those MentalClass instances are, to some degree, autonomous). For example, a MentalClass instance can decide:

❑ which Goal is to be achieved and which not,

❑ when and how the particular Goal instance is to be achieved,

❑ whether the particular Goal instance is already achieved or not,

❑ which Plan to execute, etc.

Instances of MentalSemiEntityTypes are referred to as *mental semi-entities*.

**Associations**

| /mentalAttribute: MentalProperty[*] | A set of all MentalProperties owned by the MentalSemiEntityType. The association is ordered and derived. Subsets UML Class::ownedAttribute. |
|---|---|

**Constraints** 1. The mentalAttribute meta-association refers to all ownedAttributes of the kind MentalProperty:

mentalAttribute = self.ownedAttribute->
    select(oclIsKindOf(MentalProperty))

**Notation** There is no general notation for MentalSemiEntityType. The specific subclasses of MentalSemiEntityType define their own notation.

**Rationale** MentalSemiEntityType is introduced as a common superclass to all metaclasses which can own MentalProperties.

### 12.1.8 MentalProperty

**Semantics** MentalProperty is a specialized Property (from UML) used to specify that instances of its owner (i.e. mental semi-entities) have control over instances of the MentalClasses of its type, e.g. can decide whether to believe or not (and to what extent) in a Belief, or whether and when to commit to a Goal.

The attitude of a mental semi-entity to a belief or commitment to a goal is modeled by a Belief instance, or a Goal instance, being held in a slot of the corresponding MentalProperty.

The type of a MentalProperty can be only a MentalClass.

MentalProperties can be owned only by:

❑ MentalSemiEntityTypes as attributes, or

❑ MentalAssociations as member ends.

MentalProperties (except of MentalProperties of Belief type) can own MentalConstraints (each of a different type) to allow the redefinition of MentalConstraints of their types. The redefinition rules are described in section 12.1.4.

**Note:** The Plans controlled by MentalSemiEntityTypes are modeled as owned UML Activities, and therefore use of Plans as types of MentalProperties is forbidden, even if they are specialized MentalClasses.

**Attributes**

| | |
|---|---|
| degree: ValueSpecification [0..1] | The degree of the MentalClass specified as the type of the MentalProperty. If specified, it overrides the degree value specified for the MentalClass itself. |

**Associations**

| | |
|---|---|
| association: MentalAssociation [0..1] | The MentalAssociation of which this MentalProperty is a member, if any. Redefines UML Property::association. |
| type: MentalClass[0..1] | The type of a MentalProperty. Redefines UML TypedElement::type. |
| mentalConstraint: MentalConstraint[*] | A set of MentalConstraints describing the MentalClass specified as the type. If specified, they redefine MentalConstraints specified for the MentalClass itself. Subsets UML Element::ownedElement. |

**Constraints**  1. If the type meta-association is specified, the MentalClass referred to by it cannot be a Plan:

self.type->notEmpty() implies (not self.type.oclIsKindOf(Plan))

2. Each mentalConstraint must have different kind:

self.mentalConstraint->forAll(mc1, mc2 | mc1.kind<>mc2.kind)

3. The mentalConstraints can be specified only for a ConstrainedMentalClass:

   not (self.type->notEmpty() and
       self.type.oclIsKindOf(ConstrainedMentalClass)) implies
       self.mentalConstraint->isEmpty()

**Notation**  When shown as the end of a MentalAssociation, the MentalProperty is
depicted as a UML association end, see section 12.1.9.

When shown as an attribute of an MentalSemiEntityType, the Mental-
Property is depicted as a UML attribute with the <<mental>> stereotype. If specified, the value of the meta-attribute degree is depicted as
a property string (tagged value) with the name 'degree'. See Fig. 12-6.

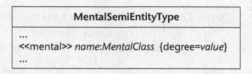

**Fig. 12-6** Notation of MentalProperty shown as an attribute

Usually, the MentalConstraints of a MentalProperty are specified as
hidden information, not shown in the diagram. However, if a user
needs to express them explicitly, the MentalConstraints can be shown
within a property string belonging to the MentalProperty. Each specified MentalConstraint has the form of a single tagged value following
the format:

  *mental_constraint ::= mental_constraint_kind '=' specification*
  *mental_constraint_kind ::= 'commit' | 'pre' | 'inv' | 'cancel' | 'post'*

The specification represents the UML Constraint's specification meta-
association (i.e. a boolean expression), and *mental_constraint_kind* is a
keyword identifying the kind of the mental constraint (see section
12.1.5 for details).

**Presentation**  The MentalProperties of a MentalSemiEntityType can be placed in a
**options**  special class compartment with stereotype <<mental>>. The stereotype <<mental>> of a particular MentalProperty is in this case omitted.
See Fig. 12-7.

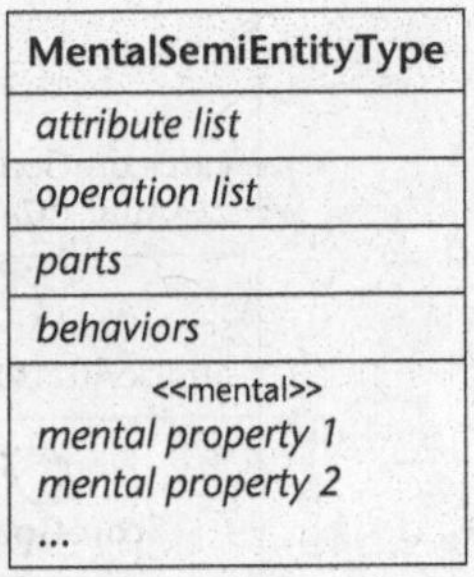

| MentalSemiEntityType |
| --- |
| *attribute list* |
| *operation list* |
| *parts* |
| *behaviors* |
| <<mental>><br>*mental property 1*<br>*mental property 2*<br>... |

**Fig. 12-7** Alternative notation of MentalProperties—placed in a common special class compartment

Another notational alternative is to group MentalProperties of one MentalSemiEntityType according to their fundamental types and to place each group into a specific class compartment. There are defined compartments <<beliefs>> for Beliefs, and <<goals>> for Goals. The stereotype <<mental>> of a particular MentalProperty is in this case omitted. See Fig. 12-8.

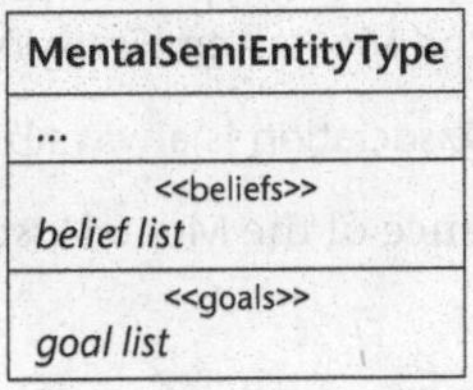

| MentalSemiEntityType |
| --- |
| ... |
| <<beliefs>><br>*belief list* |
| <<goals>><br>*goal list* |

**Fig. 12-8** Alternative notation of MentalProperties—grouped by fundamental types

**Style**  MentalConstraints are usually specified as hidden information.

**Examples**  Fig. 12-9 shows the definition of an EntityRoleType called Striker used to model a soccer striker, i.e. a player whose main job is to attack and try to score goals. The possibility to commit to these two goals is expressed by the MentalProperties named scoreGoal and attack, both of the fundamental type Goal. To commit to either of these goals, the Striker must believe that the goal is achievable. This is expressed by ownership of two MentalProperties named canScoreGoal and canAttack of the fundamental type Belief. To achieve the goals, the Striker defines two Plans called ScoreGoalPlan and AttackPlan.

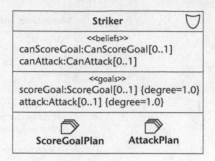

Fig. 12-9 Example of MentalProperty

Rationale   MentalProperty is introduced to specify that mental semi-entities have control over Goal and Belief instances.

## 12.1.9 MentalAssociation

Semantics   MentalAssociation is a specialized Association (from UML) between a MentalSemiEntityType and a MentalClass used to specify a MentalProperty of the MentalSemiEntityType in the form of an association end.

MentalAssociation is always binary.

An instance of the MentalAssociation is called *mental link*.

Associations

| | |
|---|---|
| memberEnd: Property[2] | Two associated Properties. This is an ordered association. Redefines UML Association::memberEnd. |
| mentalMemberEnd: MentalProperty[1] | Associated MentalProperty. Subsets MentalAssociation::memberEnd. |

Notation   MentalAssociation is depicted as a binary UML Association with the stereotype <<mental>>, see Fig. 12-10. The association end at the mentalMemberEnd's side can additionally show the value of its meta-attribute degree as a property string (tagged value) with the name 'degree'.

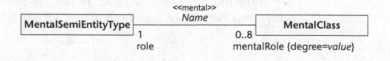

Fig. 12-10 Notation of MentalAssociation

Style   Stereotype <<mental>> of the mentalMemberEnd is usually omitted.

The MentalAssociation's stereotype can be omitted from the diagram as well, i.e. an Association between MentalSemiEntityType and a MentalClass is considered to be a MentalAssociation, if it is evident from the context.

**Examples** Fig. 12-11 shows a diagram semantically equivalent to the diagram in Fig. 12-9, but all MentalProperties are depicted as MentalAssociations.

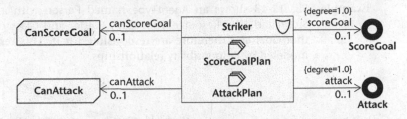

**Fig. 12-11** Example of MentalAssociation

**Rationale** MentalAssociation is introduced to enable modeling of MentalProperties in the form of association ends. It is used to specify that mental semi-entities have control over Goal and Belief instances.

## 12.1.10 Responsibility

**Semantics** Responsibility is a specialized Realization (from UML) used to model a relation between MentalClasses (called *responsibility objects*) and NamedElements (from UML) (called *responsibility subjects*) that are obligated to accomplish (or to contribute to the accomplishment of) those MentalClasses (e.g. modification of Beliefs, or achievement or maintenance of Goals, or realization of Plans).

**Associations**

| | |
|---|---|
| subject:<br>NamedElement[1..*] | The subject NamedElements responsible for object MentalClasses.<br>Redefines UML Dependency::client. |
| object:<br>MentalClass[1..*] | The set of MentalClasses the subject is responsible for.<br>Redefines UML Dependency::supplier. |

**Notation** Responsibility is depicted as a UML Realization (Dependency) relationship with the stereotype <<responsible>>. The responsibility subject (a

NamedElement) represents a client and the responsibility object (a MentalClass) is a supplier. See Fig. 12-12.

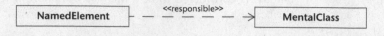

**Fig. 12-12** Notation of Responsibility

**Examples** Fig. 12-13 shows an AgentType named Person with a Goal named StoreFluid. The ResourceTypes Cup, Bottle, and Glass can all realize that Goal and therefore are responsible for it. This responsibility is modeled by Responsibility relationships.

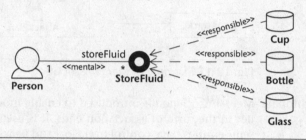

**Fig. 12-13** Example of Responsibility

**Rationale** Responsibility is introduced to model which NamedElements are responsible for (or contribute to) the accomplishment of instances of which MentalClasses.

## 12.2 Beliefs

**Overview** The *Beliefs* package defines metaclasses used to model beliefs.

**Abstract syntax** The diagram of the Beliefs package is shown in Fig. 12-14.

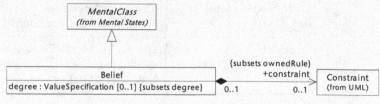

**Fig. 12-14** Beliefs—belief

## 12.2.1 Belief

**Semantics**  Belief is a specialized MentalClass used to model a state of affairs, proposition or other information relevant to the system and its mental model. If an instance of a Belief is held in a slot of a mental semi-entity's MentalProperty, it represents the information which the mental semi-entity believes, and which does not need to be objectively true. The ability of a MentalSemiEntityType to believe in beliefs of a particular type is modeled by the ownership of a MentalProperty of the corresponding type.

The belief referred to by several mental semi-entities simultaneously represents their *common belief.*

The degree meta-association of a Belief specifies the reliability or confidence in the information specified by the Belief's constraint, i.e. a degree to which it is believed that the information specified by the Belief is true. AML does not specify either the syntax or semantics of degree's values, users are free to define and use their own. For example the values can be real numbers, integers, enumeration literals, expressions, etc.

The specification of the information a Belief represents is expressed by the owned Constraint (from UML).

When inherited, the owned constraint is overridden.

It is possible to specify attributes and/or operations for a Belief, to represent its parameters and functions, which can both be used in the owned constraint as static or computed values.

**Attributes**

| | |
|---|---|
| degree: ValueSpecification [0..1] | Specification of the reliability or confidence in the information specified by the constraint meta-association, i.e. a degree to which the owning MentalSemiEntityType believes that the information specified by the Belief is true. Subsets MentalState::degree. |

**Associations**

| | |
|---|---|
| constraint: Constraint[0..1] | The specification of the information a Belief represents. Subsets UML Namespace::ownedRule. |

**Notation**  Belief is depicted as a UML Class with the stereotype <<belief>> and/or a special icon. If specified, the value of the meta-attribute degree is depicted as a property string (tagged value) with name 'degree', placed in the name compartment. The constraint, enclosed with braces ('{' '}'), is placed in a special class compartment. See Fig. 12-15.

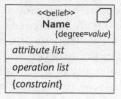

**Fig. 12-15** Notation of Belief

**Presentation** Belief can alternatively be depicted as a rectangle with beveled top-left
**options** and bottom-right corners. The stereotype icon and keyword is omitted in this case. See Fig. 12-16.

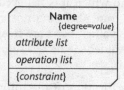

**Fig. 12-16** Alternative notation of Belief—with a special shape

If not referred to explicitly in the model, the name of a Belief can be unspecified. In this case the name compartment of such a Belief can be omitted and only the constraint is specified. See Fig. 12-17.

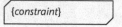

**Fig. 12-17** Alternative notation of Belief—omitted name compartment

**Style** Owned operations, receptions, internal structure of parts and connectors, ports, supported and required interfaces, specification of owned behaviors, and nested classifiers are not usually specified for Beliefs.

**Examples** Fig. 12-18 shows a Belief called NearBall, which represents the belief that ball is nearby. The attribute near specifies what distance in meters is meant by "near". Its default value is 1.5, but can be changed at run time. The constraint specifies that the distance from the ball is less or equal than the value of near.

**Rationale** Belief is introduced to model beliefs.

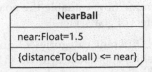

| NearBall |
|---|
| near:Float=1.5 |
| {distanceTo(ball) <= near} |

**Fig. 12-18** Example of Belief

## 12.3 Goals

**Overview** The *Goals* package defines metaclasses used to model goals.

**Abstract syntax** The diagram of the Goals package is shown in Fig. 12-19.

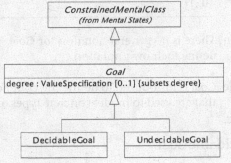

**Fig. 12-19** Goals—goal hierarchy

### 12.3.1 Goal

**Semantics** Goal is an abstract specialized ConstrainedMentalClass used to model goals, i.e. conditions or states of affairs, with which the main concern is their achievement or maintenance. The Goals can thus be used to represent objectives, needs, motivations, desires, etc.

Commitment of a mental semi-entity to a goal is modeled by containment of the corresponding Goal instance by the value of the mental semi-entity's MentalProperty.

The goal to which several mental semi-entities are committed to simultaneously represents their *common goal*.

The meta-attribute degree specifies the relative importance or appropriateness of the Goal. AML does not specify either the syntax or semantics of degree's values, users are free to define and use their own.

Goals can have attributes to specify parameters of their instances, e.g. the goal "Buy car" can have attributes carType, carColor, or maxPrice. Goals can have also operations to compute e.g. utility function(s) to determine how valuable the goal is, or operations computing the parameters of goals, etc.

**Note:** Different categories of goals used in goal-based requirements modeling approaches (KAOS [31], [146], NFR [23], [88], GBRAM [5], etc.)[30], can be specified, for instance, by special user-defined tagged values or by special naming conventions used for Goals, e.g. 'Maintain[Attack]', 'Achieve[ScoreGoal]', 'Avoid[ConcedeGoal]'. The goal categories may depend on the domain or methodology used, and therefore are not defined by AML. Users can define these themselves. See example in Fig. 12-23.

**Attributes**

| | |
|---|---|
| degree: ValueSpecification [0..1] | The relative importance of the Goal. Subsets MentalState::degree. |

**Notation** There is no general notation for Goal. The specific subclasses of Goal define their own notation.

**Rationale** Goal is introduced to define the common features of all its subclasses that are used to model concrete types of goals.

## 12.3.2 DecidableGoal

**Semantics** DecidableGoal is a specialized concrete Goal used to model goals for which there are clear-cut criteria according to which the goal-holder can decide whether the DecidableGoal (particularly its postCondition; for details see section 12.1.5) has been achieved or not.

**Note:** DecidableGoal is also called 'hard goal' or simply 'goal' in some goal-based requirements modeling approaches (TROPOS [12], [143], i* [4], [163], [164], GRL [51], [80], KAOS [31], [146], etc.).

**Notation** DecidableGoal is depicted as a UML Class with the stereotype <<dgoal>> and/or a special icon, see Fig. 12-20.

If specified, the value of the meta-attribute degree is depicted as a property string (tagged value) with the name 'degree', placed in the name compartment.

The DecidableGoal rectangle can contain special compartments <<commit>>, <<pre>>, <<inv>>, <<cancel>>, and <<post>> for the contained MentalConstraints. These compartments may be omitted and can be specified in any order.

---

[30] Such as achievement, maintenance, avoidance, optimization, improvement, accuracy, etc.

If a DecidableGoal also specifies attributes, operations, behaviors, etc. they can be depicted in standard compartments as specified in UML.

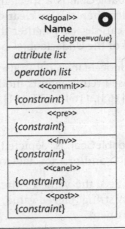

**Fig. 12-20** Notation of DecidableGoal

**Examples** Fig. 12-21 shows the detail of a DecidableGoal named InterceptBall which represents a desire of a soccer robot to intercept the ball. Keyword 'self' from the owned MentalConstraints is therefore used to refer to the soccer robot (an instance of the SoccerRobot AgentType, see Fig. 11-7). The goal is committed to whenever the ball is near the robot. In order to commit to the goal, the robot must be free and its team cannot already have the ball. If the ball moves away from the robot, while trying to intercept the ball, the robot abandons this goal. The goal is successfully accomplished when the soccer robot obtains the ball. All aforementioned conditions are modeled as owned MentalConstraints.

| InterceptBall {degree=0.8} |
| --- |
| ball:Ball |
| <<commit>> |
| {self.pitch.isNear(self,ball)} |
| <<pre>> |
| {not self.team.hasBall(ball) and self.isFree()} |
| <<cancel>> |
| {not self.pitch.isNear(self,ball)} |
| <<post>> |
| {self.haveBall(ball)} |

**Fig. 12-21** Example of DecidableGoal

**Rationale** DecidableGoal is introduced to explicitly model decidable goals.

### 12.3.3 UndecidableGoal

**Semantics** UndecidableGoal is a specialized concrete Goal used to model goals for which there are no clear-cut criteria according to which the goal-holder can decide whether the postCondition (see section 12.1.5 for details) of the UndecidableGoal is achieved or not.

**Note:** UndecidableGoal is also called 'soft goal' or 'softgoal' in some goal-based requirements modeling approaches (TROPOS [12], [143], i* [4], [163], [164], GRL [51], [80], KAOS [31], [146], NFR [23], [88], etc.).

**Notation** UndecidableGoal is depicted as a UML Class with the stereotype <<ugoal>> and/or a special icon, see Fig. 12-22.

If specified, the value of the meta-attribute degree is depicted as a property string (tagged value) with name 'degree', placed in the name compartment.

The UndecidableGoal rectangle can contain special compartments <<commit>>, <<pre>>, <<inv>>, <<cancel>>, and <<post>> for the contained MentalConstraints. These compartments may be omitted and can be specified in any order.

If an UndecidableGoal also contains attributes, operations, behaviors, etc. they can be depicted in standard compartments as specified in UML.

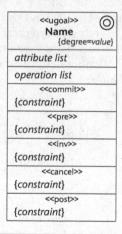

**Fig. 12-22** Notation of UndecidableGoal

**Examples** Fig. 12-23 shows the fragment of a simple problem decomposition diagram for the development of a computer game. The diagram consists solely of UndecidableGoals, where each represents a non-functional requirement. Such diagrams can be used to describe system requirements and their relationships in the form of a mental model.

UndecidableGoals are decomposed using Contribution relationships.

Classification of goals into categories (maintain, achieve, provide, or avoid) was accomplished by application of the naming convention (for details see section 12.3.1), where the category name precedes the goal's object placed in brackets.

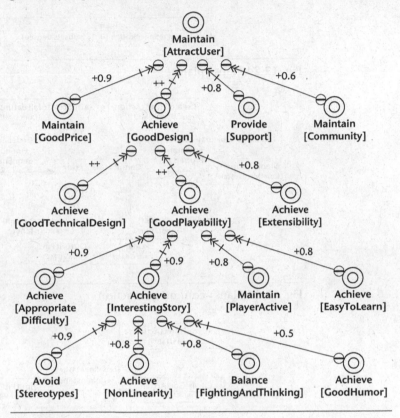

Fig. 12-23 Example of UndecidableGoal

**Rationale** UndecidableGoal is introduced to explicitly model undecidable goals.

## 12.4 Plans

**Overview** The *Plans* package defines metaclasses devoted to modeling plans.

**Abstract**  The diagrams of the Plans package are shown in figures Fig. 12-24 to
**syntax**  Fig. 12-26.

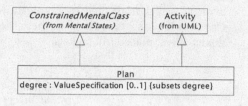

**Fig. 12-24** Plans—plan

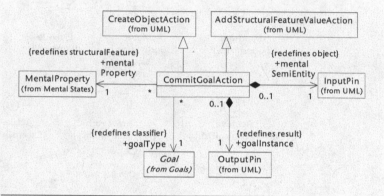

**Fig. 12-25** Plans—commit goal action

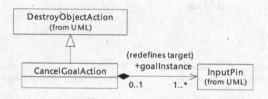

**Fig. 12-26** Plans—cancel goal action

## 12.4.1  Plan

**Semantics**  Plan is a specialized ConstrainedMentalClass and Activity (from UML),
used to model capabilities of MentalSemiEntityTypes which represents
either:

❏ predefined plans, i.e. kinds of activities a mental semi-entity's reasoning mechanism can manipulate in order to achieve Goals, or

❏ fragments of behavior from which the plans can be composed (also called *plan fragments*).

In addition to UML Activity, Plan allows the specification of commit condition, cancel condition, and invariant (for details see section 12.1.5), which can be used by reasoning mechanisms[31].

For modeling the applicability of Plans, in relation to given Goals, Beliefs and other Plans, the Contribution relationship is used.

The meta-attribute degree specifies the relative preference of the Plan. AML does not specify either the syntax or semantics of degree's values, users are free to define and use their own.

**Attributes**

| | |
|---|---|
| degree: ValueSpecification [0..1] | The relative preference of the Plan. Subsets MentalState::degree. |

**Constraints**

1. Specification of the Constraint referred to by the precondition meta-association is identical with the specification of the MentalConstraint of kind *preCondition* referred to by the mentalConstraint meta-association, if the both are specified:

   self.precondition->notEmpty() and
       self.mentalConstraint->select(kind=#preCondition)->
       notEmpty() implies self.precondition.specification =
       self.mentalConstraint->select(kind=#preCondition).specification

2. Specification of the Constraint referred to by the postcondition meta-association is identical with the specification of the MentalConstraint of kind *postCondition* referred to by the mentalConstraint meta-association, if the both are specified:

   self.postcondition->notEmpty() and
       self.mentalConstraint->select(kind=#postCondition)->
       notEmpty() implies self.postcondition.specification =
       self.mentalConstraint->
       select(kind=#postCondition).specification

3. If the context (see UML Behavior::context meta-association) for Plan is specified, it must be a MentalSemiEntityType:

   self.context->notEmpty() implies
       self.context.oclIsKindOf(MentalSemiEntityType)

---

[31] UML Activity specifies just pre-condition and post-condition.

**Notation** Plan is depicted as a UML Activity with the stereotype <<plan>> and/or a special icon, see Fig. 12-27.

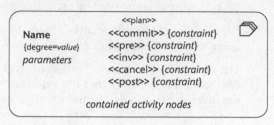

**Fig. 12-27** Notation of Plan

If specified, the value of the meta-attribute degree is depicted as a property string (tagged value) with name 'degree', placed near the Plan name.

If the mental constraints of a Plan need to be displayed explicitly, they can be shown as stereotyped Constraints (from UML) placed into the Plan's rounded rectangle. For this, the stereotypes <<commit>>, <<pre>>, <<inv>>, <<cancel>>, and <<post>> are used.

If specified, UML standard Constraints precondition and postcondition, shown as stereotyped constraints <<precondition>> and <<postcondition>> are not shown because their values are identical to the MentalConstraints of kind *preCondition* and *postCondition*.

**Style** Usually, the mental constraints of a Plan are specified as hidden information, and are not shown in the diagram.

**Examples** See Fig. 11-101, Fig. 11-120, Fig. 12-29, and Fig. 12-31.

**Rationale** Plan is introduced to model predefined plans, or fragments of plans from which the plans can be composed.

## 12.4.2 CommitGoalAction

**Semantics** CommitGoalAction is a specialized CreateObjectAction (from UML) and AddStructuralFeatureValueAction (from UML), used to model the action of commitment to a Goal.

This action allows the realization of the commitment to a Goal by instantiating the Goal and adding the created instance as a value to the MentalProperty of the mental semi-entity which commits to the Goal.

Commitment to an existing instance of a Goal can be modeled by AddStructuralFeatureValueAction (from UML) or by CreateLinkAction (from UML).

The CommitGoalAction specifies:

☐ what Goal is being instantiated (goalType meta-association),

☐ the Goal instance being created (goalInstance meta-association),

☐ the owning mental semi-entity committed to the Goal (mental-SemiEntity meta-association), and

☐ the MentalProperty, owned by the type of the owning mental semi-entity, to which the created Goal instance is added (mental-Property meta-association).

If the MentalProperty referred to by the mentalProperty meta-association is ordered, the insertAt meta-association (inherited from the AddStructuralFeatureValueAction) specifies a position at which to insert the Goal instance.

Because the value meta-association (inherited from UML WriteStructuralFeatureAction) represents the same Goal instance as is already represented by the goalInstance meta-association, the properties of the InputPin referred to by the value meta-association are ignored in CommitGoalAction, and can be omitted in its specification.

**Associations**

|  |  |
|---|---|
| goalType: Goal[1] | Instantiated Goal.<br>Redefines UML CreateObjectAction::classifier. |
| goalInstance:<br>OutputPin[1] | The OutputPin on which the created Goal instance is placed.<br>Redefines UML CreateObjectAction::result. |
| mentalSemiEntity:<br>InputPin[1] | The InputPin specifying the mental semi-entity committed to the Goal.<br>Redefines UML StructuralFeatureAction::object. |
| mentalProperty:<br>MentalProperty[1] | The MentalProperty where the created Goal instance is being placed.<br>Redefines UML StructuralFeatureAction::structuralFeature. |

**Constraints** 1. If the type of the InputPin referred to by the mentalSemiEntity meta-association is specified, it must be a MentalSemiEntityType:

self.mentalSemiEntity.type->notEmpty() implies
    self.mentalSemiEntity.type.oclIsKindOf(MentalSemiEntityType)

2. If the type of the OutputPin referred to by the goalInstance meta-association is specified, it must conform to the Goal referred to by the goalType meta-association:

self.goalInstance.type->notEmpty() implies
    self.goalInstance.type.conformsTo(self.goalType)

3. If the type of the MentalProperty referred to by the mentalProperty meta-association is specified, the Goal referred to by the goalType meta-association must conform to it:

self.mentalProperty.type->notEmpty() implies
    self.goalType.conformsTo(self.mentalProperty.type)

4. CommitGoalAction can be performed only by a mental semi-entity:

self.activity().hostClassifier().oclIsKindOf(MentalSemiEntityType)

**Notation**   CommitGoalAction is shown as a UML Action with the stereotype <<commit goal>> and/or a special icon, see Fig. 12-28.

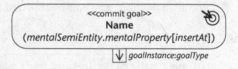

**Fig. 12-28** Notation of CommitGoalAction

Optionally, the name of the committing mental semi-entity, delimited by a period from the name of the MentalProperty referred to by the mentalProperty meta-association, may be specified in parentheses below the action's name. If the MentalProperty is ordered, the value of the insertAt meta-association can be placed after the MentalProperty's name in brackets.

If the committing mental semi-entity itself executes the CommitGoalAction, it can be identified by the keyword 'self' instead of committing mental semi-entity's name.

The created Goal instance is specified as an OutputPin. All notational variations for the UML OutputPin are allowed. The committed Goal is specified as the type of the OutputPin.

The mandatory InputPin referred to by the value meta-association has unspecified properties and is not drawn in diagrams.

**Examples**   Fig. 12-29 shows the Plan of the EntityRoleType named Striker (see Fig. 12-11 for details) to kick a ball. If the striker is near the goal of the other team, it tries to kick towards the goal by committing to the Goal called KickGoal. If the striker is not near, it tries to find a teammate who is near and not offside. If such a teammate exists, the striker tries to pass the ball to the teammate by committing to the Goal called PassBall. If such a teammate does not exist, the striker simply tries to kick the ball away by committing to the Goal called KickBallAway.

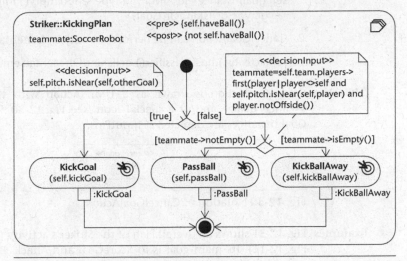

**Fig. 12-29** Example of Plan and CommitGoalAction

Another example of CommitGoalAction is in Fig. 12-31.

**Rationale**  CreateRoleAction is introduced to model commitment actions within Activities (Plans).

## 12.4.3 CancelGoalAction

**Semantics**  CancelGoalAction is a specialized DestroyObjectAction (from UML) used to model de-commitment from goals.

This action allows the realization of de-commitment from a Goal by destruction of the corresponding Goal instance.

De-commitment from an instance of a Goal that does not need to be destroyed can be modeled by RemoveStructuralFeatureValueAction (from UML) or DestroyLinkAction (from UML).

**Associations**

| goalInstance: InputPin[1..*] | The InputPins representing the Goal instances to be disposed. Redefines UML DestroyObjectAction::target. |
|---|---|

**Constraints** 1. If the types of the InputPins referred to by the goalInstance meta-association are specified, they must be Goals:

self.goalInstance->forAll(gi | gi.type.->notEmpty() implies
   gi.type.oclIsKindOf(Goal))

2. CancelGoalAction can be performed only by a mental semi-entity:

self.activity().hostClassifier().oclIsKindOf(MentalSemiEntityType)

**Notation** CancelGoalAction is drawn as a UML Action with the stereotype <<cancel goal>> and/or a special icon, see Fig. 12-30. The cancelled Goal instances are depicted as InputPins.

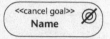

**Fig. 12-30** Notation of CancelGoalAction

**Examples** Fig. 12-31 shows an overall Plan of the Striker's activity (for details see Fig. 12-11). Its main goal is to ScoreGoal and Attack. Both Goals are committed in parallel.

If the game is interrupted, the striker has to stop its activities, and therefore both the committed Goals are stopped, until the game continues.

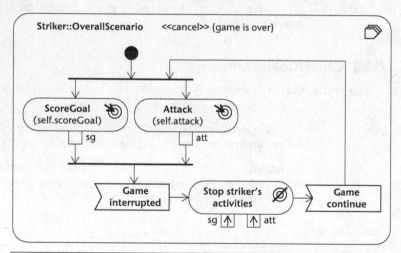

**Fig. 12-31** Example of Plan , CommitGoalAction, and CancelGoalAction

**Rationale** CancelGoalAction is introduced to model de-commitment to goals.

## 12.5 Mental Relationships

**Overview** The *Mental Relationships* package defines metaclasses used to model relationships between MentalStates which can support reasoning processes.

**Abstract syntax** The diagram of the Mental Relationships package is shown in Fig. 12-32.

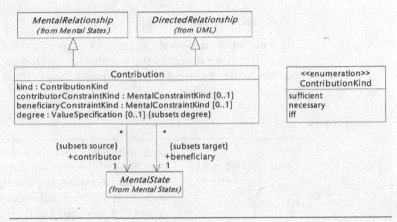

**Fig. 12-32** Mental Relationships—contribution

### 12.5.1 Contribution

**Semantics** Contribution is a specialized MentalRelationship and DirectedRelationship (from UML) used to model logical relationships between MentalStates and their MentalConstraints.

The manner in which the *contributor* of the Contribution relationship (i.e. a MentalState referred to by the contibutor meta-association) influences its *beneficiary* (i.e. a MentalState referred to by the beneficiary meta-association) is specified by values of meta-attributes of the particular Contribution.

The meta-attribute kind determines whether the contribution of the contributor's MentalConstraint of a given kind (specified by the meta-attribute contributorConstraintKind) is a necessary, sufficient, or equivalent condition for the beneficiary's MentalConstraint of a given kind (specified by the meta-attribute beneficiaryConstraintKind).

The meta-attribute contributorConstraintKind specifies the kind of a MentalConstraint of the contributor which contributes in some way to a kind of MentalConstraint of the beneficiary, specified by the beneficiaryConstraintKind meta-attribute. For example, a Contribution can specify that a postcondition of the contributor contributes in some way (e.g. in a positive and sufficient way) to the precondition of the related beneficiary. For details about possible values of the constraint kinds see section 12.1.5.

If contributor and/or beneficiary is a Belief, the contributorConstraint-Kind and/or the beneficiaryConstraintKind meta-attribute is unspecified. In this case the Belief's constraint is considered to contribute or benefit.

If the contributor and/or beneficiary is a Contribution, the contributorConstraintKind and/or the beneficiaryConstraintKind meta-attributes are also unspecified.

The meta-attribute degree can be used to specify the extent to which the contributor influences the beneficiary. AML does not specify either the syntax or semantics of degree's values, users are free to define and use their own.

**Attributes**

| | |
|---|---|
| kind: ContributionKind[1] | Determines whether the contribution of the contributor's MentalConstraint of a specified kind is a necessary, sufficient, or equivalent condition for the beneficiary's MentalConstraint of a specified kind. |
| contributorConstraint-Kind:MentalConstraint-Kind[0..1] | The kind of the contributor's MentalConstraint which contributes to the kind of the beneficiary's MentalConstraint (specified by the beneficiaryConstraintKind meta-attribute). |
| beneficiaryConstraint-Kind:MentalConstraint-Kind[0..1] | The kind of the beneficiary's MentalConstraint to which the kind of the contributor's MentalConstraint (specified by the contributorConstraintKind meta-attribute) contributes. |
| degree: ValueSpecification [0..1] | Degree of influence. Subsets MentalState::degree. |

**Associations**

| | |
|---|---|
| contributor: MentalState[1] | The contributor of the Contribution. Subsets UML DirectedRelationship::source. |
| beneficiary: MentalState[1] | The beneficiary of the Contribution. Subsets UML DirectedRelationship::target. |

**Constraints** 1. If the MentalState referred to by the contributor meta-association is a Belief or a Contribution, the contributorConstraintKind meta-attribute is unspecified:

> self.contributor.ocllsKindOf(Belief) or
> > self.contributor.ocllsKindOf(Contribution) implies
> > self.contributorConstraintKind->isEmpty()

2. If the MentalState referred to by the beneficiary meta-association is a Belief or a Contribution, the beneficiaryConstraintKind meta-attribute is unspecified:

> self.beneficiary.ocllsKindOf(Belief) or
> > self.beneficiary.ocllsKindOf(Contribution) implies
> > self.beneficiaryConstraintKind->isEmpty()

**Notation** Sufficient Contribution (i.e. kind=#sufficient) is depicted as an arrow with double arrowhead, leading from the contributor to the beneficiary. See Fig. 12-33.

Contribution's degree is depicted as a label (usually an expression) placed near the arrow line.

The value of the contributorConstraintKind is depicted as a keyword placed near the Contribution's tail. The value of the beneficiaryConstraintKind is depicted as a keyword placed near the Contribution's arrowhead. The keywords are specified in section 12.1.5.

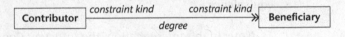

**Fig. 12-33** Notation of sufficient Contribution

Necessary Contribution (i.e. kind=#necessary) is depicted as the sufficient Contribution, but the arrow line is crossed by a short line near the arrowhead. See Fig. 12-34.

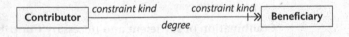

**Fig. 12-34** Notation of necessary Contribution

Equivalence (iff) Contribution (i.e. kind=#iff) is depicted by a line with arrowheads placed at each end. See Fig. 12-35.

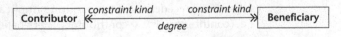

**Fig. 12-35** Notation of equivalence (iff) Contribution

**Presentation options** A graphical icon for particular MentalConstraintKind can be used instead of textual labels. Alternative notation is depicted in Fig. 12-36.

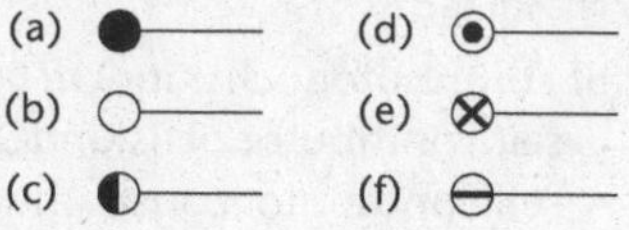

| | | | |
|---|---|---|---|
| (a) ●——— | | (d) ◉——— | |
| (b) ○——— | | (e) ⊗——— | |
| (c) ◐——— | | (f) ⊖——— | |

**Fig. 12-36** Alternative notation for MentalConstraintKind used for Contribution ends: (a) commitCondition, (b) preCondition, (c) commitPreCondition, (d) invariant, (e) cancelCondition, and (f) postCondition.

**Examples** **Contribution as a logical implication.** Contribution can be understood as a logical implication between MentalStates or their MentalConstraints (if specified). Tab. 12-3 provides interpretation of different Contribution kinds using the logical implication.

| Contribution | Logic interpretation | Description |
|---|---|---|
| C ———≫ B | $C \Rightarrow B$ | C is sufficient for B |
| C ——⊢≫ B | $C \Leftarrow B$ | C is necessary for B |
| C ≪——≫ B | $C \Leftrightarrow B$ | C is equivalent with B (C is sufficient and necessary for B) |

**Tab. 12-3** Logic interpretation of Contribution. C stands for contributor, B for beneficiary, $\Rightarrow$ denotes logical implication, and $\Leftrightarrow$ logical equivalence.

**Note:** In this interpretation, the sufficient Contribution leading from A to B is logically equal to a necessary Contribution leading from B to A. Even though this property of strictly logical interpretation may tempt one to use just one kind of Contribution in models, from the domain perspective it may be required to use both, sufficient and necessary, Contribution kinds to express the mental model in a more natural and comprehensive way.

**Combination of sufficient and necessary Contributions.** If a set of Contributions of the same kind have the same beneficiary and the value of their beneficiaryConstraintKind meta-attribute (if specified), their logical interpretations can be combined according to the following rules:

❒ contributors of all sufficient Contributions are logically OR-ed to form the antecedent[32] of the resulting implication,
i.e. (contributor$_1$ $\vee$ ... $\vee$ contributor$_n$) $\Rightarrow$ beneficiary, and

---

[32] The *antecedent* is the operand of the implication which represent the sufficient condition, and the *consequent* is the operand which represent the necessary condition, i.e. *antecedent => consequent*.

❏ contributors of all necessary Contributions are logically AND-ed to form the consequent[32] of the resulting implication, i.e. beneficiary $\Rightarrow$ (contributor$_1$ $\wedge$ ... $\wedge$ contributor$_n$).

Operator $\vee$ stands for logical OR (disjunction), and $\wedge$ represents logical AND (conjunction).

According to the aforementioned rules, the model presented in Fig. 12-37 could be interpreted as follows:

P.pre $\Rightarrow$ (G1.commpre $\wedge$ G2.commpre)
(G3.post $\vee$ B) $\Rightarrow$ P.post

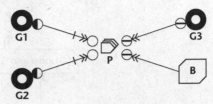

**Fig. 12-37** Example of combining sufficient and necessary Contributions

**Complex logical relationships.** Contributions in combination with Beliefs can also be used to express more complex logical expressions between MentalStates.

Fig. 12-38 shows three semantically equivalent model variants, that could be interpreted as the following logical formula:

((G1.post $\wedge$ G2.post) $\vee$ B) $\Rightarrow$ P.pre

The expression G1.post denotes postcondition of DecidableGoal G1, G2.post postcondition of the DecidableGoal G2, B1 represents constraints of the Belief B, and P.pre stands for precondition of Plan P1.

The example shows a usage of Beliefs for modeling complex conditions and their possible decomposition. Presented model variants show different levels of formula decomposition and modeling of constituents explicitly.

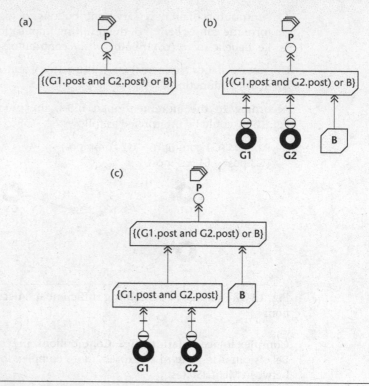

**Fig. 12-38** Example of modeling complex logical relationships between MentalStates: (a) no further decomposition of the contributing Belief, (b) a simple one-level depth decomposition of the contributing Belief, and (c) a full decomposition of the contributing Belief into its constituents modeled explicitly.

**Examples of notation and semantics for degree.** The degree meta-attribute can be specified as a numeric value—a real number from interval <-1,1>. Positive numbers represent a *positive contribution* of the contribution to the beneficiary, negative numbers represent a *negative contribution*. The larger the number is, the more degree of contribution it represents. Zero value represents an *indifferent contribution*, i.e. the contributor does not influence the beneficiary at all.

Another method of specifying the value of the degree is by using symbolic literals with predefined semantics. Tab. 12-4 provides examples of such literals, their interpretation and mapping to numeric values.

The both forms can be combined in one model.

| Value | | Interpretation | |
|---|---|---|---|
| Symbolic | Numeric | Intuitive | Modal logic |
| (empty) | | A implies C | $A \Rightarrow C$ |
| 0 | 0 | C is indifferent to A | $A \Rightarrow \Box(C \vee \neg C)$ |
| + | +0.5 | A contributes to C | $A \Rightarrow \Diamond C$ |
| ++ | +1.0 | A contributes to C strongly | $A \Rightarrow \Box C$ |
| - | -0.5 | A conflicts with C | $A \Rightarrow \Diamond \neg C$ |
| -- | -1.0 | A conflicts with C strongly | $A \Rightarrow \Box \neg C$ |

**Tab. 12-4** Examples of values of the Contribution's degree. A indicates implication antecedent and C stands for implication consequent (i.e. $A \Rightarrow C$). The implication here represents the logic interpretation of a Contribution, as defined before. The modal operator $\Diamond$ stands for "possible", and operator $\Box$ for "necessary". See [152] for details. Symbol $\neg$ denotes logical negation.

> **Note:** The formula $\Box A \Rightarrow A$ is an axiom (known also as the *axiom T*) of the basic modal logics (KT, KT4, KT5, etc.). If such logics are used to interpret the modal operators, the degrees *implies* (empty string) and *contributes strongly* ('++') are semantically equivalent.

Advanced schemas for the degree can also use more complex expressions.

Contribution as contributor or beneficiary.

The Contribution relationship can be the contributor as well as the beneficiary of another Contribution. Fig. 12-39 shows an example in which achievement of the DecidableGoal FillCoffeeMachine contributes to the precondition of the DecidableGoal PrepareCoffee, but only if the coffee machine is not damaged. Furthermore, if preparation of the coffee (by accomplishment of the PrepareCoffee DecidableGoal) causes it to be drunk (by committing to the Drink DecidableGoal, which represents drinking of a prepared beverage), it is deduced that a person committed to these goals may like coffee.

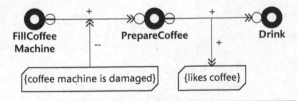

**Fig. 12-39** Example of contribution to Contribution, and contributing Contribution

**Real-world examples.** Fig. 12-40 shows a causal analysis of the Plan PassBallPlan. The diagram depicts the necessary conditions for the

Plan execution, as well as the consequences of its successful accomplishment.

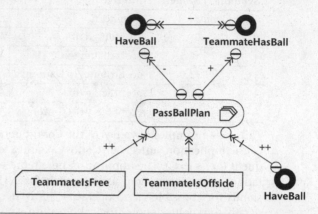

**Fig. 12-40** Example of Contribution used in causal analysis

The diagram from Fig. 12-40 should be interpreted as a set of the following logical formulas:

PassBallPlan.pre $\Rightarrow$ $\Box$TeammateIsFree
PassBallPlan.pre $\Rightarrow$ $\Box\neg$TeammateIsOffside
PassBallPlan.pre $\Rightarrow$ $\Box$HaveBall.post
PassBallPlan.post $\Rightarrow$ $\Diamond\neg$HaveBall.post
PassBallPlan.post $\Rightarrow$ $\Diamond$TeammateHasBall.post
HaveBall.post $\Rightarrow$ $\Box\neg$TeammateHasBall.post
TeammateHasBall.post $\Rightarrow$ $\Box\neg$HaveBall.post

Fig. 12-41 shows an example of the problem decomposition model aimed at specifying how to win a soccer game. The main Decidable-Goal of a soccer player WinGame is decomposed into other Decidable-Goals and Beliefs by means of Contribution relationships.

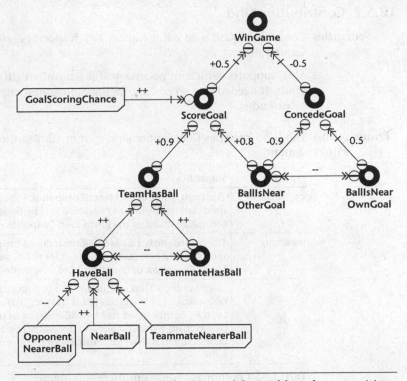

**Fig. 12-41** Example of Contribution used for problem decomposition analysis

Indifferent Contribution is used to explicitly model independence of MentalStates and their MentalConstraints. Fig. 12-42 shows an example which specifies that scoring a goal (specified by the ScoreGoal's post-condition) is independent of the Belief that the player is younger than 18 years.

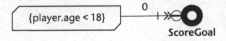

**Fig. 12-42** Example of indifferent Contribution

Another example of the Contribution can be found in Fig. 12-23.

**Rationale** Contribution is introduced to model logical relationships between MentalStates and their MentalConstraints.

## 12.5.2 ContributionKind

**Semantics** ContributionKind is an enumeration which specifies possible kinds of Contributions.

AML supports sufficient, necessary and equivalent (iff) contribution kinds. If needed, the set of ContributionKind enumeration literals can be extended.

**Enumeration** Tab. 12-5 specifies ContributionKind's enumeration literals and their
**values** semantics.

| Value | Semantics |
|---|---|
| *sufficient* | The contributor or its MentalConstraint of the given kind (if specified) is a sufficient condition for the beneficiary or its MentalConstraint of the given kind (if specified). |
| *necessary* | The contributor or its MentalConstraint of the given kind (if specified) is a necessary condition for the beneficiary or its MentalConstraint of the given kind (if specified). |
| *iff* | (if and only if) The contributor and beneficiary or their MentalConstraints of the given kinds (if specified) are equivalent, i.e. the contributor or its MentalConstraint of the given kind (if specified) is a sufficient and necessary condition for the beneficiary or its MentalConstraint of the given kind (if specified). |

**Tab. 12-5** ContributionKind's enumeration literals

**Rationale** ContributionKind is introduced to define possible kinds of Contributions.

# Chapter 13

# Ontologies

**Overview** The *Ontologies* package defines the metaclasses used to model ontologies. AML allows the specification of class-level as well as instance-level ontologies.

**Package structure** Fig. 13-1 depicts the package diagram of the Ontologies package.

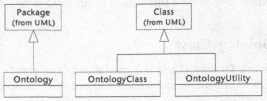

**Fig. 13-1** Ontologies—package structure

## 13.1 Basic Ontologies

**Overview** The *Basic Ontologies* package defines the generic means for modeling of ontologies in AML, namely, ontology classes and their instances, relationships, constraints, and ontology utilities. Ontology models are structured by means of the ontology packages.

**Abstract syntax** The diagram of the Basic Ontologies package is shown in Fig. 13-2.

```
Package              Class
(from UML)          (from UML)
    △                   △
    |          |--------|--------|
    |          |                 |
 Ontology  OntologyClass   OntologyUtility
```

**Fig. 13-2** Basic Ontologies—all elements

## 13.1.1 Ontology

**Semantics**  Ontology is a specialized Package (from UML) used to specify a single ontology. By utilizing the features inherited from UML Package (package nesting, element import, package merge, etc.), Ontologies can be logically structured.

**Notation**  Ontology is depicted as a UML Package with the stereotype <<ontology>> and/or a special icon, see Fig. 13-3.

**Fig. 13-3** Notation of Ontology

**Style**  The ontology stereotype is usually displayed as decoration (a small icon placed in upper-right corner) of the original UML Package symbol.

**Examples**  Fig. 13-4 shows an example of importing and merging of ontologies in the form of a package diagram.

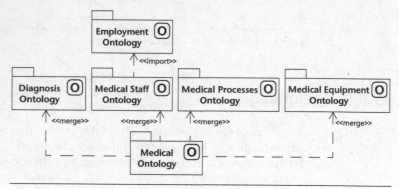

**Fig. 13-4** Example of Ontology package diagram

**Rationale**  Ontology is introduced to specify a single ontology.

## 13.1.2 OntologyClass

**Semantics**  OntologyClass is a specialized Class (from UML) used to represent an ontology class (called also ontology concept or frame).

Attributes and operations of the OntologyClass represent its slots. Ontology functions, actions, and predicates belonging to a concept modeled by an OntologyClass are modeled by its operations.

OntologyClass can use all types of relationships allowed for UML Class (Association, Generalization, Dependency, etc.) with their standard UML semantics.

Even if UML predefines the "facet" used for attributes and operations (i.e. the form of metainformation that can be specified for them, for example, name, multiplicity, list of parameters, return value, or standard tagged values), the user is allowed to extend this metainformation by adding specific tagged values.

OntologyClass can also be used as an AssociationClass.

**Notation** OntologyClass is depicted as a UML Class with the stereotype <<oclass>> and/or a special icon, see Fig. 13-5.

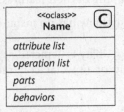

**Fig. 13-5** Notation of OntologyClass

**Examples** Fig. 13-6 shows a fragment of the Medical Staff Ontology built up from several OntologyClasses.

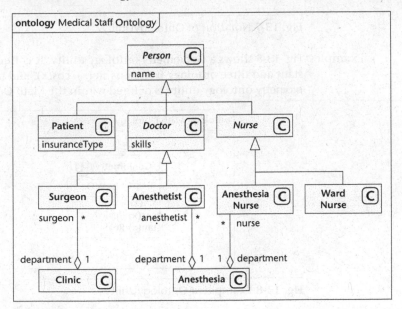

**Fig. 13-6** Example of OntologyClass

**Rationale**  OntologyClass is introduced to model an ontology class (also called concept or frame).

### 13.1.3  OntologyUtility

**Semantics**  OntologyUtility is a specialized Class (from UML) used to cluster global *ontology constants*, *ontology variables*, and *ontology functions/actions/predicates* modeled as owned features. The features of an OntologyUtility can be used by (referred to by) other elements within the owning and importing Ontologies.

There can be more than one OntologyUtility classes within one Ontology. In such a way different OntologyUtilities provide clusters for logical grouping of their features.

OntologyUtility has no instances, all its features are class-scoped.

**Notation**  OntologyUtility is depicted as a UML Class with the stereotype <<outility>> and/or a special icon, see Fig. 13-7.

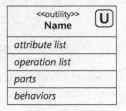

**Fig. 13-7** Notation of OntologyUtility

**Examples**  Fig. 13-8 shows a Goniometry ontology utility. It contains the PI constant and three ontology functions sin(x), cos(x), and tan(x). The Goniometry ontology utility is defined within the Math Ontology.

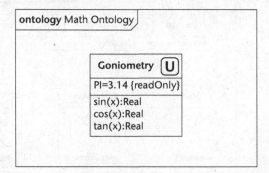

**Fig. 13-8** Example of OntologyUtility

**Rationale**  OntologyUtility is introduced to cluster global ontology constants, ontology variables, and ontology functions/actions/predicates.

# Chapter 14

# Model Management

**Overview** The *Model Management* package defines the generic-purpose model-ing constructs which can be used to structure AML models and thus manage their complexity and understandability.

**Package structure** The package diagram of the Model Management package is depicted in Fig. 14-1.

**Fig. 14-1** Model Management—package structure

## 14.1 Contexts

**Overview** The *Contexts* package defines the metaclasses used to logically struc-ture models according to situations that can occur during a system's lifetime and to model elements involved in handling those situa-tions.

**Abstract syntax** The diagram of the Contexts package is shown in Fig. 14-2.

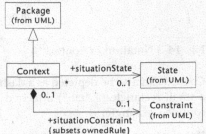

**Fig. 14-2** Contexts—context

### 14.1.1 Context

**Semantics**  Context is a specialized Package (from UML) used to contain a part of the model relevant for a particular situation. The situation is specified either as a Constraint (from UML) or an explicitly modeled State (from UML) associated with the Context.

**Associations**

| | |
|---|---|
| situationState: State[0..1] | The State determining the situation for the Context. |
| situationConstraint: Constraint[0..1] | The Constraint determining the situation for the Context.<br>Subsets UML Namespace::ownedRule. |

**Constraints**  1. Either the situationState or the situationConstraint meta-association can be specified:

    self.situationState->notEmpty() xor
        self.situationContext->notEmpty()

**Notation**  Context is depicted as a UML Package with the stereotype <<context>> and/or a special icon, see Fig. 14-3.

The name of the State referred to by the situationState meta-association, or the specification of the Constraint referred to by the situationConstraint meta-association may be placed after or below the Context's name.

If the situation is specified as a State, it uses the following format:

    '[' *state_name* ']'

The *state_name* represents the name of the State referred.

If the situation is specified as a Constraint, it uses the syntax of Constraint as defined in UML—a text string in braces ('{' '}').

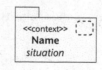

**Fig. 14-3** Notation of Context

**Presentation options**  Context can also be depicted as a dashed large rounded rectangle with a small rectangle (a "tab") attached to the top left side of the large rounded rectangle.

If the members of the Context are not shown, the name and the situation is placed within the large rounded rectangle, see Fig. 14-4 (a).

If the members of the Context are shown within the large rounded rectangle, the name and the situation is placed within the tab, see Fig. 14-4 (b). The visibility of a Context member may be indicated as for UML Package. Members may also be shown by branching lines ("nesting" relationship) to member elements, drawn outside the package, for details see [104].

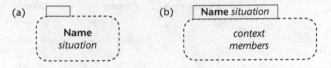

**Fig. 14-4** Alternative notations of Context: (a) members are hidden, (b) members are shown.

**Examples** Fig. 14-5 shows the Context used to describe the substitution of soccer players. It contains the algorithm of substitution, interaction of entities taking part in substitution, as well as definition of BehaviorFragments defining the substitution-specific Capabilities of affected EntityRoleTypes.

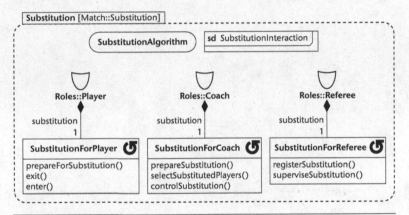

**Fig. 14-5** Example of defining Context

The Usage and ElementImport relationships (both from UML) can be used to model participation of elements in Contexts. Fig. 14-6 demonstrates application of the Usage relationships to depict dependency of EntityRoleTypes on particular Contexts. Each Context may define the Capabilities, Interactions, provided and used services, StateMachines, Activities, social relationships, etc. of the related EntityRoleTypes, specified for the referred situation. The EntityRoleTypes (and possibly also other modeling elements) are then composed of situation-specific parts. This kind of situation-based decomposition enables to specify complex behavior and structural features of modeling elements in a flexible and comprehensive way.

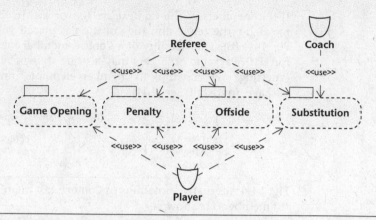

**Fig. 14-6** Example of using Contexts

**Rationale**   Context is introduced to offer the possibility to logically structure models according to the situations which can occur during a system's lifetime and to model elements involved in handling those situations.

# Chapter 15

# UML Extension for AML

**Overview** The *UML Extension for AML* package adds the meta-properties defined in the AML Kernel package to the standard UML 2.0 Superstructure metaclasses. It is a non-conservative extension of UML, and is an optional part of the language.

**Abstract syntax** The diagram of the UML Extension for AML is shown in Fig. 15-1.

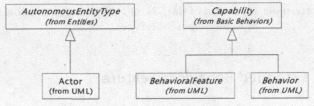

**Fig. 15-1** UML Extensions for AML—UML element extensions

## 15.1 Extended Actor

**Semantics** Actor, being a specialized AutonomousEntityType, can:

- ❑ own MentalProperties,
- ❑ have Capabilities,
- ❑ be decomposed into BehaviorFragments,
- ❑ provide and/or use services (see section 11.4),
- ❑ observe and/or effect its environment (see section 11.5),
- ❑ play entity roles (see section 10.5),
- ❑ participate in social relationships (see section 10.5), and
- ❑ specify values of the meta-attributes defined by the Socialized-SemiEntityType.

**Examples** Fig. 15-2 shows an Actor called Player which represents a user of an RPG (Role Playing Game) computer game. Its goal, to win the game, is modeled by a MentalAssociation with the WinGame DecidableGoal. Additionally, the Player can either play an entity role of a hero (modeled by the Hero EntityRoleType) or a creature (modeled by the Creature EntityRoleType).

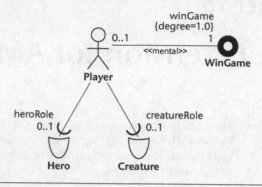

**Fig. 15-2** Example of extended Actor

**Rationale** Extension of UML Actor is introduced to allow the modeling of Actors as AutonomousEntityTypes.

## 15.2 Extended BehavioralFeature

**Semantics** BehavioralFeature, being a specialized Capability, can in addition to UML BehavioralFeature also specify meta-associations: inputs, outputs, pre-conditions, and post-conditions.

**Notation** See section 11.1.2.

**Examples** The Operation[33] (from UML) shoot() of the SoccerRobot AgentType specifies pre- and post-conditions, see Fig. 15-3.

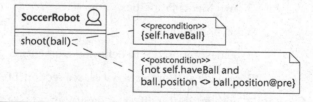

**Fig. 15-3** Example of extended BehavioralFeature

---

[33] Operation is a specialized BehavioralFeature.

The pre-condition constrains the soccer robot invoking the Operation such that it must have the ball, and the post-condition specifies that after successful execution of the shoot() Operation, the soccer robot no longer possesses the ball and the ball will have changed its position.

**Rationale** The extension of BehavioralFeature is introduced to unify common meta-attributes of BehavioralFeature and Behavior in order to refer to them uniformly e.g. while reasoning.

## 15.3 Extended Behavior

**Semantics** Behavior, being a specialized Capability, can in addition to UML Behavior also specify meta-associations: inputs, outputs, pre-conditions, and post-conditions.

**Notation** See sections 11.1.2 and 12.4.1.

**Examples** The Activity (from UML) called SubstitutionAlgorithm, shown also in Fig. 14-5, can specify the pre- and post-conditions, see Fig. 15-4.

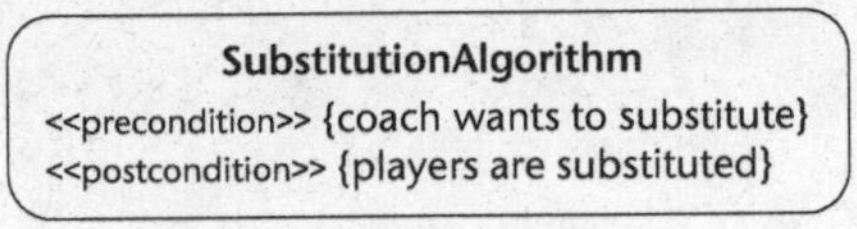

> **SubstitutionAlgorithm**
> <<precondition>> {coach wants to substitute}
> <<postcondition>> {players are substituted}

**Fig. 15-4** Example of extended Behavior

For other examples see Fig. 11-101 and Fig. 12-29.

**Rationale** Extension of Behavior is introduced to unify common meta-attributes of BehavioralFeature and Behavior in order to refer to them uniformly e.g. while reasoning.

# Chapter 16

# Diagrams

## 16.1 Diagram Frames

AML extends the UML 2.0 notation of the diagram frames by:

❑ an alternative syntax of the heading of the diagram frame, and

❑ the possibility to explicitly specify the list of template parameters for diagram frames which represent templates.

Fig. 16-1 depicts the notation of the AML diagram frame.

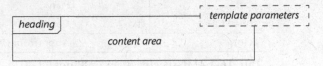

**Fig. 16-1** Diagram frame notation

**Heading** The heading of the diagram frame has the following syntax:

*heading* ::= [*kind*] [*owner*] ['::' *diagram-name*] [*property-string*]

The *kind* is the type and the *owner* is the name (also possibly containing parameters, the type of the return value, binding information, etc.) of the namespace enclosing, or the model element owning, elements in the diagram (as defined by UML [104]). The *diagram-name* is the name of the diagram and the *property-string* specifies the tagged values of the namespace enclosing, or the model element owning, elements in the diagram.

If needed, the set of MentalConstraintKind enumeration literals can be extended.

AML extends the set of UML diagram frame kinds, see Tab. 16-1. If needed, this set can be extended also by other diagram frame kinds (e.g. for new modeling elements added by users).

| Name | Short form | Type of owner |
|------|-----------|---------------|
| agent | | AgentType |
| resource | res | ResourceType |
| environment | env | EnvironmentType |
| organization unit | orgu | OrganizationUnitType |
| role | | EntityRoleType |
| agent execution environment | aee | AgentExecutionEnvironment |
| ontology | ont | Ontology |
| ontology class | oclass | OntologyClass |
| behavior fragment | bf | BehaviorFragment |
| interaction protocol | ip | InteractionProtocol |
| service specification | sspec | ServiceSpecification |
| service protocol | sp | ServiceProtocol |
| perceptor type | pct | PerceptorType |
| effector type | eft | EffectorType |
| plan | | Plan |
| context | ctx | Context |
| actor | | Actor (from UML) |

**Tab. 16-1** AML-specific diagram kinds

**Template parameters**  AML frames representing the templates (parameterized elements) can explicitly specify the list of TemplateParameters (from UML) of the represented element. The list of TemplateParameters is placed in a dashed rectangle in the upper right corner of the diagram frame.

To enable logical grouping of the TemplateParameters, their subsets can be depicted in the form of stereotyped lists, or placed into separate compartments. Both possible notations are depicted in Fig. 16-2. The stereotypes of parameter lists (i.e. <<stereotype X>> and <<stereotype Y>> in the figure) identify application of the subsequent TemplateParameters.

(a)                        (b)

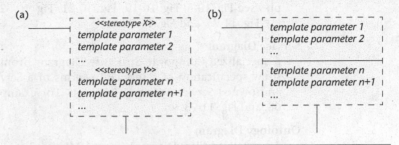

**Fig. 16-2** Grouping of template parameters: (a) template parameters in a stereotyped list, and (b) template parameters in compartments.

## 16.2 Diagram Types

AML extends the set of diagram types defined by UML with the following diagram types:

**Mental Diagram**

A specialized Class Diagram (from UML) used to capture mental attitudes of mental semi-entities in terms of MentalStates, i.e. Goals, Plans, Beliefs and MentalRelationships. Mental Diagrams can be owned either by an MentalSemiEntityType to express its mental model, or by a Package (from UML) to express a shared mental model. For examples see Fig. 12-37 to Fig. 12-42.

**Goal-Based Requirements Diagram**

A specialized Mental Diagram used to capture goal-based requirements. It usually contains specification of the system stakeholder's mental attitudes concerning the system modeled, and their relationships to the other elements of the system model. For an example see Fig. 12-23.

**Society Diagram**

A specialized Class Diagram (from UML) used to capture the global view of the multi-agent system's architecture in terms of EntityTypes (e.g. AgentTypes, ResourceTypes, EnvironmentTypes, OrganizationUnitTypes), EntityRoleTypes, and their relationships (e.g. all kinds of UML relationships, SocialAssociations, PlayAssociations, Perceives and Effects dependencies, ServiceProvisions and ServiceUsages). For examples see Fig. 10-11, Fig. 10-20, Fig. 10-33, Fig. 10-37, and Fig. 10-40.

**Entity Diagram**

A specialized Composite Structure Diagram (from UML) used to capture the details of the internal structure of an EntityType (in terms of its owned Features, Behaviors and Ports), played EntityRoleTypes, and related ServiceProvisions and ServiceUsages. For examples see Fig. 10-5, Fig. 10-19, Fig. 10-21, Fig. 10-32, Fig. 11-7 part (a), Fig. 11-75, and Fig. 11-98.

### Service Diagram

A specialized Composite Structure Diagram (from UML) used to show specification of a service in terms of a ServiceSpecification and owned ServiceInteractionProtocols. For examples see Fig. 11-68, and Fig. 11-73.

### Ontology Diagram

A specialized Class Diagram (from UML) used to show a specification of an ontology in terms of Ontologies, OntologyUtilities and OntologyClasses together with their mutual relationships. For examples see Fig. 13-4, Fig. 13-6, and Fig. 13-8.

### Behavior Decomposition Diagram

A specialized Class Diagram (from UML) used to show BehavorFragments, owned Capabilities, and their mutual relationships. For an example see Fig. 11-7 part (b).

### Protocol Sequence Diagram

A specialized Sequence Diagram (from UML) used to show the specification of an InteractionProtocol in the form of a Sequence Diagram. For an example see Fig. 11-48.

### Protocol Communication Diagram

A specialized Communication Diagram (from UML) used to show the specification of an InteractionProtocol in the form of a Communication Diagram. For an example see Fig. 11-49.

### Service Protocol Sequence Diagram

A specialized Protocol Sequence Diagram used to show the specification of a ServiceProtocol in the form of Sequence Diagram. For an example see Fig. 11-71.

### Service Protocol Communication Diagram

A specialized Protocol Communication Diagram used to show the specification of a ServiceProtocol in the form of Communication Diagram. For an example see Fig. 11-72.

### MAS Deployment Diagram

A specialized Deployment Diagram (from UML) used to show deployment of a multi-agent system to a physical environment and structural aspects of mobility. For examples see Fig. 10-47, Fig. 10-48, Fig. 10-55, and Fig. 11-117.

Please note that this taxonomy provides a logical organization for the various major kinds of diagrams. However, it does not preclude the mixing of different kinds of diagram types, as one might do when combining structural and behavioral elements (for instance, showing a state machine nested inside an internal structure). Consequently, the distinction between the various kinds of diagram types are not strictly enforced.

All the specialized Class Diagrams and the Entity Diagram can have two forms: the type and the instance. The instance variations of the diagrams are identified by the word 'Object' in their names, for example, Mental Object Diagram, or Society Object Diagram.

The diagram hierarchy is depicted in Fig. 16-3.

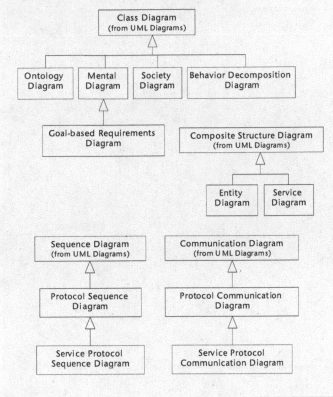

**Fig. 16-3** Taxonomy of AML diagrams

# Chapter 17

# Extension of OCL

## 17.1 New Operators

Formal models of MAS usually use different types of modal family logics to describe the system. Our intention is to allow such expressions to be used within OCL expressions.

AML defines a set of operators used to extend the OCL Standard Library [100] to include expressions belonging to modal logic, deontic logic, temporal logic, dynamic logic, epistemic logic, BDI logic, etc. For details see [147] and [152].

Tab. 17-1 summarizes operators added to OCL.

| Operator | Semantics | Known as |
|---|---|---|
| **Modal Logic** | | |
| possible($p$ : *Boolean*) : *Boolean* | $p$ is possible. | $\Diamond p$ |
| necessary($p$ : *Boolean*) : *Boolean* | $p$ is necessary. | $\Box p$ |
| **Deontic Logic** | | |
| obliged($p$ : *Boolean*) : *Boolean* | $p$ is obliged. | Obl$p$ |
| permitted($p$ : *Boolean*) : *Boolean* | $p$ is permitted. | Per$p$ |
| **Temporal Logic** | | |
| until($p$ : *Boolean,q* : *Boolean*) : *Boolean* | $p$ holds until $q$ is valid. | $p$U$q$ |
| past($p$ : *Boolean*) : *Boolean* | $q$ held in past. | P$q$ |
| future($p$ : *Boolean*) : *Boolean* | $p$ holds sometimes in the future. | F$p$ |
| afuture($p$ : *Boolean*) : *Boolean* | $p$ holds always in the future. | G$p$ |
| next($p$ : *Boolean*) : *Boolean* | $p$ holds in the next moment. | X$p$, O$p$ |
| **Dynamic Logic and KARO** | | |
| e.ability($c$ : *Capability*) : *Boolean* | Mental semi-entity $e$ is able to perform the capability $c$. | $A_e c$ |

**Tab. 17-1** New OCL operators (1/2)

| Operator | Semantics | Known as |
|---|---|---|
| e.opportunity(c : Capability, p : Boolean) : Boolean | Mental semi-entity e has the opportunity to perform the capability c, and doing so leads to p. | $<do_e c>p$ |
| e.possibility(c : Capability, p : Boolean) : Boolean | If the opportunity to do c is indeed present, doing so leads to p. | $[do_e c]p$ |
| e.pracPoss(c : Capability, p : Boolean) : Boolean | Mental semi-entity e has the opportunity and the ability to perform c, and doing so leads to p. | $PracPoss_e$ $(c, p)$ |
| e.can(c : Capability, p : Boolean) : Boolean | Mental semi-entity e knows that performing c constitutes a practical possibility to bring about p. | $Can_e(c, p)$ |
| **Epistemic Logic** | | |
| e.knows(p : Boolean) : Boolean | Mental semi-entity e knows that p is true. | $eKp$, $K_e\,p$ |
| G.cknows(p : Boolean) : Boolean | p is a common knowledge among mental semi-entities in the set G. | $E_G\,p$ |
| e.uncertain(p : Boolean) : Boolean | Mental semi-entity e is uncertain of the truth of p. e neither believes p nor its negation, but believes that p is more likely to be true than its negation. | |
| **BDI Logic** | | |
| e.believes(p : Boolean) : Boolean | Mental semi-entity e believes that p is true. | $eBelp$, $Bel_e\,p$ |
| e.desires(p : Boolean) : Boolean | Mental semi-entity e desires p to become true. | $eDesp$ |
| e.intends(p : Boolean) : Boolean | Mental semi-entity e intends p to become true and will plan to bring it about. | $eIntp$ |
| **Other operators** | | |
| e.happens(c : Capability) : Boolean | Mental semi-entity e currently preforms the capability c. | |
| e.done(c : Capability) : Boolean | Mental semi-entity e has just finished the execution of the capability c. | |
| e.achieved(g : Goal) : Boolean | Mental semi-entity e has just achieved the goal g. | |

**Tab. 17-1** New OCL operators (2/2)

**Examples** In the following example the expression utilizing the extension to OCL has been used to specify that possession of the ball can lead to scoring a goal.

> (TeamHasBall.post) implies (possible(ScoreGoal.post))

DecidableGoals TeamHasBall and ScoreGoal are described in Fig. 12-41.

Another example states that if an agent believes that its team does not possess the ball, it switches to the defending strategy.

> (self.believe(not TeamHasBall.post)) implies
>     (next(self.happens(Strategy::defend())))

BehaviorFragment Strategy and its Capability defend() is described in Fig. 11-7.

# Part IV

# Final Remarks

This part provides a summary of the achieved results and outlines the possible directions for the further development and application of AML.

# Chapter 18

# Conclusions

## 18.1 Context of the Work

Agent-oriented software engineering is a new software engineering paradigm that has appeared in recent years. It is a promising approach to the development of distributed, open, heterogeneous, highly dynamic, and intelligent systems. One of the current areas of interest is the specification and dissemination of agent-based development methodologies that provide software engineers with the means to create organized, repeatable and high-quality process for the development of multi-agent systems.

One very important aspect of a methodology, directly influencing its applicability and usability, is the set of underlying concepts used to represent and model the developed system. These concepts must be reflected by both the methodology process and used modeling language(s). In order to capture specific features of agent-based systems, specific modeling languages and supporting methodologies must also be created.

Therefore, the work of AOSE is now largely concentrated on the following tasks:

❑ **Definition of a unified, general-purpose MAS metamodel(s).**
The metamodel is intended to specify the fundamental architectonic, behavioral, and mental concepts used to specify an abstract MAS.

❑ **Specification of unified general-purpose MAS modeling language(s).**
Based on the concepts from MAS metamodel(s), an agent-oriented modeling language is defined. It is used to model MAS applications in a concrete syntax and semantics.

❑ **Creation of MAS development methodologies.**
MAS development methodologies lead developers in the analysis,

design, construction, deployment, testing, administration, etc. of systems based on MAS concepts.

## 18.2 Solution

**Goals of the work**   This work is situated within the context of the aforementioned AOSE's tasks. The goal was to design and specify a semi-formal visual modeling language for specifying, modeling and documenting systems in terms of concepts drawn from MAS theory. The Agent Modeling Language (AML)—the result of this work—was required to overcome the deficiencies of the current state-of-the-art and practice in the area of MAS modeling languages, namely: insufficient documentation of modeling languages, the use of proprietary and/or non-intuitive modeling constructs, limited scope, mutual incompatibility, insufficient support by CASE tools, etc. AML is intended to be a ready-to-use, complete and highly expressive modeling language suitable for the industrial development of real-world software solutions based on multi-agent technologies. Further requirements put on AML are specified in Chapter 3.

**Analysis of agent-oriented modeling languages**   The starting point for the development of our modeling language was to obtain the necessary know-how from the area of MAS and agent-oriented modeling in particular. Apart from studying the relevant theories, specification and modeling approaches, abstract MAS models, technologies, and available agent-based solutions, the main source of inspiration was drawn from existing agent-oriented modeling languages. The most relevant ones have been identified herein, and by their analysis we have produced a detailed appraisal of their scope, underlying concepts, used modeling techniques and mechanisms, strengths, and weaknesses. A short summary of the selected agent-oriented modeling languages, each of which is a significant contributor to the area of agent-oriented modeling, is provided in Chapter 2.

**Stating requirements**   Enlightened by the discovered facts, we set forth the generally applicable quality criteria of a MAS modeling language, which were then used as the fundamental requirements in designing AML. These are discussed in Chapter 3. The stated requirements are specified in a sufficiently generic manner that they can be used as general rules for designing any (software) modeling and specification language.

**Conceptual MAS metamodel**   Based on analysis of the modeled MAS aspect, we defined the basic MAS modeling concepts and created the MAS metamodel, which forms a conceptual basis for the design of AML. The conceptual MAS metamodel is described in Chapter 5. Even though the metamodel is relatively simple, it can sufficiently explain the underlying AML concepts.

**AML**  In combination with the UML 2.0 metamodel, we used the previously defined MAS concepts to define the AML modeling constructs. The abstract syntax and semantics of AML are specified in the AML metamodel. Based on the metamodel we also defined the language's notation, used to specify its concrete syntax. The AML metamodel and notation represent the core of the language specification.

We also extended the basic set of UML diagram types with additional ones, to provide agent-specific views of the system model. Another achievement of AML is the definition of a set of operators extending the OCL Standard Library [100] with operators from modal logic, deontic logic, temporal logic, dynamic logic, epistemic logic, BDI logic, etc. These operators allow the specification of OCL constraints based on different types of modal family logics, that provide more natural, and commonly used, means for specification of MASs.

The fundamental AML modeling principles and the rational behind them are discussed in Chapter 6, and a detailed specification of the language is provided in Part III.

In addition to the AML core language specification (i.e. the metamodel and notation), we have also defined two UML profiles, the *UML 1.\* Profile for AML* and the *UML 2.0 Profile for AML*, to specify AML as standard extensions of UML 1.\* and 2.0 respectively. The description of the AML profiles can be found in [18].

## 18.3 Challenges

During our work we had to cope with several fundamental problems, and we were also frequently forced to create detours to apparent dead ends. Here follows a summary of the most critical problems and dead ends.

One of the problems we faced from the beginning was the sheer **complexity of the problem domain**. DAI, MAS, and AOSE in particular, are interdisciplinary areas influenced by many other scientific and engineering disciplines, such as artificial intelligence, artificial life, social sciences, software engineering, computer science, biology, economics, robotics, etc. In each of these disciplines we identified a large number of theories and engineering approaches relevant to the context of AML. As a consequence, we had to study many theories, theoretical MAS models, specification and modeling languages (used in software engineering, artificial intelligence, computer science, logic, etc.), principles and selected areas of sociology, AI, robotics, some system engineering solutions, technologies, etc. For example, we learned the details of more than 40 different specification languages.

The second problem was **conceptual divergency of used AML sources**. Unfortunately, many of the AML sources use different principles, concepts and techniques. To harmonize such divergent approaches into a homogenous, consistent framework of AML concepts and metamodel was a very complex task requiring a considerable amount of conceptual and analytical work.

Another challenge was to **harmonize MAS concepts with object-oriented modeling mechanisms used in UML**. In order to utilize the well-defined UML modeling framework for modeling MASs, two paradigms, object-oriented and agent-oriented, had to be harmonized. We based our solution on the proposition that the agent-oriented paradigm is an extension of the object-oriented paradigm. In a simplified view, agents represent special objects with additional features, such as autonomy, situatedness, reactivity, proactiveness, social ability, etc. By identifying the "essence of agent orientation" and expressing it in terms of concrete technical concepts, we were able to design the AML modeling mechanisms and incorporate them into the UML metamodel. However, this process was not trivial.

In certain cases **the default UML semantics is in contrast to MAS principles** (e.g. the coupling of a message reception with the triggered behavior). It was necessary to identify these cases and provide modifications to the UML semantics and/or to provide certain modeling "workarounds" (e.g. to provide alternative ways of modeling the same concept). To be able to identify such problems and to design their solutions properly, we had to understand all nuances of the UML semantics and also elaborate the AML modeling mechanisms at a very fine level of detail. This amounted to an enormous volume of work because, for instance, the UML 2.0 Superstructure Specification [104] is approximately 800 pages, and the UML metamodel itself contains 295 metaclasses.

In the design of AML we often faced the problem of **contrary requirements** and finding balanced, satisfactory solutions. For instance, we had to decide between completeness (i.e. coverage of as many aspects of MAS as possible, resulting in a large number of modeling elements) vs. simplicity (i.e. providing few comprehensible easy-to-use modeling elements), precise semantics vs. understandability, generic (i.e. independent of any particular theory, software development process or implementation environment,) vs. applicable in modeling real technologies (i.e. technology-specific), formal specification (represented e.g. by mathematical expressions with non-trivial semantics) vs. semi-formal visual language (using easy-to-learn, but possibly ambiguous and/or imprecise, pictorial notation), etc.

Last but not least, an additional problem faced in designing AML was the **complexity of the AML specification**. Many concepts had to be organized into one consistent modeling framework and properly documented. The metamodel contains 86 metaclasses, from which 71 are concrete, i.e. they represent tangible modeling elements that can be used in user's models, and therefore additionally must define notations.

## 18.4 Results

**Goal achievement summary**  Let us at this point analyze the accomplishments of the goals stated in section 1.2.

The most crucial accomplishment is that we have achieved the central goal of the work to define a semi-formal visual modeling language—AML—for specifying, modeling and documenting systems in terms of concepts drawn from MAS theory.

AML represents a consistent framework for modeling applications that embody and/or exhibit characteristics of multi-agent systems. It integrates best modeling practices and concepts from existing agent oriented modeling and specification languages (they are listed in Chapter 4) into a unique framework built on the foundations of UML 2.0 and OCL 2.0. AML is also specified in accordance with the OMG modeling frameworks MOF 2.0 and *Model-Driven Architecture* (*MDA*).

The structure of the language definition combined with the MDA/MOF/UML "metamodeling technology" (UML profiles, first-class metamodel extension, etc.) gives AML the advantage of natural extensibility and customizability. Depending on the user's needs and skills, the language extensions can be created at several levels, namely: metamodel extension, AML profile extension, and concrete model extension.

Due to the specification of UML profiles for AML, the language can be easily and flexibly implemented within UML 1.* and UML 2.0 CASE tools and other technologies based on UML and XMI.

AML provides a rich set of modeling constructs for complex specification systems from different perspectives. AML covers a considerable number of system views, each of which represents a single aspect of MAS, that together allow the creation of complex and precise models. Modeling the static structure, dynamics and behavior of fundamental MAS entities (i.e. agents, resources and environments), social aspects, MAS deployment and mobility, capabilities, behavior decomposition, communicative interactions, services, observations and effecting interactions, mental aspects (i.e. beliefs, goals, plans, and their relationships), ontologies, and contexts are all covered by AML. Regarding the scope and feature set, AML is currently the most complete published agent-oriented modeling language.

Despite the considerably large language specification, AML is internally consistent from the conceptual, semantic and syntactic perspectives.

The AML specification [18] provides a comprehensive description of the language's syntax and semantics, and also demonstrates practical usage of AML's modeling constructs by means of comprehensive examples. The specification of the language achieves the quality level of OMG standards. There is no other such in-depth and extensive specification of an agent-oriented modeling language yet available.

We feel confident that AML is sufficiently detailed, comprehensive and tangible to be a useful tool for software architects building systems based on, or exhibiting attributes of, multi-agent technologies. In this respect we anticipate that AML may form a significant contribution to the effort of bringing about widespread adoption of intelligent agents across varied commercial market sectors.

**Beyond the goals** It is also worth mentioning that we have gone beyond the originally stated objectives to achieve the additional important results mentioned below:

**CASE tools:** In order to provide developers with AML-based modeling tools, and also practically prove the declared straightforward implementation of AML in UML CASE tools, we have implemented UML profiles for AML in three CASE tools: UML 2.0-based Enterprise Architect, UML 2.0-based StarUML, and UML 1.5-based IBM Rational Rose, see section 7.1.

Furthermore, the implementation in Enterprise Architect was extended by the LS/TS code generator and was incorporated into the commercial agent-based software development and runtime suite Living Systems Technology Suite, as one of its tools called LS/TS Modeler. A very important feature of the code generator is that apart from relatively straightforward generation of code from the static structure diagrams (implemented by most UML code generators), it also supports code generation from UML behavioral models, i.e. activities, state machines, and interactions.

As a "side effect" of the LS/TS implementation we have also designed a common metamodel of the previously mentioned UML 2.0 behavior models. We perceive this as a very important achievement from a theoretical perspective because we proved that it is possible to create a common metamodel of UML 2.0 activities, state machines, and interactions, unifying their operational semantics. It is therefore possible to transform a model of any of these kinds to a model of another kind, without altering its semantics.

The implementation of the code generator itself was developed by a team of programers from Whitestein Technologies who were provided with the requirements specification, analysis, and the tool design. Apart from the analytical work we also undertook the tool's testing and overall project management.

Implementations of AML in CASE tools have proved that AML can be automated by means of its relatively easy integration into UML 1.* and 2.* based CASE tools. AML implementation can in this way extend the functionality of existing UML-based CASE tools with the means to model MAS applications and to combine agent-specific modeling mechanisms with "orthodox" object-oriented models. These facts indirectly point out the appropriateness and usefulness of the AML language architecture, the provided extension mechanisms, as well as the CASE tool support.

**Methodology:** Besides AML we have also defined a software development methodology based on AML. The methodology, called ADEM, is a comprehensive agent-based system development methodology with a special focus on modeling aspects. ADEM provides guidelines for the use of AML in the context of a MAS development process, by extending and making use of the best practices of AOSE. ADEM is a coherent and extensible methodology based on RUP, which utilizes concepts drawn from MAS theory, as specified by AML. The methodology follows the SME approach in order to provide flexibility in defining concrete methods customized to specific conditions of particular system development projects.

**AML in projects:** AML has already been successfully applied as a language for modeling requirements, analysis and design of applications in several research and commercial software development projects. The applications were built in various domains, e.g. planning of surgical operations, simulation of artificial societies, and distributed network management systems. These projects tested AML under real-world conditions and proved that it is a useful tool for modeling complex, concurrent, distributed and intelligent systems. Furthermore, AML extensibility mechanisms allowed customizing of the language for designing applications deployed with various target implementation technologies.

**Standardization activities:** An important means of disseminating AML ideas into the (agent-oriented) software engineering community was our participation in the related international standardization activities. Our active involvement in the work of FIPA Modeling Technical Committee, FIPA Methodology Technical Committee, AgentLink Agent-Oriented Software Engineering Technical Forum Group, and OMG Agents Special Interest Group, has provided several opportunities to present AML and related ideas to forums of AOSE specialists and to gather valuable feedback which has been taken into account in the language design and specification.

## 18.5 Summary of Original Contribution

A summary of original contributions to the field of agent-oriented modeling follows:

❑ AML is the most complete published agent-oriented modeling language available to date. It covers modeling of the static structure, dynamics and behavior of fundamental MAS entities (i.e. agents, resources and environments), social aspects, MAS deployment and mobility, capabilities, behavior decomposition, communicative interactions, services, observations and effecting interactions, mental aspects (i.e. beliefs, goals, plans, and their relationships), ontologies, and contexts.

❑ AML is one of the most completely specified and well documented agent-oriented modeling languages. It is defined in the same way as the UML 2.0 Superstructure Specification (yet more precisely and consistently), exploiting the metamodeling possibilities of the UML 2.0 Infrastructure Specification [103] and MOF 2.0 [99]. The specification of AML is probably the most extensive specification of an agent-oriented modeling language. It defines metamodel, semantics, constraints, notation (including alternative notation), usage examples, and rationale for each defined modeling element type. For instance, as we have practically demonstrated in the case of the LS/TS Modeler, the language specification provides a sufficient level of detail such as to be directly used as an implementation specification of AML-based CASE tools.

❑ From the technical point of view, AML provides several innovative modeling approaches that do not appear in other MAS modeling languages. For instance:

  • using specialized UML structural features to model different aspects of MAS entities (see section 6.1.2 for details)

  • explicit modeling of environments as complex entities (see section 10.4 for details),

  • modeling entity roles as complex behaviored, socialized and mental semi-entities (see sections 6.3 and 10.5.6 for details),

  • unique modeling of MAS deployment and mobility (see sections 6.4, 10.6, and 11.6 for details),

  • effective visual modeling of mental aspects having the semantics of formal modal logic (see section 6.7 and chapter 12 for details),

  • unique idea of situation-based modeling supported by the explicit structuring of a model into contexts (see sections 6.9 and 14.1 for details), etc.

# Chapter 19

# Further Work

## 19.1 Improvements of AML

**Continuous improvements** Despite our confidence in the current state of AML and generally positive feedback from the AOSE community, we realize that AML is not yet complete. It is subject to continuous reviews and improvements which lead to enhancements of the language itself, its documentation, and related artifacts. Continuous, iterative improvement of AML, e.g. by providing flexible incorporation of user's findings and change requests into the language specification, can satisfy its users and therefore support dissemination and widespread use of AML.

**Directions of improvements** According to the feedback from official AML reviewers, informal reactions from the AOSE community, and also practical experiences obtained from projects at Whitestein Technologies, we anticipate possible enhancements of AML in the following directions:

❏ **Revision of the AML specification.**
The current version of the AML specification [18] should be updated in order to provide more comprehensive description of the semantics, improved notation of certain modeling elements, and more examples. Our main goal is to improve understandability of the specification.

❏ **Improvements of existing modeling mechanisms.**
Some of the AML packages could be enhanced in order to provide more comprehensive modeling mechanisms based on concepts found in other specification languages. In the first instance, we are going to improve the following packages:

* Ontologies—to provide more advanced modeling of ontologies based on concepts drawn from *Ontology Definition Metamodel (ODM)* [101], *Web Ontology Language (OWL)* [110,132], *DARPA Agent Markup Language (DAML)* [30,43], *Ontology Inference Layer (OIL)* [41,43,97], and possibly also other ontology specification languages.

- Services—to allow specification of services compatible with *Web Services* [149] and *OWL-based Web Service Ontology* (*OWL-S*) [84].

❏ **Extension of the scope.**

In order to extend the scope of applicability, AML should support additional aspects of MAS. The next foreseen extension is Security and its interconnection with existing AML packages, such as Entities, MAS Deployment, Communicative Interactions, Observations and Effecting Interactions, and Mobility. Other extensions of AML are possible in the future.

❏ **Defining a simplified version of AML.**

On one hand, the relatively large number of elements in the current AML specification could cause problems with its learning and correct application by users. On the other hand, the number of elements cannot be considerably reduced while retaining the current scope of the language. To help users (mainly new users) with learning and applying AML, we propose to define a consistent subset of AML modeling constructs, called *AML-lite*, intended to incorporate only the well-known and commonly used MAS concepts, such as agent, (entity) role, social relationships, communication interaction, or agent execution environment, without specifying their details (such as specific meta-attributes). AML users then would establish themselves by learning and using AML-lite, and after obtaining a certain level of experience would move to the "full" AML.

❏ **Defining a formal model of AML concepts.**

In order to formalize and precisely describe the concepts used in AML, we plan to create a formal model of the conceptual MAS metamodel described in Chapter 5. We have yet to decide on the formal specification language to be used, but the current top candidate is Object-Z [131].

## 19.2 Broader Application of AML

**AML as a pattern modeling language**  There is no unified means of visually modeling the structural and behavioral aspects in specifications of *agent design patterns* (for more information see [1], [6], [36], [37], [72], [73], [71], [75], [118], and [154]). Agent design pattern specifications usually use UML class diagrams to model structures, and UML state machines, activity and sequence diagrams (possibly extended by AUML), to model the pattern dynamics. Since UML models, and object-oriented models in general, are insufficient and/or inappropriate to model MAS-specific features (a discussion on this topic can be found e.g. in [9]), specific agent-oriented languages should be applied here. Another reason for the diversity of employed agent pattern modeling languages is caused by the tendency of the pattern designers from a community of users of a specific agent-oriented language to also use that particular language in the specification of their patterns. An example is the use of TROPOS [12,143] in the agent design patterns defined in [75].

Software developers wanting to use libraries of agent design patterns have, therefore, some problems in learning and properly applying particular patterns, because they may be specified in various languages using different notations and semantics. In reality, this overhead coupled with the necessity of learning several modeling languages is generally unacceptable. The result is clear: agent design patterns are not commonly used in practice.

AML, with its considerably large scope, can efficiently replace the modeling languages currently used for agent design patterns and can become a standardized modeling language used for the specification of agent design patterns. Furthermore, AML provides specially designed modeling mechanisms to capture MAS-specific aspects which are usually subjects of specialized agent design pattern libraries, for instance, AML modeling of MAS deployment and mobility can be used in the specification of *mobility patterns* [126], or AML modeling of social aspects can be used for modeling *organizational patterns* [75] and *social patterns* [37].

**AML profile extensions and modeling frameworks**  Bringing generic AML closer to specific modeling techniques, implementation environments, technologies, development processes, etc. may require its customization. The mechanism of creating the AML profile extensions, described in Chapter 4, can be effectively used for this purpose. We intend to develop AML-based UML profiles and respective *modeling frameworks*[34] for selected MAS-related specification standards (e.g. OWL [110,132], OWL-S [84], Web Services [149], FIPA content languages [46]), MAS abstract models (e.g. FIPA Abstract Architecture [46]), and agent platforms (LS/TS [81], JADE [61], etc.). This is a necessary step toward the practical use of AML as a modeling language for designing real-world software systems.

**Extension of the CASE tools support**  We also intend to continue with providing and extending CASE tool support for AML in the following ways:

☐ Improvement of the LS/TS Modeler to add more features, for instance, new modeling tools (LS/TS design model consistency and completeness checkers, element creation wizards, etc.), or update of the code generator.

---

[34] *Modeling framework* is a set of predefined model elements that are needed to model a certain kind of system. The purpose of a specific framework can be to define the architecture of systems of a certain kind or to provide a set of reusable components. Frameworks are used as templates when creating a new model.

❏ Implementation of *MDA-style model transformation*[35] in the LS/TS Modeler, used for (semi)automatic generation of some model parts from other parts, e.g. generation of society models from ontologies and interactions, or MAS deployment models from society models.

❏ Implementation of reverse engineering of the LS/TS applications into AML models. This functionality would provide developers with complete AML to LS/TS round-trip engineering integration.

❏ Implementation of AML profile extensions and round-trip-engineering tools for other MAS technologies, for instance, agent platforms JADE, JACK, or Cougaar.

❏ Implementation of the UML profile for AML, related modeling tools (e.g. model consistency and completeness checkers), and code generation and/or reverse engineering tools also into other CASE tools providing automation interfaces. Possible candidates are: IBM Rational XDE Modeler for .NET and Eclipse, IBM Software Modeler/Architect, Poseidon for UML, Visual Paradigm for UML, etc.

**AML in other method- ologies**   There is also the possibility to integrate AML into existing agent-based methodologies as their common underlying modeling language. Currently, a number of methodologies either do not provide their own modeling languages (MASSIVE, Gaia, ROADMAP, ADELFE, Styx, Cougaar Design Methodology, etc.) or use proprietary modeling languages (OPM/MAS, AOR, CAMLE, PASSI, etc.). Their underlying specification/modeling languages could be replaced by AML, in order to utilize its modeling possibilities and also to guarantee compatibility of artifacts built by different methodologies.

**Dissemination of AML**   We expect to disseminate AML and its principles throughout the broader community of software engineers as an important task which could result in better acceptance of our work and improvements of the practices of AOSE in general. We will focus on the following activities:

❏ **Application AML in software development projects.**
   One of the main goals is integration of AML into software development projects. Even if AML has been used, or is in use, in sever-

---

[35] *MDA-style model transformation* provide a way of converting model elements from one type to another. This will typically involve converting *Platform-Independent Model* (*PIM*) elements to *Platform-Specific Model* (*PSM*) elements. For example, separate transformations could convert a PIM-model to a Java model, a C++ model and a C# model. Or a class model could be transformed to a DDL model, in which each class element is converted to a table element with the appropriate database type, and with attributes converted to columns and associations converted to foreign key associations. For details about *Model-Driven Architecture* (*MDA*) see [98].

al projects, we need to test it within the context of further projects with different setups varying in size, application domain, skills of project members, technologies used, etc. In this context, a very positive fact is that Whitestein Technologies is using AML (and ADEM) in current and forthcoming agent-oriented software development projects, mainly in the domains of telecommunications and logistics. In addition to commercial application of AML, several individuals and groups from the academic area have already expressed their interest in the application of AML in their software development projects and research work in the area of AOSE.

❏ **Preparing AML examples.**
To support the education of AML users, we are also preparing several practical examples of modeling. The examples will demonstrate usage of AML in modeling selected problems of MAS requirements capture, analysis and design. In addition to these relatively small examples, we will also prepare some comprehensive case studies which will demonstrate complete step-by-step modeling of MAS applications from different domains.

❏ **Provide training and consulting.**
To educate software engineers in AML we plan to provide in-house as well as external training courses and consulting.

❏ **Further publications.**
We plan to discuss several aspects of AML in a series of additional presentations, conference papers, journal articles, and possibly also books. We will continue to provide users of AML and interested people with more information about AML, related artifacts and tools via the official AML/ADEM web page:

*http://www.whitestein.com/pages/solutions/meth.html*


## 19.3  Assurance of Future Work

AML and related work has already become an important part of the research, and also commercial, activities of Whitestein Technologies, tightly coupled with the strategic goals of the company to provide high-quality agent-based technologies and customer solutions. We will do our best to assure that these activities are provided with sufficient resources, effort, and enthusiasm, to allow AML to continue along the successful path on which it has started since its creation and first publication in December 2004.

# Bibliography

[1] Agent Factory web page. URL: http://mozart.csai.unipa.it/af/

[2] Agent-Oriented Software Engineering TFG web page.
URL: http://www.pa.icar.cnr.it/~cossentino/al3tf2/default.html

[3] AgentLink web page. URL: http://www.agentlink.org/

[4] E. Alencar, J. Castro, G. Cysneiros, and J. Mylopoulos. From Early Requirements Modeled by the i* Technique to Later Requirements Modeled in Precise UML. In *Anais do III Workshop em Engenharia de Requisitos*, pages 92–109, Rio de Janeiro, Brazil, July 2000.

[5] A.I. Anton. *Goal Identification and Refinement in the Specification of Software-Based Information Systems.* PhD thesis, Georgia Institute of Technology, Atlanta, GA, June 1997.

[6] Y. Aridor and D.B. Lange. Agent Design Patterns: Elements of Agent Application Design. In *Second International Conference on Autonomous Agents (Agents'98)*, pages 108–115. ACM Press, 1998.

[7] AUML web page. URL: http://www.auml.org

[8] B. Bauer. UML Class Diagrams: Revisited in the Context of Agent-Based Systems. In M. Wooldridge, G. Weiss, and P. Ciancarini, editors, *Proceedings of the Second International Workshop on Agent-Oriented Software Engineering (AOSE-2001)*, pages 101–118, Montreal, Canada, May 2001. Springer.

[9] B. Bauer, J.P. Müller, and J. Odell. An Extension of UML by Protocols for Multi-agent Interaction. In *Proceedings of the International Conference on Multi-Agent Systems (ICMAS'00)*, pages 207–214, Boston, MA, USA, July 2000.

[10] B. Bauer, J.P. Müller, and J. Odell. Agent UML: A Formalism for Specifying Multiagent Interaction. In P. Ciancarini and M. Wooldridge, editors, *Agent-Oriented Software Engineering*, pages 91–103. Springer-Verlag, 2001.

[11] C. Bernon, V. Camps, M.P. Gleizes, and G. Picard. Designing Agents' Behaviours and Interactions within the Framework of ADELFE Methodology. In *Proceedings of the Fourth International Workshop: Engineering Societies in the Agents World (ESAW'03)*, pages 156–169, Imperial College London, UK, October 2003. Springer-Verlag.

[12] P. Bresciani, P. Giorgini, F. Giunchiglia, J. Mylopoulos, and A. Perini. TROPOS: An Agent-Oriented Software Development Methodology. *Autonomous Agents and Multi-Agent Systems*, 2(3):203–236, May 2004.

[13] S. Brinkkemper. Method Engineering: Engineering of Information Systems Development Methods and Tools. *Information and Software Technology*, 38(4):275–280, 1996.

[14] B. Burmeister. Models and Methodology for Agent-Oriented Analysis and Design. In K. Fischer, editor, *Working notes of the KI'96 Workshop on Agent-Oriented Programming and Distributed Systems*, June 1996.

[15] G. Bush, S. Cranefield, and M. Purvis. The Styx Agent Methodology. Technical Report 02, University of Otago, Dunedin, New Zealand, 2001.

[16] R. Cervenka. *Modeling Multi-Agent Systems*. PhD thesis, Comenius University in Bratislava, 2006.

[17] R. Cervenka, D. Greenwood and I. Trencansky. The AML Approach to Modeling Autonomic Systems. In P. Dini, P. Ayed, C. Dini, and Y. Berbers, editors, *International Conference on Autonomic and Autonomous Systems (ICAS 2006)*, Silicon Valley, California, USA, July 19–21 2006. IEEE Computer Society.

[18] R. Cervenka and I. Trencansky. Agent Modeling Language: Language Specification. Version 0.9. Technical report, Whitestein Technologies, December 2004. URL: http://www.whitestein.com/pages/solutions/meth.html

[19] R. Cervenka and I. Trencansky. Agent-Oriented Development Methodology. Overview. Version 0.9. Technical report, Whitestein Technologies, February 2005.

[20] R. Cervenka, I. Trencansky, and M. Calisti. Modeling Social Aspects of Multi-Agent Systems. The AML Approach. In J.P. Muller and F. Zambonelli, editors, *The Fourth International Joint Conference on Autonomous Agents & Multi Agent Systems (AAMAS 05). Workshop 7: Agent-Oriented Software Engineering (AOSE)*, pages 85–96, Universiteit Utrecht, The Netherlands, July 25–29 2005.

[21] R. Cervenka, I. Trencansky, and M. Calisti. Modeling Social Aspects of Multi-Agent Systems: The AML Approach. In J.P. Muller and F. Zambonelli, editors, *Agent-Oriented Software Engineering VI: 6th International Workshop, AOSE 2005*, LNCS 3950, pages 28–39, Springer-Verlag, February 2006.

[22] R. Cervenka, I. Trencansky, M. Calisti, and D. Greenwood. AML: Agent Modeling Language. Toward Industry-Grade Agent-Based Modeling. In J. Odell, P. Giorgini, and J.P. Muller, editors, *Agent-Oriented Software Engineering V: 5th International Workshop, AOSE 2004*, LNCS 3382, page 31–46, Springer-Verlag, January 2005.

[23] L. Chung, B. A. Nixon, E. Yu, and J. Mylopoulos. *Non-Functional Requirements in Software Engineering*. Kluwer Academic Publishing, 2000.

[24] M. Cossentino. Different Perspectives in Designing Multi-Agent Systems. In *AGES'02 Workshop at NODe02*, Erfurt, October 2002.

[25] M. Cossentino and C. Potts. A CASE Tool Supported Methodology for the Design of Multi-Agent Systems. In *Proceedings of the 2002 International Conference on Software Engineering Research and Practice (SERP'02)*, Las Vegas, NV, USA, June 2002.

[26] M. Cossentino, L. Sabatucci, and A. Chella. A Possible Approach to the Development of Robotic Multi-Agent Systems. In *IEEE/WIC Conference on Intelligent Agent Technology (IAT'03)*, Halifax, Canada, October 2003.

[27] Cougaar web page. URL: http://www.cougaar.org/

[28] S. Cranefield, S. Haustein, and M. Purvis. UML-Based Ontology Modelling for Software Agents. In *Proceedings of the Workshop on Ontologies in Agent, 2001*, May 2001.

[29] S. Cronholm and P.J. Agerfalk. On the Concept of Method in Information Systems Development. *Linköping Electronic Articles in Computer and Information Science*, 4 (1999)(019), October 1999.

[30] DAML web page. URL: http://www.daml.org/

[31] A. Dardenne, A. van Lamsweerde, and S. Fickas. Goal-Directed Requirements Acquisition. *Science of Computer Programming*, 20:3–50, 1993.

[32] S.A. DeLoach. Multiagent Systems Engineering: A Methodology and Language for Designing Agent Systems. In *Proceedings fo the Agent-Oriented Information Systems '99 (AOIS'99)*, Seattle, WA, May 1999.

[33] S.A. DeLoach, M.F. Wood, and C. H. Sparkman. Multiagent Systems Engineering. *International Journal of Software Engineering and Knowledge Engineering*, 11(3):231–258, 2001.

[34] R. Depke, R. Heckel, and J.M. Küster. Improving the Agent-Oriented Modeling Process by Roles. In *Proceedings of the Fifth International Conference on Autonomous Agents*, pages 640–647, Montreal, Canada, May/June 2001. ACM.

[35] M. d'Inverno and M. Luck. *Understanding Agent Systems*. Springer-Verlag, 2001.

[36] T.T. Do, M. Kolp, T.T.H. Hoang, and A. Pirotte. A Framework for Design Patterns in Tropos. In *Proceedings of the 17th Brazilian Symposium on Software Engineering (SBES 2003)*, Maunas, Brazil, October 2003.

[37] T.T. Do, M. Kolp, and A. Pirotte. Social Patterns for Designing Multiagent Systems. In *Proceedings of the Fifteenth International Conference on Software Engineering & Knowledge Engineering (SEKE'2003)*, pages 103–110, July 2003.

[38] Enterprise Architect web page.
URL: http://www.sparxsystems.com.au/products/ea.html

[39] H.E. Eriksson and M. Penker. *Business Modeling with UML: Business Patterns at Work*. John Wiley Sons, 1999.

[40]  R. Evans, P. Kearny, J. Stark, G. Caire, F. Garijo, G.J. Sanz, F. Leal, P. Chainho, and P. Massonet. MESSAGE: Methodology for Engineering Systems of Software Agents. Methodology for Agent-Oriented Software Engineering. Technical Report Eurescom project P907, EDIN 0223-0907, EURESCOM, September 2001.

[41]  D. Fensel, I. Horrocks, F. van Harmelen, S. Decker, M. Erdmann, and M. Klein. OIL in a Nutshell. In Dieng, R. et al., editor, *Knowledge Acquisition, Modeling, and Management. Proceedings of the European Knowledge Acquisition Conference (EKAW-2000)*. Lecture Notes in Artificial Intelligence, Springer-Verlag, October 2000.

[42]  J. Ferber and O. Gutknecht. A Meta-Model for the Analysis and Design of Organizations in Multi-Agent Systems. In *3rd Int. Conference on Multi-Agent Systems (ICMAS'98)*, pages 128–135. IEEE Computer Society, 1998.

[43]  R. Fikes and D.L. McGuinness. An Axiomatic Semantics for RDF, RDF-S, and DAML+OIL. December 2001.
      URL: http://www.w3.org/TR/2001/NOTE-daml+oilaxioms-20011218

[44]  FIPA Methodology Technical Committee. Working Area web page.
      URL: http://www.pa.icar.cnr.it/~cossentino/FIPAmeth/

[45]  FIPA Modeling Technical Committee web page.
      URL: http://www.fipa.org/activities/modeling.html

[46]  FIPA specifications repository web page.
      URL: http://www.fipa.org/repository/index.html

[47]  FIPA web page. URL: http://www.fipa.org/

[48]  S. Flake, C. Geiger, and J.M. Küster. Towards UML-based Analysis and Design of Multi-Agent Systems. In *Proceedings of International NAISO Symposium on Information Science Innovations in Engineering of Natural and Artificial Intelligent Systems (ENAIS'2001)*, pages 695–701, Dubai, March 2001. ICSC Academic Press.

[49]  M.L. Ginsberg. Knowledge Interchange Format: The KIF of Death. *AI Magazine*, 12(3):57–63, 1991.

[50]  N. Glaser. Conceptual Modelling of Multi-Agent Systems (The CoMoMAS Engineering Environment). In *Kluwer Series on Multiagent Systems, Artificial Societies, and Simulated Organizations*, volume 4. Kluwer, May 2002.

[51]  Goal Oriented Requirement Language (GRL) web page.
      URL: http://www.cs.toronto.edu/km/GRL

[52]  J.J. Gomez-Sanz and R. Fuentes. Agent Oriented Software Engineering with IN-GENIAS. In *Fourth Iberoamerican Workshop on Multi-Agent Systems (Iberagents 2002) - Agent Technology and Software Engineering*, Spain, November 2002. University of Malaga.

[53]  O. Gutknecht, J. Ferber, and F. Michel. Integrating Tools and Infrastructures for Generic Multi-Agent Systems. In *Proc. of the Fifth International Conference on Autonomous Agents (AA 2001)*, Montreal, Quebec, Canada, May 2001.

[54] M.P. Huget. Agent UML Notation for Multiagent System Design. *IEEE Internet Computing*, 8(4):63–71, 2004.

[55] M.P. Huget, I. Reinharts-Berger, D. Dori, O. Shehory, and A. Sturm. Modeling-Notation Source: OPM/MAS.
URL: http://www.auml.org/auml/documents/OPM.pdf

[56] IBM Corp. Rational Unified Process. Version 2003.06.13.

[57] IBM Rational Rose web page.
URL: http://www.ibm.com/software/awdtools/developer/modeler/

[58] C. Iglesias, M. Garijo, J.C. Gonzalez, and J.R. Velasco. Analysis and Design of Multiagent Systems Using MAS-CommonKADS. In M.P. Singh, A. Rao, and M.J. Wooldridge, editors, *Intelligent Agents IV*, LNAI 1365, pages 313–326. Springer-Verlag, 1998.

[59] INGENIAS web page. URL: http://grasia.fdi.ucm.es/ingenias/

[60] ISLANDER web page. URL: http://e-institutor.iiia.csic.es/islander/islander.html

[61] JADE web page. URL: http://jade.tilab.com/

[62] Java RoboCup Simulator web page.
URL: http://www.ifi.unizh.ch/ailab/people/nitschke/RoboCup.html

[63] N.R. Jennings. On Agent-Based Software Engineering. *Artificial Intelligence*, 117(2):277–296, 2000.

[64] N.R. Jennings, P. Faratin, A.R. Lomuscio, S. Parsons, M.J. Wooldridge, and C. Sierra. Automated Negotiation: Prospects, Methods and Challenges. *Journal of Group Decision and Negotiation*, 10(2):199–215, 2001.

[65] N.R. Jennings, K. Sycara, and M. Wooldridge. A Roadmap of Agent Research and Development. *Journal of Autonomous Agents and Multi-Agent Systems*, 1(1):7–38, 1998.

[66] N.R. Jennings and M. Wooldridge. Software Agents. *IEEE Review*, 42(1):17–21, January 1996.

[67] C.M. Jonker, M. Klush, and J. Treur. Design of Collaborative Information Agents. In M. Klush and L. Kerschberg, editors, *Cooperative Information Agents IV. Proceedings of CIA 2000*, pages 262–283. Springer-Verlag, July 2000.

[68] T. Juan, A. Pearce, and L. Sterling. ROADMAP: Extending the Gaia Methodology for Complex Open Systems. In *Proceedings of the First International Joint Conference on Autonomous Agents and Multi-Agent Systems (AAMAS 2002)*, Bologna, Italy, July 2002.

[69] M. Kang, L.Wang, and K. Taguchi. Modelling Mobile Agent Applications in UML 2.0 Activity Diagrams. In *Proceedings of the 3rd International Workshop on Software Engineering for Large-Scale Multi-Agent Systems, SELMAS'2004*, pages 104–111, Edinburg, United Kingdom, May 2004.

[70] L. Keller. Service Level Agreement Management - Phase 1. SLAM. Analysis and Design. Technical Report wt.r&c.slam.M1.phase1, v1.3, Whitestein Technologies, August 2004.

[71] E.A. Kendall, P.V.M. Krishna, C.V. Pathak, and C.B. Suresh. Patterns of Intelligent and Mobile Agents. In *Proc. of the second international conference on Autonomous agents*, pages 92–99, 1998.

[72] E.A. Kendall, M.T. Malkoun, and C. Jiang. Multiagent Systems Design Based on Object Oriented Patterns. *Journal of Object Oriented Programming*, June 1997.

[73] E.A. Kendall, M.T. Malkoun, and C. Jiang. A Methodology for Developing Agent-Based Systems for Enterprise Integration. In C. Zhang and D. Luckose, editors, *Proceedings of the First Australian Workshop on DAI. Lecture Notes on Artificial Intelligence*, Canberra, ACT, Australia, November 1995. Springer-Verlag.

[74] D. Kinny and M. Georgeff. Modelling and Design of Multiagent Systems. In J.P. Müller, M.J. Wooldridge, and N.R. Jennings, editors, *Intelligent Agents III: Proceedings of the Third International Workshop on Agent Theories, Architectures, and Languages (ATAL-96)*, LNAI 1193. Springer-Verlag, August 1996.

[75] M. Kolp, P. Giorgini, and J. Mylopoulos. Organizational Patterns for Early Requirements Analysis. In *Proceedings of the 15th International Conference on Advanced Information Systems Engineering (CAiSE'03)*, Velden, Austria, June 2003.

[76] J.L. Koning, M.P. Huget, J. Wei, and X. Wang. Extended Modeling Languages for Interaction Protocol Design. In M. Wooldridge, G. Weiss, and P. Ciancarini, editors, *Proceedings of the Second International Workshop On Agent-Oriented Software Engineering (AOSE-2001)*, pages 93–100, Montreal, Canada, May 2001. Springer.

[77] J. Lind. *MASSIVE: Software Engineering for Multiagent Systems*. PhD thesis, University of the Saarland, 2000.

[78] J. Lind. Issues in Agent-Oriented Software Engineering. In P. Ciancarini and M. Wooldridge, editors, *Agent-Oriented Software Engineering: First International Workshop, AOSE 2000. Lecture Notes in Artificial Intelligence*, Vol. 1957, pages 45–58. Springer-Verlag, 2001.

[79] O. Lindland, G. Sindre, and A. Solvberg. Understanding Quality in Conceptual Modelling. *IEEE Software*, 11(2):42–49, March 1994.

[80] L. Liu and E. Yu. From Requirements to Architectural Design—Using Goals and Scenarios. In *Software Requirements to Architectures Workshop (STRAW 2001)*, Toronto, Canada, May 2001.

[81] Living Systems Technology Suite (LS/TS) web page. URL: http://www.whitestein.com/pages/solutions/ls ts.html

[82] M.P. Luck, P. McBurney, and Ch. Preist. *Agent Technology: Enabling Next Generation Computing (A Roadmap for Agent-Based Computing)*, AgentLink II, January 2003.

[83] M.P. Luck, editor. *Agent Technology Roadmap: Overview and Consultation Report. Agent Based Computing.* University of Southampton on behalf of AgentLink III, December 2004.

[84] D. Martin (ed.). OWL-S 1.0 Release. URL: http://www.daml.org/services/

[85] V.Mascardi. *Logic-Based Specification Environments for Multi-Agent Systems.* PhD thesis, Università degli Studi di Genova, May 2002.

[86] MESSAGE web page.
URL: http://www.eurescom.de/public/projects/P900-series/p907/

[87] MiS20 - Robotic Soccer web page. URL: http://hmi.ewi.utwente.nl/MiS20/

[88] J. Mylopoulos, L. Chung, and B. Nixon. Representing and Using Nonfunctional Requirements: A Process-Oriented Approach. *IEEE Trans. on Sofware Engineering*, 18 No. 6:483–497, June 1992.

[89] N. Nopper. Living Agents Runtime System (LARS) - The Agent Platform for Business Applications. In *AgentLink News 5*, pages 5–8. AgentLink, May 2000.

[90] J. Odell. A Primer to Method Engineering. In S. Brinkkemper, K. Lyytinen, and R.J. Welke, editors, *Method Engineering Principles of Method Construction and Tool Support.* Chapman & Hall, London, 1996.

[91] J. Odell, M. Nodine, and R. Levy. A Metamodel for Agents, Roles, and Groups. In J. Odell, P. Giorgini, and J.P. Muller, editors, *Agent-Oriented Software Engineering V: 5th International Workshop, AOSE 2004.* Springer-Verlag, January 2005.

[92] J. Odell, H.V.D. Parunak, and B. Bauer. Extending UML for Agents. In G. Wagner, Y. Lesperance, and E. Yu, editors, *Proceedings of the Agent-Oriented Information Systems Workshop at the 17th National Conference on Artificial Intelligence*, pages 3–17, Austin, Texas, July 2000. ICue Publishing.

[93] J. Odell, H.V.D. Parunak, and B. Bauer. Representing Agent Interaction Protocols in UML. In P. Ciancarini and M. Wooldridge, editors, *Proceedings on the First International Workshop on Agent-Oriented Software Engineering (AOSE 2000)*, pages 121–140, Limerick, Ireland, June 2000. Springer.

[94] J. Odell, H.V.D. Parunak, S. Brueckner, and M. Fleischer. Temporal Aspects of Dynamic Role Assignment. In P. Giorgini, G. Muller, and J. Odell, editors, *Agent-Oriented Software Engineering (AOSE) IV*, LNCS 2935, Berlin, 2004. Springer-Verlag.

[95] J. Odell, H.V.D. Parunak, and M. Fleischer. The Role of Roles in Designing Effective Agent Organizations. In A. Garcia, C. Lucena, F. Zambonelli, A. Omicini, and J. Castro, editors, *Software Engineering for Large-Scale Multi-Agent Systems, Lecture Notes on Computer Science volume 2603*, pages 27–28, Berlin, 2003. Springer.

[96] J. Odell, H.V.D. Parunak, M. Fleischer, and S. Brueckner. Modeling Agents and their Environment. In *Proceedings of AOSE 2002*, pages 16–31, Bologna, Italy, July 2002. Springer.

[97]  OIL web page. URL: http://www.ontoknowledge.org/oil/

[98]  OMG. MDA Guide. Version 1.0.1, omg/2003-06-01, June 2003.

[99]  OMG. Meta Object Facility (MOF) Core Specification. Version 2.0, formal/06-01-01, January 2006.

[100]  OMG. Object Constraint Language. Version 2.0, formal/06-05-01, May 2006.

[101]  OMG. Ontology Definition Metamodel Specification. ptc/06-10-11, October 2006.

[102]  OMG. Unified Modeling Language Specification. Version 1.5, formal/03-03-01, March 2003.

[103]  OMG. Unified Modeling Language: Infrastructure. Version 2.0, formal/05-07-05, March 2006.

[104]  OMG. Unified Modeling Language: Superstructure. Version 2.0, formal/05-07-04, August 2005.

[105]  OMG. Software Process Engineering Metamodel Specification. Version 1.1, for-mal/05-01-06, January 2005.

[106]  OMG. XML Metadata Interchange (XMI) Specification. Version 2.0, formal/03-05-02, May 2005.

[107]  OMG Agent Platform Special Interest Group web page.
URL: http://www.objs.com/agent/

[108]  OMG Analysis & Design Task Force. Request for Information on Modeling Agent-based Systems. ad/2004-08-05, 25 August 2004.

[109]  A. Omicini. Societies and Infrastructures in the Analysis and Design of Agent Based Systems. In P. Ciancarini and M. Wooldridge, editors, *Agent-Oriented Software Engineering Proceedings of the First International Workshop (AOSE-2000)*, pages 185–194, Limerick, Ireland, June 2000. Springer-Verlag.

[110]  OWL web page. URL: http://www.w3.org/TR/2002/WD-owl-guide-20021104/

[111]  L. Padgham and M. Winikoff. Prometheus: A Methodology for Developing Intelligent Agents. In *Proceedings of the First International Joint Conference on Autonomous Agents and Multi-Agent Systems (AAMAS 2002)*, Bologna, Italy, July 2002.

[112]  L. Padgham and M. Winikoff. *Developing Intelligent Agent Systems. A practical guide*. John Wiley & Sons Ltd, 2004.

[113]  H.V.D. Parunak and J.J. Odell. Represening Social Structures in UML. In M. Wooldridge, G. Weiss, and P. Ciancarini, editors, *Proceedings of the Second International Workshop on Agent-Oriented Software Engineering (AOSE-2001)*, pages 17–31, Montreal, Canada, May 2001. Springer.

[114] J. Pavon and J. Gomez-Sanz. Agent Oriented Software Engineering with INGE-NIAS. In V. Maik, J. Muller, and M. Pchouek, editors, *Multi-Agent Systems and Applications III: 3rd International Central and Eastern European Conference on Multi-Agent Systems, CEEMAS 2003*, LNCS 2691/2003, page 394. Springer-Verlag, August 2003.

[115] J. Pena, R. Corchuelo, and J. Arjona. A Top-Down Approach for MAS Protocol Descriptions. In *Proceedings of the 2003 ACM Symposium on Applied Computing (SAC 2003)*, pages 45–49, Melbourne, FL, USA, March 2003. ACM.

[116] A. Poggi, G. Rimassa, P. Turci, J. Odell, H. Mouratidis, and G. Manson. Modeling Deployment and Mobility Issues in Multiagent Systems using AUML. In P. Giorgini, J.P. Muller, and J. Odell, editors, *Agent-Oriented Software Engineering (AOSE) IV*, LNCS 2935. Springer-Verlag, December 2003.

[117] Prometheus Design Tool web page.
URL: http://www.cs.rmit.edu.au/agents/pdt/

[118] O.F. Rana and C.A. Biancheri. A Petri Net Model of the Meeting Design Pattern for Mobile-Stationary Agent Interaction. In *Proc. of the 32nd Hawaii International Conference on System Sciences*, 1999.

[119] A.S. Rao and M.P. Georgeff. Modeling Rational Agents within a BDI Architecture. In J.F. Allen, R. Fikes, and E. Sandewall, editors, *KR'91: Principles of Knowledge Representation and Reasoning*, pages 473–484. Morgan Kaufmann, San Mateo, California, 1991.

[120] RELATIONSHIP. A Vocabulary for Describing Relationships Between People.
URL: http://purl.org/vocab/relationship/

[121] E.B. Reuter. The Social Attitude. *Journal of Applied Sociology*, 8(1923):97–101, 1923.

[122] RoboCup Soccer Simulator web page. URL: http://sserver.sourceforge.net/

[123] C. Rolland. A Primer for Method Engineering. In *Proceedings of the INFORSID Conf. (INFormatique des Organisations et Systems d'Information et de Decision)*, pages 10–13, Toulouse, France, June 1997.

[124] M. Saeki. Software Specification & Design Methods and Method Engineering. *International Journal of Software Engineering and Knowledge Engineering*, 1994.

[125] L. Shan and H. Zhu. CAMLE: A Caste-Centric Agent Modelling Language and Environment. In *Proceedings of the 3rd International Workshop on Software Engineering for Large-Scale Multi-Agent Systems, SELMAS'2004*, Edinburg, United Kingdom, May 2004.

[126] A. Silva and J. Delgado. The Agent Pattern for Mobile Agent Systems. In *European Conference on Pattern Languages of Programming and Computing*, Bad Irsee, Germany, 1998.

[127] V.T. Silva, R. Choren, and C. Lucena. A UML Based Approach for Modeling and Implementing Multi-Agent Systems. In *Proceedings of the Third International Joint Conference on Autonomous Agents and Multiagent Systems - Volume 2 (AA-MAS'04)*, pages 914–921. IEEE Computer Society, July 2004.

[128] V.T. Silva, A. Garcia, A. Brandao, C. Chavez, C. Lucena, and P. Alencar. Taming Agents and Objects in Software Engineering. In A. Garcia, C. Lucena, J. Castro, A. Omicini, and F. Zambonelli, editors, *Software Engineering for Large-Scale Multi-Agent Systems: Research Issues and Practical Applications*, volume LNCS 2603, pages 1–25. Springer-Verlag, April 2003.

[129] V.T. Silva and C. Lucena. Extending the UML Sequence Diagram to Model the Dynamic Aspects of Multi-Agent Systems. Technical Report MCC 15/03, PUC-Rio, Rio de Janeiro, Brazil, 2003.

[130] V.T. Silva and C. Lucena. From a Conceptual Framework for Agents and Objects to a Multi-Agent System Modeling Language. In *Autonomous Agents and Multi-Agent Systems*, volume 9, pages 145–189. Springer Science+Business Media B.V., July 2004.

[131] G. Smith. *The Object-Z Specification Language*. Advances in Formal Methods Series. Kluwer Academic Publishers, 2000.

[132] M.K. Smith, D. McGuinness, R. Volz, and C. Welty. Web Ontology Language (OWL), Guide Version 1.0, W3C Working Draft.
URL: http://www.w3.org/TR/2002/WD-owl-guide-20021104/

[133] C.H. Sparkman, S.A. DeLoach, and A.L. Self. Automated Derivation of Complex Agent Architectures from Analysis Specifications. In M. Wooldridge, G. Weiss, and P. Ciancarini, editors, *Proceedings of the Second International Workshop On Agent-Oriented Software Engineering (AOSE-2001)*, pages 77–84, Montreal, Canada, May 2001. Springer.

[134] M. Spit, K. Lieberherr, and S. Brinkkemper. Integrating Adaptiveness into Object-Oriented Analysis and Design Methods – a Situational Method Engineering Approach. Technical Report NU-CCS-95-05, Northeastern University, February 1995.

[135] StarUML web page. URL: http://staruml.sourceforge.net/

[136] A. Sturm, D. Dori, and O. Shehory. Single-Model Method for Specifying Multi-Agent Systems. In *2nd International Joint Conference on Autonomous Agents and Multiagent Systems (AAMAS-2003)*, Melbourne, Australia, July 2003.

[137] W. Sutandiyo, M.B. Chhetri, S. Krishnaswamy, and S.W. Loke. From m-GAIA to Grasshopper: Engineering Mobile Agent Applications. In G. Kotsis, S. Bressan, and I.K. Ibrahim, editors, *iiWAS'2003 - The Fifth International Conference on Information Integrationand Web-based Applications Services*. Austrian Computer Society, 15-17 September 2003.

[138] W.B. Teeuw and H. van den Berg. On the Quality of Conceptual Models. In *16th International Conference on Conceptual Modeling*, Los Angeles, CA, 3–6 November 1997. URL: http://osm7.cs.byu.edu/ER97/workshop4/tvdb.html

[139] J.-P. Tolvanen. *Incremental Method Engineering with Modeling Tools. Theoretical Principles and Empirical Evidence*. PhD thesis, Jyväskylä studies in computer science, economics and statistics 47, University of Jyväskylä, Finland, 1998.

[140] I. Trencansky and R. Cervenka. Agent Modeling Language (AML): A Comprehensive Approach to Modeling MAS. *Informatica*, 29(4):391–400, 2005.
URL: http://ai.ijs.si/informatica/

[141] I. Trencansky and R. Cervenka. Agent Modeling Language (AML): Toward Industry-Grade Agent-Based Modeling. Presented at Agent Link III–Technical Forum II, Agent-Oriented Software Engineering TFG, Ljuljana, February, 28–March 1, 2005.
URL: http://www.pa.icar.cnr.it/~cossentino/al3tf2/docs/aml_trencansky.pdf

[142] I. Trencansky, R. Cervenka, and D. Greenwood. Applying a UML-based Agent Modeling Language to the Autonomic Computing Domain. In *OOPSLA'06: Companion to the 21st ACM SIGPLAN Conference on Object-Oriented Programming Languages, Systems, and Applications*, pages 521–529, Portland, Oregon, USA, October 22–26 2006. ACM Press.

[143] Tropos web page. URL: http://www.cs.toronto.edu/km/tropos/

[144] W.M. Turski and T.S.E. Maibaum. *The Specification of Computer Programs*. Addison-Wesley, 1987.

[145] A. Tveit. A Survey of Agent-Oriented Software Engineering. In *Proceedings of the First NTNU Computer Science Graduate Student Conference*. Norwegian University of Science and Technology, May 2001.
URL: http://csgsc.idi.ntnu.no/2001/pages/papers/atveit.pdf

[146] A. van Lamsweerde. Requirements Engineering in the Year 00: A Research Perspective. In *ICSE 2000: 22nd International Conference on Software Engineering*, pages 5–19. ACM Press, June 2000.

[147] B. van Linder, J.-J. Ch. Meyer, and W. van der Hoek. Formalizing Motivational Attitudes of Agents Using the KARO Framework. Technical Report UU-CS (Ext. r. no. 1997-06), Utrecht, the Netherlands: Utrecht University: Information and Computing Sciences, 1997.

[148] K. Van Slooten and B. Hodes. Characterising IS Development Project. In *IFIP WG 8.1 Conference on Method Engineering*, pages 29–44. Chapman & Hall, 1996.

[149] W3C. Web Services Activity web page. URL: http://www.w3.org/2002/ws/

[150] G. Wagner. A UML Profile for External AOR Models. In *Proceedings of the Third International Workshop on Agent-Oriented Software Engineering (AOSE-2002)*, LNAI 2585, pages 99–110, Bologna, Italy, July 2002. Springer-Verlag.

[151] G. Wagner. The Agent-Object-Relationship Meta-Model: Towards a Unified Conceptual View of State and Behavior. *Information Systems*, 28(5):475–504, 2003.

[152] G.Weiss. Multiagent Systems—A Modern Approach to Distributed Artificial Intelligence. *The MIT Press*, 3rd edition, 2001.

[153] G. Weiss. Agent Orientation in Software Engineering. *Knowledge Engineering Review*, 16(4):349–373, 2002.

[154] M. Weiss. On the Use of Patterns in Agent System Design. In *AOIS at AAMAS'02*, Bologna, Italy, 2002.

[155] G.J. Wickler. *Using Expressive and Flexible Action Representation to Reason about Capabilities for Intelligent Agent Cooperation*. PhD thesis, University of Edinburgh, 1999.

[156] Wikipedia web page. URL: http://en.wikipedia.org/

[157] K. Wistrand and F. Karlsson. Method Components – Rationale Revealed. In A. Persson and J. Stirna, editors, *Lecture Notes in Computer Science*, Volume 3084/2004, pages 189–201. Springer-Verlag, August 2004.

[158] M. Wooldridge. Agent-Based Software Engineering. *IEE Proceedings on Software Engineering*, 144(1):26–37, 1997.

[159] M. Wooldridge and P. Ciancarini. Agent-Oriented Software Engineering: The State of the Art. In *Handbook of Software Engineering and Knowledge Engineering*. World Scientific Publishing Co., 2001.

[160] M. Wooldridge and N.R. Jennings. Intelligent Agents: Theory and Practice. *The Knowledge Engineering Review*, 10(2):115–152, 1995.

[161] M. Wooldridge, N.R. Jennings, and D. Kinny. The Gaia Methodology for Agent-Oriented Analysis and Design. *Journal of Autonomous Agents and Multi-Agent Systems*, 3(3):285–312, 2000.

[162] Q. Yan, L. Shan, X. Mao, and Z. Qi. RoMAS: A Role-Based Modeling Method for Multi-Agent System. In J.P. Li, J. Liu, N. Zhong, J. Yen, and J. Zhao, editors, *Proceedings of the Second Internacional Conference on Active Media Technology (ICANT2003)*, pages 156–161, Chongqing, China, May 2003. Chinese Electronical Industry Society, Logistical Engineering University, World Scientific.

[163] E. Yu. *Modelling Strategic Relationships for Process Reengineering*. PhD thesis, Department of Computer Science, University of Toronto, Canada, 1995.

[164] E. Yu. Towards Modelling and Reasoning Support for Early-Phase Requirements Engineering. In *Proceedings of IEEE International Symposium on Requirements Engineering RE'97*, Washington DC, January 1997. IEEE.

[165] E. Yu and J. Mylopoulos. Understanding "Why" in Software Process Modelling, Analysis, and Design. In *Proceedings of 16th International Conference on Software Engineering*, pages 159–168, May 1994.

[166] E. Yu and J. Mylopoulos. From ER to 'A-R' – Modeling Strategic Actor Relationships for Business Process Reengineering. *Int. J. of Intelligent and Cooperative Information Systems*, 4(23):125–144, 1995.

[167] F. Zambonelli, N.R. Jennings, and M. Wooldridge. Organizational Rules as an Abstraction for the Analysis and Design of Multi-agent Systems. *Journal of Knowledge and Software Engineering*, 11:303–328, 2001.

[168] F. Zambonelli, N.R. Jennings, and M. Wooldridge. Developing Multiagent Systems: The Gaia Methodology. *ACM Trans. on Software Engineering and Methodology*, 12(3):317–370, 2003.

[169] H. Zhu. Developing Formal Specifications of MAS in SLABS: A Case Study of Evolutionary Multi-Agent Ecosystem. In P. Giorgini, Y. Lesperance, G. Wagner, and E.S.K. Yu, editors, *Agent-Oriented Information Systems (AOIS '02). Proceedings of the Fourth International Bi-Conference Workshop on Agent-Oriented Information Systems (AOIS-2002 at AAMAS-02)*, Bologna, Italy, July 2002.

# List of Acronyms

| | |
|---|---|
| acl | Agent Communication Language |
| cl | Content Language |
| ADEM | Agent-Oriented Development Methodology |
| AI | Artificial Intelligence |
| AML | Agent Modeling Language |
| AOR | Agent-Object-Relationship |
| AORML | AOR Modeling Language |
| AOSE | Agent-Oriented Software Engineering |
| AUML | Agent UML |
| BDI | Belief-Desire-Intention |
| CAME | Computer-Aided Method Engineering |
| CAMLE | A Caste-Centric Agent Modelling Language and Environment |
| CASE | Computer-Aided Software Engineering |
| CDL | Capability Description Language |
| DAI | Distributed Artificial Intelligence |
| DAML | DARPA Agent Markup Language |
| DARPA | Defense Advanced Research Projects Agency |
| EA | Enterprise Architect |
| ER | Entity-Relationship |
| FIPA | Foundation for Intelligent Physical Agents |
| GBRAM | Goal-Based Requirements Analysis Method |
| GRL | Goal-oriented Requirement Language |
| GUI | Graphical User Interface |
| IDE | Integrated Development Environment |
| KAOS | Knowledge Acquisition in autOmated Specification |
| LS/TS | Living Systems Technology Suite |
| MAS | Multi-Agent System |
| MAS-ML | Multi-Agent System Modeling |
| MASSIVE | MultiAgent SystemS Iterative View Engineering |
| MDA | Model-Driven Architecture |
| MESSAGE | Methodology for Engineering Systems of Software Agents |
| MOF | Meta Object Facility |
| NFR | Non-Functional Requirements |
| OCL | Object Constraint Language |
| OIL | Ontology Inference Layer |

| OMG | Object Management Group |
| OOSE | Object-Oriented Software Engineering |
| OPM | Object-Process Methodology |
| OWL | Web Ontology Language |
| OWL-S | OWL-based Web Service Ontology |
| PASSI | Process for Agent Societies Specification and Implementation |
| RFI | Request for Information |
| ROADMAP | Role Oriented Analysis and Design for Multi-Agent Programming |
| RUP | Rational Unified Process |
| SMART | Structured and Modular Agents and Relationship Types |
| SME | Situational Method Engineering |
| SPEM | Software Process Engineering Metamodel Specification |
| TAMAX | TAP1 Agent Modeling And eXchange format |
| TAO | Taming Agents and Objects |
| UML | Unified Modeling Language |
| XMI | XML Metadata Interchange |
| XML | eXtensible Markup Language |

# Index